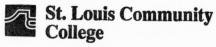

MASSACRE
on the
Lordsburg Road

NUMBER FIFTEEN:
The Elma Dill Russell Spencer Series
in the West and Southwest

The Southwestern Territories in 1883

MASSACRE
on the
Lordsburg Road

A Tragedy of the Apache Wars

MARC SIMMONS

Texas A&M University Press
College Station

The paper used in this book meets the minimum requirements
of the American National Standard for Permanence of Paper
for Printed Library Materials, Z39.48-1984. Binding materials
have been chosen for durability.

Library of Congress Cataloging-in-Publication Data

Simmons, Marc.
    Massacre on the Lordsburg road : a tragedy of the Apache wars /
Marc Simmons.
        p.   cm. — (The Elma Dill Russell series in the West and
Southwest ; no. 15)
    Includes bibliographical references and index.
    ISBN 0-89096-772-5
    1. Apaches Indians—Wars, 1883–1886. 2. McComas family—
Assassination. 3. McComas family—Captivity, 1883. 4. Indian
captivities—New Mexico—Lordsburg. 5. Crook, George, 1829–1890.
6. United States. Army. Cavalry, 5th. I. Title. II. Series.
E83.88.S56   1997
973.8'4—dc21   97-19530
                                                            CIP

For
Janaloo Hill
Faithful Keeper of the Past

❦ Contents ❧

Illustrations

☙ Preface ❧

It was more than a century ago that Judge Hamilton C. McComas and his wife Juniata were slain by Apache raiders and their blue-eyed, six-year-old son Charley was carried into captivity. The tragic incident occurred on the desolate road between Lordsburg and Silver City, in the southwestern corner of the New Mexico Territory, at approximately noon on March 28, 1883. The shattering news made headlines everywhere and stunned the American people.

Those killed by Indians on the western frontier usually were nobodies—poor pioneer emigrants, cowboys, trappers, prospectors, hardrock miners, mail couriers, government scouts, and soldiers. Often such people ended up in unmarked graves at trailside and were remembered only as statistics in the large tally of casualties produced by the westward movement. In the McComas case, however, the victims were socially and politically prominent, and their deaths caused widespread consternation.

A second element that attracted public attention, of course, was the uncertainty of little Charley's fate. A child in distress inevitably brings forth an outpouring of concern and sympathy. Was he still alive? If so, could he be rescued? And who was to go after the Apaches and attempt that ticklish and dangerous job? Those questions were on many lips in the spring of 1883.

The McComas massacre has not been an easy story to plumb. It frequently receives passing mention in general histories of the Apache wars, but seldom is much detail given. A summary in a few paragraphs is about all the reader can expect to find. For more than a dozen years, I followed the historical tracks without making significant progress. I needed to know the circumstances of the McComases' lives prior to their rendezvous with death on the Lordsburg Road, so as to understand what brought them there.

My challenge, in this respect, had a configuration similar to the plot of Thornton Wilder's 1928 Pulitzer Prize–winning novel, *The Bridge of San Luis*

Rey. In that best-selling book, it will be recalled, a suspension bridge high in the Peruvian Andes one day broke and sent five travelers plummeting into the gulf below. The author's narrative examines the background of the fatal accident to determine "why this happened to *those* five."

In the same way, but acting as a historian, I wanted to illuminate the antecedents of my massacre to show how it all came about and to follow up with a look at the aftermath, especially the effects upon those who were in some way involved. Usually pioneers who died at the hands of Indians were rather quickly forgotten, and their personal histories remain untold. But I wondered if something more could not be done with the McComas couple. Owing to their importance, the lateness of their murders at the tag end of the Indian wars, and the publicity generated by the prolonged search for Charley McComas, it seemed likely that a coherent picture of the entire affair could yet be drawn.

Then in the autumn of 1992, I had an extraordinary piece of luck. I dropped by one of my favorite antiquarian bookshops, Parker's Books of the West, located two blocks up Palace Avenue from the central plaza in Santa Fe, New Mexico. Amanda Evans was at the front desk and, upon seeing me, she exclaimed: "Oh, I've been hoping you would come in. I have a question for you."

Like lawyers and doctors, historians are accustomed to being assailed by questions wherever they go. My policy is to respond politely, because I've learned that sometimes the simplest queries can lead me to a jackpot in the way of historical information. This proved to be one of those rare instances.

"We had a lady from California visit the shop several weeks ago," Amanda said. "She was asking for books on the McComas massacre. I told her there really weren't any, but that in one of your books on New Mexico you had something to say about it. I couldn't remember which one, so I offered to find out from you and mail her a copy."

"Yes," I replied, "I published a short sketch on the McComas affair some years ago in my little book, *Ranchers, Ramblers, and Renegades.* But why is she interested?"

"Oh, she says that she is a great-granddaughter of the McComases," answered Amanda.

My eyes grew wide, and my jaw fell. "Good gosh! Do you know how long historians have searched for a McComas descendant? I hope you haven't lost that woman's address."

Amanda hadn't. She pulled it right up on her computer. As I walked out clutching a slip of paper that held the address, I had the strongest feeling that a new alignment of stars was suddenly working in my favor. Something surely would come of this.

Was there a body of McComas family papers? And—equally important—if there were, would I be allowed to see them? There exists a strange phenomenon that I've never been able to explain: many, many people who have personal documents of a historical nature suddenly become very possessive and secretive when they discover that an author or scholar has an interest in them. They automatically assume that the papers, which may have lain neglected in their attic for years, have enormous monetary value, and that this value somehow will be diminished if others are allowed to copy them or even see them. Such a situation is the researcher's worst nightmare. He knows there are documents that he should examine, if his study is to have any claim to completeness. But he is denied access.

I wrote a straightforward letter to the address in California given me by Amanda Evans. Then I held my breath and waited. Two weeks later a brown envelope arrived in the mail. Inside were photocopies of the McComas family papers, few in number, but each one valuable, even critical, to my massacre book. For once my correspondent had turned out to be not only amenable and generous but downright eager to see my study advance, so that she could learn more about her own family history. Rather than a nightmare, I was granted a dream come true.

Carolyn Kimme-Smith, as it happened, was the granddaughter of Ada McComas, who died in 1963. Twelve-year-old Ada and her younger sister Mary had been left behind in Silver City with a neighbor on the day in 1883 when Papa, Mama, and little brother Charley had climbed into a buckboard and ridden off to keep their appointment with doom on the Lordsburg Road. Mrs. Kimme-Smith had vivid memories of her elderly grandmother and great-aunt, and recollections of their sufferings as a result of their tragedy. These she shared with me in a series of personal letters written over the next two years. Also, a collection of family photographs, mostly dating from the 1870s, was placed at my disposal.

From that point forward, my good fortune seemed to multiply. New data and offers of assistance sprouted like daffodils in spring. For example, James J. McBride, recently retired from the U.S. Air Force, came to me one afternoon and asked if he could help me on some project, as he was beginning to dabble in southwestern history. Immediately I set him to reading early newspapers on microfilm, and in no time at all he was hooked on the McComas story. During a personal business trip to Chicago, Jim even took time to track down some elusive references to Judge McComas, who had spent part of his early career in Illinois. Later Jim and his wife Barbara negotiated and photographed the faint stagecoach road through Thompson Canyon that had been traveled by the McComases just before they encountered the Apaches.

Another couple who volunteered to lend assistance was Mary and Mel Cottom, accomplished genealogists of Manhattan, Kansas. Not only did they plow archival furrows in search of McComas family background, but also they read and copied issues of several St. Louis newspapers containing coverage of the massacre and the army pursuit of the Indians. In obtaining microfilm materials, they were courteously aided by the dedicated staff of the Interlibrary Loan Department, Farrell Library, Kansas State University in Manhattan.

In the early stages of writing, I telephoned my old friend Janaloo Hill (to whom this book is dedicated). She and her husband Manny Hough are the owners and last two residents of the mining ghost town of Shakespeare, where Judge McComas landed when he first came to New Mexico from St. Louis. I asked Janaloo if she could shed any light on my story, and she replied affirmatively, in two respects.

First, she proposed to send me the transcript of a tape-recorded interview by Julius Caesar Brock shortly before his death in 1952. As a teenager, Brock had been one of the first persons to discover the blood-stained McComas corpses beside their buckboard. Moreover, he just barely missed getting killed by the same band of Apaches. Janaloo remembered the old pioneer clearly and described for me his quirky behavior.

Her second offer proved even more exciting. Long ago, Brock's daughter had guided Janaloo to the massacre site, now in a remote area and completely unmarked. From what I learned, it appeared likely that Janaloo was the only person in New Mexico today who knew the location. "Next time you are in this corner of the state," she declared, "stop by and I'll take you there. I'm certain I can find it again."

My luck was still coursing in a mighty stream, because an opportunity to use her guide service came shortly afterward. Fellow freelance historian Mark L. Gardner called from his home in Cascade, Colorado, to say that he had just gotten a commission to write a history of Fort Bowie National Historic Site in southeastern Arizona. He was planning to drive his pickup down for a tour of the place and would be passing through Santa Fe. I could climb aboard there and tag along, if I had some McComas business to take care of in the area. Indeed I did!

Fort Bowie in the 1880s had been a major staging point for the pursuit of

Apache marauders. After touring the remote ruins and making a quick side trip to archives in Tucson, Mark and I drove back to New Mexico. At Shakespeare, we met Janaloo and Manny, who told us to follow them in their ranch pickup; if the primitive road were passable, we might make it to the massacre site. The late February morning had dawned cold and gray. A stiff wind bore occasional swirls of snowflakes and sleet, adding a mournful note to our errand.

Janaloo's memory was sharp, and we went right to the piece of ground where Hamilton and Juniata McComas had fallen. Just beyond rose the craggy battlements of the Burro Mountains, and in their center the mouth of Thompson Canyon yawned dark and sinister. The wild scene was haunted. None of us doubted that. Human blood had been spilled here, and a tragic chapter in history written.

Later in the day, we continued on to Silver City, which I already had mined for McComas material on previous visits. But I needed to recheck something I had seen in the records of the Grant County Courthouse. Mark followed me in, and while I dug out my reference, he wandered into the open vault of the county clerk. A few minutes later, he emerged carrying a narrow cardboard file box, old and grimy.

"Look here," he announced excitedly. "Do you know about this? It was sitting out of the way, back in a corner."

I glanced at the browned label pasted to the box and saw a single word written in purple ink: "McComas." It was the probate file for the judge's estate, buried in the vault all these many years and never seen by scholars, as best I could tell. I would have missed it myself but for the keen eye of Mark Gardner. That little bundle of documents yielded almost as much information as the McComas family papers that had come to me from California.

Somewhere midway through my project, I began to realize that I was the recipient of extraordinary favors. Whenever I faced a problem or needed help, the heavens seemed to open magically, and important leads or even an entire body of material, like the probate file, would fall straight into my lap. I'd experienced nothing similar in the writing of thirty previous books. For those, I had been forced to confront the usual obstacles met by historians when they go prowling for sources. I can perhaps be pardoned, therefore, for thinking that the spirits of the McComas couple, wanting their story belatedly told, regularly were intervening on my behalf, to see that I got what I needed. As I made progress in piecing the tale together, something else soon became apparent.

No one at the time understood fully all the circumstances that led to the massacre of Judge McComas and his wife and the kidnapping of their son. Many contemporary people saw a fragment of the picture, but none possessed enough knowledge of surrounding events to form a complete picture. A century later, after swimming in the pool of historical data that I had accumulated, I was able to draw the outline and fill in most of the major details. One day it occurred to me that I was the only person ever to grasp the full dimensions of what had happened to the McComas family. Naturally, when my book appeared, the circumstances would be revealed to all, and old uncertainties laid to rest. But until then, I alone kept the story in my head and shouldered the responsibility for preserving it.

Readers who may be curious about how I was able to assemble enough evidence to allow me to write a lengthy narrative on a subject that long has been mired in obscurity and confusion should consult the endnotes that identify my sources. They reveal that innumerable widely scattered and miscellaneous particles of fact, like random chips from the block of history, were gathered, analyzed, and ordered in the process of reconstructing what happened on the Lordsburg Road.

A central aim was to try to show Hamilton C. McComas and Juniata McComas as flesh-and-blood human beings, as living individuals. In attempting to accomplish that, I included some small details about their lives that, in any other context, probably would have been ignored. Their inclusion here, I think, adds to our understanding of what kind of people they really were. In actual fact, the McComases' personal histories would not have been worth writing had they not died in such a dramatic way. But, given that climactic circumstance, the rather mundane course of their early lives assumes unexpected significance.

One more point ought to be made, by way of a disclaimer. Regrettably, my McComas account, as I have narrated it here, cannot be fine-tuned. There exist too many loose ends that must be left dangling and gaps that have to be filled by surmise. Even so, I was astounded by the quantity of what still could be recovered.

The result, then, is a kind of case study, tracing the white man's version of a single incident in our Indian wars. But it incorporates, where possible, references to the Apaches' side of the story. Their slant, however, is not easily fathomed, for a variety of reasons.

To this day, Apaches claim that history has misrepresented them or at least not related events as they saw them. To some degree, of course, that is true. Since the white man wrote the history books, the contents were his to compose. The Apache, lacking a system of writing, was dependent upon memory for preservation of the tribal past. But human memory is weak and limited, and anyway Apache oral traditions paid no attention to chronology or went much beyond warrior exploits. One aging Apache in the 1930s remarked: "We don't remember our grandparents' time, just as white men don't." Yes, but the whites had their printed sources to consult.

Long afterward, when Apaches were asked about the McComas affair, they responded with what they thought their old enemies wanted to hear. Or they simply doctored the facts to protect themselves and their tribe. The Apache, in his conquered state, became a master of obfuscation. Some high-ranking army officers phrased it more bluntly, saying that he was a liar when it suited him. But at bottom the problem was that both desert-bred Apaches and frontier Americans operated by different sets of rules and viewed the function of history in their own unique ways.

As will be seen, several Indian accounts have been recorded that purport to tell how Judge and Mrs. McComas died and what the Indians did with their child captive, Charley. The reliability of all of these is in doubt, but then so are the written recollections of many whites who, according to Arizona historian Frank C. Lockwood, seldom could get their stories straight enough to correspond with those of other eyewitnesses. All of this simply means that any modern historian dealing with a topic related to the Apaches must tread warily and maintain a persistent skepticism.

With regard to obtaining the Indian perspective, I had another small experience of the mysteriously magical sort that no longer were unexpected. Early on, I had taken note of a ten-year-old Apache boy named Haozous, who as a warrior apprentice had been with Chato's war party that attacked the McComases. Sam Haozous, as he became known, lived until 1957.

One afternoon I was reading in a regional magazine about world-renowned Indian sculptor Allan Houser, whose art studio was located only a mile or so from my own home in the Galisteo Badlands of central New Mexico. Houser, I knew, was a Chiricahua Apache, but the magazine article added an eye-popping detail. His last name had been Anglicized to make it more pronounceable. The original surname had been Haozous, and Allan Houser was the son of Sam Haozous!

I wasted no time in arranging an interview with Mr. Houser. He candidly recalled his father's reminiscences of the 1883 raid and remarked how the McComas episode had left its mark on his people. Hearing an Apache speak of that long-ago event made it seem close and very real. A few short months after my talk with him, Allan Houser died at age eighty.

Many well-publicized chapters in the history of the American West have been told and retold so often that, through over-familiarity, they have lost their punch. The McComas saga, however, has a freshness and special poignancy about it, reminding us that there is still much frontier history which we are only now beginning to discover.

One word of explanation about my spelling preferences. For the spelling of three names, the historical record is inconsistent. In personal letters, the judge wrote his son's name as Charley, and I have followed his lead even though other family members and newspapers more often spelled it Charlie. Apache war leader Chato is sometimes rendered as Chatto, and his lieutenant Bonito as Benito. In both cases, I have chosen to use the first spelling.

In addition to those persons whose help I already have acknowledged, I wish to express my thanks for the assistance of the following: the late Dan L. Thrapp and Gregory Franzwa, both of Tucson; Lynda Sánchez, Lincoln, New Mexico; Shirley Hurd, who combed archives and photographed the McComas grave marker in Fort Scott, Kansas; Susan Berry of the Silver City Museum; Professor Dale Giese of Western New Mexico University, Silver City; Albert Ward and Dr. Jack Zipper of Albuquerque; Susie Henderson, Cerrillos, New Mexico; and the Allan Houser family. I owe a special debt of gratitude to Rebecca Bustamante for assistance in preparing the final manuscript and added thanks to John P. Wilson of Las Cruces.

Marc Simmons
Cerrillos, N.M.
May 15, 1995

MASSACRE
on the
Lordsburg Road

Chapter One

A Proper Beginning

The family of Hamilton C. McComas was one to be reckoned with in that part of Virginia that lay beyond the Blue Ridge Mountains. The earliest McComases are believed to have descended from Pennsylvania and Maryland in one of the successive waves of Scotch-Irish frontiersmen and settlers that flowed southwestward through the great Valley of Virginia during the initial half of the eighteenth century.[1]

These first comers are remembered as tall, robust, uncouth, restless folk, something in the nature of country bumpkins. The stylish, rich plantation owners in the Tidewater to the east regarded them with disdain, even while acknowledging that they were enterprising and pious, most being staunch Presbyterians. These settlers were natural-born fighters, too, as skilled in handling a long rifle as they were in using an ax. Easily and quickly, they displaced the Indians who had first claim on the land.

Within a few short generations, as the wilderness receded westward and disappeared, at least some offspring of the old frontier folk lost their rough edges, absorbed formal learning, and even began to play major roles in professional and state affairs. The McComases were among those select families of western Virginia who emerged as leaders in the political, judicial, and military spheres.

Elisha McComas, grandfather of Hamilton, is listed as a pioneer of Cabell County, Virginia. Beginning as a farmer, he afterwards, in what proved to be a long, vigorous, and productive life, had a varied career in public service. As a member of the Virginia Assembly, he is reported to have served thirteen terms in the House of Delegates, during the years after 1809. He also is credited with serving as a Gentleman Justice on Cabell County's first court, perhaps thereby setting a precedent for numbers of his descendants who would be attracted to the legal profession.

Military life, too, engaged Elisha McComas, who enrolled in the Virginia Militia. During the War of 1812, he held the rank of colonel in the 120th Regiment, a unit that sent detachments to aid in the defense of Fort Meigs, Ohio, and to fight British invaders along the Atlantic seaboard. By 1822, he had been commissioned a brigadier general, with the result that, even after retirement, he always was addressed respectfully as General McComas.[2]

Elisha married Annie French, and they raised seven children. Among the siblings, the two oldest sons, William (father of Hamilton) and David, achieved the greatest prominence. David McComas won fame as a brilliant jurist, was active in the Whig Party, and sat for five sessions in the Virginia State Senate, beginning in 1830. On March 28, 1831, he delivered an impassioned speech before that body, upholding the right of South Carolina to secede from the Union. Thirty years later, just prior to the outbreak of the Civil War, his speech was published and circulated widely. In the last decades of his life, he presided as a judge of the General Court of the State of Virginia and, in addition, served on the Eighteenth Circuit Court.

William, the eldest son of Elisha and Annie McComas, was born in 1793, two years before his brother David. He received his education in private schools and at Emory and Henry College, subsequently becoming both a practicing attorney and an ordained Methodist minister. (Many of the Scotch-Irish Presbyterians converted to the Methodist and Baptist denominations after emigrating to Virginia.) William, like his brother, won a seat in the Virginia State Senate (1830–33). He went on to be elected under the Whig banner as representative in Washington to the 23rd Congress and the 24th Congress. From humble beginnings, the McComases had advanced within two generations to become people of substance and reputation—members of that peculiarly American class of citizens who were the boomers, movers, and achievers of the nineteenth century.[3]

During the War of 1812, on February 24 of that year, William McComas took as his wife Mildred Ward, whose grandfather had been a soldier in the American Revolution and whose father was a colonel of the Virginia Militia. The couple started their family young, William being only nineteen at the time of his marriage, and over the next thirty years, they produced eleven children. The last, a daughter named Irene, was born in 1843, just ten years before her mother's death. In the union of McComas and Ward, two sturdy bloodlines intermingled and furnished the developing nation what it needed most: industrious and worthy men and women who were filled with civic pride.

The eighth child of this marriage, and the fourth son, was christened Hamilton Calhoun McComas. The boy was born in Parkersburg, Virginia, on November 9, 1831. It is a reasonable guess that his first name commemorated Alexander Hamilton, secretary of the treasury of the United States, and his middle name John C. Calhoun, the South Carolina statesman who then was serving as the nation's vice president. That supposition is supported by the fact that an older brother, James Madison, and a younger one, Benjamin Jefferson, also bore the names of American patriots.[4]

We know that "Ham" was a nickname by which the family addressed Hamilton Calhoun as a boy. In later life, his closest associates seem to have called him by his first two initials, and that too may have been a custom that started when he was young. The few personal letters that remain from his hand, even those sent to his own children, invariably are signed "H. C. McComas."

About his boyhood and education, relatively little is known. It was claimed later that he had displayed an interest in the law at a youthful age, which is not surprising given the fact that so many of his kin were affiliated with the legal system. Since his father had gone to college and it is recorded that an older brother, Elisha Wesley McComas, went to Ohio for his education, we must suppose that H. C., too, was given a fair measure of formal schooling.[5] If so, it was interrupted at age seventeen when he enlisted in the army during the Mexican War.

Some months elapsed after the outbreak of the conflict, but a call for troops finally reached Virginia. H. C.'s twenty-five-year-old brother, Elisha, took the lead in raising a company from Cabell County, which was mustered into the United States service on February 23, 1847, at Newport Barracks.[6] Elisha, with the rank of captain, commanded the unit, while his younger brother, William Wirt, was first lieutenant. In the ranks were two more siblings, James Madison and Hamilton Calhoun. When their Company C of the Eleventh U.S. Infantry departed for New Orleans to join the main army, the McComases, with four names on the official roster, were well represented.[7]

New Orleans served as one of the principal ports of embarkation for the Mexican theater, and there the Eleventh Infantry became part of the Veracruz Expedition led by Gen. Winfield Scott. What followed was the naval invasion of Mexico's Gulf coast and the march of Scott's army overland, ultimately to conquer Mexico City. The young men of the McComas clan, as near as we can determine, were in the thick of the fighting. One of them, Capt. Elisha Wesley, was wounded and even held briefly as a prisoner of war.[8] If H. C. or any of his brothers kept a diary or wrote newsy letters home telling of their wartime experiences, these regrettably have not come to light.

By all reports, Company C of the Eleventh Infantry returned home to Cabell County, Virginia, to a heroes' welcome. Assuming that there were the customary downtown parade and patriotic speeches, the McComas brothers, looking toward professional careers and public service in politics, could not but have benefited from having briefly donned the mantles of soldier-celebrities.

It was about this time—that is, the late 1840s—that H. C. entered into serious study of the law. Since both his father, William, and his uncle David were lawyers, he would have gotten plenty of guidance in his reading, which ought to have included such standard works as the Virginia *Statutes*, James Kent's *Commentaries on the American Law,* and Sir William Blackstone's old standby, *Commentaries on the Law of England.* The aspiring young man evidently applied himself to the task with commendable industry, for by 1852 he had been admitted to the bar, at the young age of twenty-one.[9]

Soon afterward, he left family and home to strike out on his own. Novice attorney Hamilton Calhoun McComas migrated to the Midwest, settling in small-town Illinois. The move in part can be ascribed, perhaps, to plain Scotch-Irish restlessness, for it was the first of several major relocations that H. C. would undertake in the course of his life, the last being the fatal one to the New Mexico Territory. But for his first independent plunge into the world, why he chose Illinois and who might have influenced him in making that decision are questions that cannot now be answered.

For his principal place of residence, he fixed upon the town of Monticello, the seat of Piatt County in east central Illinois. From what we know, it was a quiet, steady-going, rural community with the ordinary thoroughfares and commonplace cross streets lined with typical midwestern residences, some grand and some modest. At its center stood a plain two-story courthouse surmounted by a domed cupola. The lawns on the courthouse square during election time attracted "stump speakers," or candidates for political office who alternately charmed and infuriated large crowds with their oratory.

On July 30, 1858, attorney Abraham Lincoln from nearby Springfield came to town in his campaign to unseat Illinois Democrat Stephen A. Douglas in the U.S. Senate. When Lincoln arrived at the square by carriage from the train station, onlookers noted that his face appeared gaunt and haggard. Nevertheless, he descended from the conveyance "with a kind of hop, skip, and a jump," then mounted the open platform under the trees and spoke with force and dignity for half an hour.[10]

Was H. C. McComas among the throng that greeted the future president on that sunny summer day? According to a McComas family tradition, he had a brief formal association with Abe in the legal profession, but the claim has not been verified.[11] Lincoln's circuit practice, which brought him to all the state and federal courts in central Illinois, involved a variety of litigation, from debt collection and land titles to railroad suits and an occasional murder case. As an attorney practicing within the Lincoln orbit, H. C. would have had plenty of opportunity to cross paths with him and develop at least a passing acquaintance.

For an ambitious and energetic young lawyer seeking to rise and make his mark in the world, H. C.'s selection of Monticello as a place to launch his career seems oddly off target. Although it was a county seat, the place otherwise was outside the mainstream, having a population of less than one thousand and catering mainly to surrounding farmers who formed the backbone of the regional economy.

It may be that he viewed it as a town of promise and anticipated that, as it grew, he could hang onto the municipal coattails and prosper as well. The New York newspaper editor, Horace Greeley, traveling through Illinois at mid-century, had found the state on the move. "There are new blocks in her cities," he wrote, "new dwellings in every village, new breakings on this or that edge of almost every prairie."[12] That go-ahead spirit and headlong rush for development would have appealed to McComas, as he contemplated his future.

In any case, by 1856, if not before, H. C. had formed a law partnership with one T. Milligan. The firm advertised its legal services in the professional directory appearing in the weekly *Monticello Times*.[13] Using such advertising was a custom H. C. followed, through a succession of partners, right up to his fatal encounter with the Apaches in 1883. At the time of his death, a notice for the firm of McComas & Wright was running in the *Silver City Enterprise*.

In late 1857 or early 1858, H. C.'s elder brother, Elisha Wesley, followed him to Illinois but settled in Chicago rather than rural Monticello. Two years earlier, Elisha W. McComas had been elected lieutenant-governor of Virginia on the Democratic ticket that brought Henry A. Wise to the office of governor. Wise, known as "a true gentleman, a man of the world, and something of a scholar," also was a brilliant orator who reserved his sharpest barbs for northern abolitionists.[14]

Whatever amity originally had existed between the governor and lieutenant-governor seems to have dissolved by early 1857, when Elisha W. McComas resigned from office. Publicly, he gave as the reasons ill health and a desire to seek a better climate in the West. But close friends said that the resignation was prompted by a severe disagreement with Governor Wise over the conduct of the firebrand abolitionist, John Brown, who recently had slain five proslavery men in Kansas, in an incident known as the Pottawatomie Massacre. That very well could have been the case, for the McComases were known for taking strong stands, and, as in this instance, even sacrificing careers, on principle.[15]

So, Elisha Wesley packed his valise, bid farewell to family, and took the train for Illinois. In Chicago, he established a law practice and quickly became known as a leader of the bar. It was his role in the Jumpertz case that gave him a reputation far beyond the state boundaries. A man by that name, it seems, was charged with murdering a certain Sophia Werner and chopping her into small pieces, which he packed into a trunk and shipped by express. In a trial that made national headlines, McComas successfully defended Mr. Jumpertz and won his release.[16]

In some manner, Elisha Wesley made the acquaintance of Chicago industrialist Cyrus H. McCormick, inventor of the automatic reaper. In 1860, McCormick purchased and combined the city's two largest newspapers, the *Herald* and the *Times.* In announcing the new paper, he declared its motto to be "Principles, not men!" And he named as the first editor "ex-governor" E. W. McComas, who also was identified as a former Virginia journalist. (Until his death, McComas always was addressed by the respectful title of governor, even though he served only as lieutenant-governor.) The *Chicago Times and Herald* became an exponent of Southern Democracy and a defender of States' Rights, positions squarely in line with Elisha Wesley's beliefs and background. He also was in accord with McCormick's moral declaration: "Nothing will be allowed in these columns that will cause a blush to the most rigidly pure."[17]

McComas and his wife, Arianna Holderby (she too was a native of Cabell County, Virginia, and they were married in 1843), moved in Chicago's loftiest social circles. Even in the days of his editorship, he maintained his private law practice; between the two roles, he was able to meet nearly everyone of importance. Illinois Sen. Stephen A. Douglas was considered an intimate friend, and when Douglas died in 1861, Elisha Wesley wrote and published a tribute generally acknowledged to be the most beautiful and widely read. Shortly afterward, he was selected to deliver Chicago's official address of welcome to England's Prince of Wales on his visit to the city, during a tour of the country.[18]

This extended reference to the career of H. C. McComas's older brother is given here for two reasons. First, it reaffirms the statement made earlier about the prominence of the McComas name, a fact which guaranteed that H. C.'s gory death in 1883 would make headlines across America. And second, among the brothers, Elisha Wesley appears to have been closest to H. C. At least, their later careers by design intersected, first in Illinois and later in Fort Scott, Kansas.

On June 1, 1859, at age twenty-seven, H. C. McComas finally married. Virtually nothing is known of the circumstances or background of his wife, Louisa K. Pratt, except that she was a twenty-year-old native of Pickaway, Ohio, and came from a good family. Within a year, she bore their first son, David, probably named for H. C.'s outspoken uncle back in Virginia. Their second son, born in 1862, took the name of H. C.'s father, William.[19] A quarter-century later, McComas was on the way to meet his eldest son in New Mexico's Pyramid Mountains when Chato's Apaches ended his life.

It is not unreasonable to assume that outwardly the McComases presented the appearance of being an idyllic couple. From a well-connected family, he was tall, dignified, and professionally successful. Although direct evidence is lacking, it seems a safe bet that she was attractive and intelligent, the model helpmate for a bright young lawyer on his way up. However, given what was to follow—an indiscretion on the part of Louisa McComas that resulted in termination of their marriage—one would have to conclude that, under the domestic surface, things were not as placid as they appeared. The dissolution of the marriage, when it came, proved to be simply one more casualty of the Civil War.

Those McComases still in Virginia were the first ones to feel the chilling effects of the coming storm. As noted, in 1831 David McComas had delivered a ringing speech before the State Senate defending the right of South Carolina to secede from the Union. Now, in early 1861, with the country on the point of breaking up over sectionalism and slavery, Virginia Secessionists dusted off the old McComas speech, republished it, and gave it wide circulation.[20]

When the Virginia legislature authorized the calling of a secession convention, to meet at Richmond on February 13, David McComas was selected as a delegate, as was his brother William (H. C.'s father). At the opening session, William won appointment to the convention's Committee on Federal Relations, where the crucial decisions were made. He was one of only four men from western Virginia named to the committee, as Unionist sentiment remained strong in that region of the state. In fact, William broke with his brother and voted against the secession ordinance, which led Virginia out of the Union and into the Confederacy.[21]

The McComases, like so many other families of the day, were divided in their loyalties and sentiments. Thus, when war broke out, brother opposed brother, and fathers saw sons defect to the opposing side. William McComas watched as two sons joined the Confederate Army. Youngest son Benjamin Jefferson served under Jubal Early, was captured at Cedar Creek, and sat out the rest of the war in a Yankee prison camp. Another son, William Wirt, who was a practicing physician, raised a company of Virginia volunteers to fight for the South and was killed in action at South Mills in 1862.[22]

Economic and political friction long had existed between residents of eastern and western Virginia. Under the stresses of the Civil War, the differences became intolerable, owing particularly to the pro-Union stance of many westerners. In 1863, the latter broke away, formed the new entity of West Virginia, and secured admission to the United States as the thirty-fifth state. The McComases' Cabell County ended up just inside the boundary of West Virginia— that is, it rested directly on the border between warring North and South.

Although he was far away in Illinois, H. C. McComas did not remain untouched by these events. He maintained close contact with the family, including, one may assume, occasional return visits to Cabell County. Then, on September 4, 1862, more than a year after the outbreak of war, H. C. took up arms in defense of the Union. He was the only member of his immediate family to do so. He joined a newly formed regiment, the 107th Illinois Infantry, called into being by the state governor.[23]

This unit, composed of four companies from McComas's own Piatt County and six additional companies from neighboring De Witt County, was mustered in at Camp Butler, outside the state capital, Springfield. It was then the custom for volunteer soldiers to select their own officers, and H. C. was elected lieutenant colonel of the regiment. As things turned out, his was to be a very short period of service.

The colonel and commander of the regiment, the man who had organized it under a commission from the Illinois governor, was Thomas Snell of De Witt County. Apparently he considered the unit his personal fiefdom and, through the army sutler, began diverting military supplies for his own profit. His misconduct soon was revealed, and he was dismissed from the service. That left Lt. Col. H. C. McComas as acting commander.

Snell, it seems, blamed McComas for his downfall, and very probably McComas indeed was responsible. H. C. was in the best position to discover the regimental commander's wrongdoing and, being a strict moralist and a competent lawyer himself, would have had no hesitation in blowing the whistle. By doing so, however, he made an implacable enemy.

Back to De Witt County went the disgraced Thomas Snell, but not to a quiet retirement. In his embittered state, he launched a private campaign to get his nemesis removed from command of the 107th Infantry. Of Snell, H. C. wrote, "He has (with his potent ability to do mischief) been pursuing me at home . . . with every character of falsehood and misrepresentation that disappointed malignancy can invent."[24] Those strong words confirm the depth of estrangement between the two men.

Specifically, Colonel Snell held public meetings and wrote letters to his former soldiers, attempting to discredit McComas and saying that it was not fitting for De Witt County men to be led by someone who was not their own. In other words, McComas, coming from next-door Piatt County, was a "foreigner." That argument, silly as it was, proved effective in stirring up dissension in the ranks. By now the regiment had been moved south into Kentucky, closer to the war zone; here H. C. began to assess more clearly the strong feelings among the troops and to realize that these feelings were impairing his ability to lead.

H. C.'s superior, the military commander of Kentucky, was Gen. Jeremiah T. Boyle, who was the son of a chief justice of the Kentucky court of appeals. In civilian life, Boyle had been a well-educated attorney.[25] On January 25, 1863, McComas, from his encampment with the regiment at Mumfordsville, Kentucky, sent General Boyle at his headquarters in Louisville a letter of resignation. In it, he summarized his problems with Snell; in concluding, he expressed the belief that, owing to "the malign influences that unfortunately surround this regiment, we are doomed to inefficiency and ultimately, in all probability, to disgrace."[26]

Clearly, H. C. recognized that his promotion to full colonel and permanent commander of the regiment was going to be blocked by Snell's machinations. Of equal weight, as a man with a prickly sense of honor, he wanted no part of a unit that seemed destined to disgrace itself. Here was a McComas again, acting on principle. H. C. felt impelled to resign for the reasons he gave Boyle, but, at the simplest level, his resignation, as he explained to the general, was the best way to settle this whole question. General Boyle must have agreed, for, on the following February 6, he allowed McComas to relinquish his commission and the command of the 107th Illinois Infantry.[27]

In his detailed letter to the general, H. C. had mentioned that, if his resignation were accepted, he intended in the future to reenter military service, but in a different capacity, so that "I can have an equal chance with other officers."[28] When that was written, he no doubt meant what he said. Upon returning home to Monticello, Illinois, however, he soon met with a shock in his domestic life that would alter all his plans drastically.

While he was away in the military service of his country, wife Louisa had developed a romantic liaison with his law partner, Milligan. Since, as the old saying goes, a husband is always the last to know, it is probably fair to assume that the scandalous situation was a common topic of town gossip. The revelation must have staggered the prim and proper H. C. McComas.

Of angry and tearful scenes that may have passed between husband and wife, there is no record. The matter ended when H. C. divorced Louisa, for the stated reason of adultery. Presumably he dissolved his partnership with Milligan at the same time. In nineteenth-century small-town America, such an episode would have been regarded as shameful in the extreme, the more so since the woman was mother of two small children. Undoubtedly it left permanent scars on all persons involved. It is known, for example, that twenty years after the event, Louisa was still using the last name of McComas, indicating that she never had remarried. Perhaps she was unable to live down the indiscretions of her young adulthood.[29]

Inasmuch as husbands in those days were considered ultimately to be responsible for the orderly rule of their households, they often received a large share of the blame for any disruption. That was certainly what happened in H. C.'s case. His parents back in West Virginia took him to task in no uncertain terms. He already had earned their displeasure for joining the Union Army while his brothers were under arms in the South. Now they even found him at fault for Louisa's misconduct. The correct southern thing for him to do would have been to leave his wife and children with them when he marched off to war. But since he had left them unchaperoned in the wicked North, well— this was the result. H. C.'s reaction to the criticism has to be imagined, since none of his personal papers contains a reference to this traumatic affair.[30]

In looking back at the turning points in H. C. McComas's life that led him along an irregular course toward his untimely fate in New Mexico, we cannot help wondering to what degree his divorce eventually contributed to that tragic outcome. The question is unanswerable now. On the other hand, something else dating from his Illinois years very definitely had an influence on his later career in the Southwest. That was his friendship with John Boyle.

The evidence that the two men began an association about the time of the Civil War, if not before, is entirely circumstantial but nevertheless quite compelling. John Boyle was born on his grandparents' farm in Crawford County, Illinois (southeast of McComas's Piatt County), on August 16, 1839, and attended school at Paris, Illinois. At about the age of twenty, after reading law, he was admitted to the bar of the Danville Circuit Court and the Illinois Supreme Court. As a young lawyer practicing in the eastern counties of the state just prior to the Civil War, he would have had abundant opportunity to associate with H. C. McComas. Boyle's ancestors were from Virginia and had migrated to Kentucky, where his grandfather became chief justice of the state. With their shared Virginia background, powerful family connections, and legal vocations, Boyle and McComas would have had much in common.[31]

Shortly before the outbreak of Civil War hostilities, Boyle went down to Kentucky, where he heard the news of the firing on Fort Sumter (April 12, 1861). Immediately he joined the Union movement to keep Kentucky loyal and assisted in the raising of troops. Upon enlistment in the military, he landed in the 11th Brigade of the Army of Ohio, and, along with his uncle, Gen. Jeremiah T. Boyle, he saw action at the bloody battle of Shiloh in early April 1862. The following month, when his one-year enlistment was up, he accepted a commission as a captain in the 9th Regiment of the Kentucky Volunteer Cavalry.

By August, John Boyle held the rank of lieutenant colonel. He was made adjutant general of U.S. Volunteers in Kentucky, becoming the chief administrative officer for the state troops. His rapid rise surely must have been traceable to favoritism shown by his uncle, who was commander of all of Kentucky's military forces. As mentioned above, General Boyle was H. C. McComas's superior and the man to whom he submitted his resignation, ending his brief interlude of service. The correspondence over this matter is the first documentation to appear, so far, linking the McComas and Boyle names. But, as we have seen, probably John Boyle and H. C. had been acquainted for some time prior to the war.[32]

After the collapse and surrender of the Confederacy, John Boyle entered law practice with his uncle Jeremiah, who was just beginning to engage in railroad development and to show interest in the acquisition of western lands. Within a few years, the general was to amass a large personal fortune; in the process, he doubtless served as the primary influence leading his nephew to indulge in mining and land speculation in the far Southwest.[33]

In 1866 John Boyle returned to Paris, Illinois, with a wife he had married at Memphis in 1863, and opened a law office. In 1868 he won a four-year term as state's attorney for the 27th Judicial District. When his tenure was up in 1874, he and his family moved to St. Louis, a city located more favorably for the western business ventures that increasingly absorbed his attention. It was there, a few years later, that he unknowingly would start H. C. McComas on the road leading to his fatal encounter with renegade Apaches.[34]

During the three years following the close of the Civil War, McComas lived quietly in Monticello, practicing law and playing an active role in civic affairs. For example, in late 1866, he was on a committee of three persons selected to decide upon a location for a new county jail. Again, he served on a committee with the aim of buying land for a county poor farm. Those were small matters, but they pointed to something a bit larger: a county judgeship.[35] H. C. seems to have relished both the office and the title that went with it. Although his tenure was less than two years, he proudly used the title "Judge" for the remainder of his life.

It seems likely that, at his divorce, he obtained custody of his two small sons, David and William, and probably engaged a housekeeper to serve as a surrogate mother. It was possibly also during this period that his cousin Charles C. McComas settled in Decatur, twenty-five miles from Monticello. Like so many others of his family, Charles was acknowledged as a distinguished lawyer. In the following decade, he attained the office of Illinois state's attorney (1872–76). Shortly afterward, he moved to the New Mexico Territory; at the time of H. C.'s death, he was practicing law in Albuquerque and holding a seat in the territorial legislature.[36]

❧ In 1868, Hamilton C. McComas closed out his affairs in Monticello and transferred his residence 350 miles southwest to Fort Scott, Kansas, close to the Missouri line. One story claims that the move occurred after H. C. resigned his judgeship over the case of a prisoner tried for murder. The jury had brought in a guilty verdict, and McComas, disagreeing, resigned rather than sign the death warrant.[37] But his leaving also may have had a business motive, since shortly we find him listed as one of the attorneys in the famous Osage Ceded Lands case. About the change, there surely was, too, an element of "starting over," of putting behind him the unpleasant memories of his failed Illinois marriage. As it turned out, Fort Scott would afford him splendid opportunities for beginning a new life and launching another family.

The Osage Ceded Lands case involved a reservation tract of prime country, measuring thirty by fifty miles, that sprawled west of Fort Scott. As an early-day source candidly phrased the situation: "The enjoyment of that property was solemnly guaranteed to the Osage tribe by one of those pie-crust treaties which so often disgraced our government."[38] By sleight of hand, the lands were ceded to the United States in January 1867 and were to be sold to settlers, with the proceeds to be used for the benefit of the Indians. In reality, numerous white squatters already had moved inside the boundaries and were ready to assert claims under the Homestead Act.

A problem arose, however, when the governor of Kansas, citing authority

Judge Hamilton C. McComas. In McComas Family Papers,
courtesy Carolyn Kimme-Smith, Los Angeles, California

given him by the Department of Interior, began granting large sections of the
so-called Ceded Lands to two companies, the Leavenworth, Lawrence &
Galveston Railway and the Missouri, Kansas & Texas Railway, as a bonus for
building railroads in his state. Infuriated settlers and would-be settlers called
mass meetings, organized resistance societies, and pledged to carry the matter
into the courts, on the presumption that only Congress could dispose of Indian lands.[39]

The Settlers Protective Association emerged as the chief body protesting
the railroad grants. Its members decided that they wanted as the group's attorneys no "loud-mouthed pettifoggers" but rather keen-witted and aggressive
lawyers, each a specialist in his own area of the law. Those engaged included

former Gov. Wilson Shannon of Ohio, Judge William Lawrence of Ohio, Jeremiah S. Black of Pennsylvania, John E. McKeighan of Fort Scott, and Hamilton C. McComas, lately of Illinois.[40]

It was said at the time that no case ever tried in the West showed a greater array of real learning and talent than was displayed during the several years this one was in litigation. McComas became one of the chief spokesmen for the association's legal team and in the process earned such plaudits that, ever after, his accomplishments were not mentioned without some reference to his participation in the Osage Ceded Lands case. This was another instance of his electing to swim in a small pond but nevertheless making the most of the opportunities available to win prominence and assume a leadership role.

Fort Scott, where H. C. had chosen to reconstruct his life, was a small, energetic midwestern town struggling to dispel post–Civil War gloom and generate enthusiasm for an anticipated brighter future. The town's name was derived from an adjacent U.S. military post established in 1842. The town site, on the south bank of the Marmaton River, lay nestled in a natural amphitheater formed by a half-circle of green-robed hills, an altogether inviting setting for a community.

While agriculture was the mainstay of Fort Scott's postwar economy, the ambitious town fathers encouraged manufacturing and talked hopefully of seeing their home become the "Pittsburgh of Kansas." McComas, upon his arrival, observed a small but diversified industrial base encompassing mills of several kinds—a sawmill, flour mills, a planing mill, and, soon afterward, the Fort Scott Woolen Mills. There was a city brewery, two foundries, a sickle factory, a nursery company, and the Pioneer Wagon Manufactory, in which owner J. A. Bryant turned out the sturdy and popular "Bryant" wagon. Newspapers, schools, fraternal lodges, and an unusually high number of churches provided the finer embellishments for Fort Scott's civic life.[41]

In short, Fort Scott, although provincial in the extreme, seemed to be a place on the move, where community spirit and the rhetoric of boosterism were joined in a chorus of optimism. Hamilton C. McComas found the atmosphere to his liking, and he began to put down roots. One of his first moves was the establishment of a new law partnership with John E. McKeighan, a fellow attorney in the Osage Ceded Lands Case. Since his previous partner, back in Monticello, had caused him such grief, H. C. must have taken this step with some wariness. Apparently the two men found that they worked well together, however, and over the next decade a durable friendship developed. When McComas's body was returned to Fort Scott in 1883, McKeighan served as one of the pallbearers at his funeral.

Within a year of H. C.'s arrival, the first of several McComas family members followed him to Fort Scott, no doubt drawn by his warm recommendations of the place. Alice McComas Reid, daughter of Elisha Wesley McComas, with her husband, William R. Reid, settled at Fort Scott in 1869. They had married in Chicago and remained there when Elisha Wesley, soon after the end of the war, gave up his newspaper work and returned to West Virginia to care for the affairs of his ailing father, William. After the death of William, Elisha Wesley stayed in the East until 1868, when he took his family to live on farming properties he had acquired in Nebraska, near Omaha.

Soon afterward, Elisha Wesley prevailed upon his daughter Alice and his son-in-law to abandon Chicago and try their hand at farming in the prairie West. Their relocation to Nebraska, however, was not a success. As an early record explained it, "Farm life and the complete isolation of the frontier were not congenial surroundings for Mr. & Mrs. Reid and after a year of hardship, in 1869, they moved to Fort Scott, Kansas."[42] Within a year, Elisha Wesley, for reasons of his own, also concluded that a Nebraska existence was uncongenial; and, probably with the encouragement of his brother H. C., he followed Alice to Fort Scott.

On March 17, 1869, occurred unquestionably the most important event in the middle period of Hamilton C. McComas's life. On that date, in Fort Scott's Congregational Church, he married Juniata Maria Ware. He was thirty-nine years old, she twenty-three. Despite his age, the marriageable ladies of the town sensibly considered him a good catch. "The Judge," as he usually was known, stood six feet and one inch tall, was well proportioned, had a bright and inquisitive eye, and carried himself like a gentleman. A photographic portrait taken in his Fort Scott years, probably soon after his wedding, shows a wide sensitive mouth and a neatly barbered chin-beard. It is plausible to assume that the female population of Fort Scott regarded McComas as a handsome man. In addition, he had an attractive personality. Those acquainted with him described H. C. as warm-hearted and a staunch and faithful friend. Mining man Oscar W. Williams, who worked with him later in New Mexico, said that he was "active and enterprising in spirit, suave and genial in manners."[43] The *Fort Scott Evening Herald,* receiving word of his death in an Indian raid, eulogized McComas as "a companionable gentleman, full of native wit and good humor, rarely if ever giving a token of anger."[44] In sum, those who knew Hamilton C. McComas personally thought well of him. As the *Evening Herald* put it, "He was deservedly popular."

So Juniata M. Ware landed Judge McComas. Unknowingly, at the same time she placed herself on a path leading to a terrible and premature death on a dusty road in far-away New Mexico. But on the happy day of her marriage, there was no foreshadowing of that. Rather, as the new wife of a prominent jurist, she would have been looking forward to running a household and living an altogether pleasant, proper, and uneventful life.

Hiram B. Ware, Juniata's father, came from old Puritan stock and was raised at New Portland, Maine. At age fourteen, he went to sea on a whaler, shipping out of Nantucket and spending the next five years sailing the Pacific as far as China. Men later remembered him as a boy of dauntless spirit and remarkable courage.[45]

Hiram returned to the United States to marry Amanda Melvina Holbrook of Columbia Green, Connecticut, in 1840. The couple settled in nearby Hartford, where he opened a harness and saddlery business. A year later their first child, Eugene Fitch Ware, was born; his middle name was given him in honor

Juniata McComas. A Fort Scott photograph from the early 1870s.
Courtesy Silver City Museum, Silver City, New Mexico

of the famous American inventor, John Fitch, whom Hiram greatly admired.[46] Eugene would grow up to become the poet laureate of Kansas, a state senator, and a U.S. Pension Commissioner in Washington. He also would play a key role in the attempt to rescue his nephew Charley McComas from Apache captivity.

While Eugene was still of school age, his parents decided to seek their fortune in the West. Traveling by stagecoach and steamboat, the family emigrated to Burlington, Iowa, where Hiram resumed his former trade of harness maker. In that place were born two more sons, Charles L. (usually called Charley) and Robert, along with a single daughter, Juniata, whose birthday was March 4, 1846.[47] (Thus, in the month of March, she was born, married, and died.)

Eugene F. Ware, coming from a strong abolitionist family, joined the Union Army at the outbreak of the Civil War. He was still in his teens. After serving in a pair of short-lived volunteer units, he was enrolled in first the 4th and then the 7th Iowa Cavalry, rising to the rank of captain in the latter regiment. Late in the war, he saw duty on the Great Plains, where he and fellow troopers were charged with keeping the overland trails open and free of Indian raids. From that experience came the best known of his several books, *The Indian War of 1864*. He was mustered out of the army in 1866.[48]

Immediately Eugene returned home and took a strenuous newspaper job on the *Burlington Hawk Eye*. Having contracted malaria during military service, however, his health deteriorated alarmingly. A local physician dosed him successively with quinine, arsenic, and strychnine, none of which seemed to effect improvement. The doctor then urged the gaunt and weakened young man to move farther west and live in the open air, in hopes that the change would provide a healthful tonic. Ware bade good-bye to his family and hitched a ride on a pioneer wagon headed for southeastern Kansas. Unknown to him, his choice of destination was to play a crucial role in the ultimate fate of his dear sister Juniata.[49]

Young Ware rode south of Fort Scott into the future Cherokee County, an area just being opened for settlement. His first act was to stake a claim at the head of Deer Creek and break to the plow twenty acres of prairie. Obviously his health had taken a turn for the better. Later he filed on a full section of land closer to Fort Scott, which he called the "Sun Gold Section." Having done that, he returned to Iowa, spoke glowingly of his newfound home, and easily persuaded his entire family to relocate in Kansas.

The father, Hiram Ware, started still another harness shop, this one in Fort Scott. But after five years, he began moving out to the Sun Gold Section to farm during the crop season, returning only to spend the slow winter months in the comfort of town.[50] In these seemingly mundane shiftings about of the Ware family, one can perceive, in hindsight, a dark and deadly thread weaving its way undetected through the web of their lives. At the time, however, no-one saw any portent of tragedy in the rather simple fact that Hamilton C. McComas of Illinois established his new residence in Fort Scott at about the same time that the likable Wares arrived from Iowa.

Juniata Ware seems to have slipped naturally into the unhurried pace of life in Fort Scott. "A bright girl, always well informed, a great reader"—so one early-day writer characterized her.[51] All of the Wares leaned toward reading. Her brother Eugene built a large personal collection of books and late in life provided for the founding of the Fort Scott Library. At the time of Juniata's murder in New Mexico, her Silver City home was liberally stocked with books, including volumes of history, philosophy, religion, essays, and especially po-etry.[52] Quite likely she had the quiet, serious air of a bookish person.

And something else. She was possessed of a strict piety. It was said of her mother Amanda that she was "a typical frail, devout New England Congrega-tionalist"; the father, Hiram, was no less a devoted member of the same church.[53] At age sixteen, Juniata was formally united with Dr. Salter's Congregational-ist Church in Burlington, Iowa. After moving with her parents to Kansas, she helped to form the First Congregationalist Church of Fort Scott and remained a stalwart and active member until 1876, when the McComases moved to St. Louis. In that city, she united with Dr. C. L. Goodell's church, upon present-ing a letter from her Ft. Scott minister. Her name was still "standing" there at the time of her death.[54]

Religion was the preoccupation of many nineteenth-century women, just as politics was of many men. So Juniata Ware McComas's intense church-going cannot be considered all that unusual. In fact, the church offered re-spectable middle-class females one of the few creative outlets available to them. Foreign visitors often remarked upon the prudery of the average American woman, and it is true that too much time spent at the foot of a pulpit listening to Puritan thunderings easily could induce priggishness and a sanctimonious attitude. But there is nothing in the historical record to cause us to judge Juniata a prude. What little is known of her personality, rather, suggests that she was merely proper, a little formal, and probably endowed with some mea-sure of traditional New England reserve.

Of her physical appearance, the best evidence comes from a photograph taken at Fort Scott, sometime in the early 1870s. She is clad in a dark dress ornamented with a lacy white jabot, like a bib, and an ivory cameo at her throat. On her head, almost covering the dark curls, is a small brimmed hat with tucking. The eyes are wide and light, the mouth straight and unsmiling, and the ear prominent. She gives every indication of being a woman of purpose, determination, and even courage. Juniata McComas was slight and petite, wearing a dress about size eight, according to her great-granddaughter, who inherited one of her garments.[55] Their differences in height must have made a notable impression—the tall, rangy Judge McComas and the small, demure Juniata.

We know that, in Silver City, Juniata McComas generally went by the nickname of Jennie, so it is reasonable to suppose she had been called that all along, perhaps even since childhood.[56] Jennie has something of a playful ring to it, supporting the conclusion that its bearer was not a dour or humorless individual. Whatever her personal traits, H. C. McComas would have found them attractive. He wished no more marital disasters such as he had experienced in Monticello.

Precisely how H. C. met his intended bride remains unexplained. But a credible surmise is that the introduction came through her brother, Eugene Fitch Ware. His homesteading and the attendant farm work had completely restored his health, and this allowed him to contemplate making a larger mark on the world. He bought a copy of the Kansas *Statutes* (edition of 1868) and began reading it by the window of his cabin.

Upon assisting some of his neighbors with their legal problems, Ware decided that he needed to expand his studies. He drove to nearby Fort Scott, approached a friendly attorney, and upon his recommendation purchased, for six dollars, *Walker's American Law.* He read that, followed by *Kent's Commentaries* and other works. When he thought he had acquired enough knowledge of the law, his friend the attorney, who had been lending him books, arranged for the setting up of a committee of examination, which spent an afternoon quizzing him. The committee report was favorable, and he was admitted to the bar of Fort Scott.[57]

Shortly afterward, in 1871, Eugene joined the firm of McComas and McKeighan as a salaried law clerk. That fact suggests that the unnamed "friendly attorney" who had been serving as his mentor for some time was none other than his brother-in-law of two years, H. C. McComas. Did their early association lead to H. C.'s initial meeting with the sister, Juniata? We do not know. In any event, Eugene came into the firm in the midst of the Osage Ceded Lands case, gained valuable practical experience, and later, after his brother Charles also passed the bar, opened his own office, Ware and Ware.[58]

Following their wedding, H. C. and Juniata set up housekeeping in Fort

Scott. The McComas sons, David and William, lived with the couple, as did a black servant, Roxey Scott, who was in her twenties. The boys remained quite close to their father up to the time of his death. At some point, according to a much later family recollection, the pair attended a Jesuit academy, where they received a sound education. As H. C.'s second family began to expand, he may have found it convenient to ship the offspring of his first marriage away to boarding school.[59]

On New Year's Day, 1870, Juniata gave H. C. a new son, Frederick. No mention of the child has come to light in any account of the McComas family, probably because he lived for such a short time. He died the following August 27 and was interred in Fort Scott's Evergreen Cemetery, where his parents were laid to rest thirteen years later. The cemetery's burial ledger and the 1870 census provide the only record of little Frederick's brief existence.[60] The sorrow experienced by the McComases on this occasion can only be imagined.

As Christmas Day of that year rolled around, however, a second child was born, a daughter, Ada. Three years later, in May 1873, Juniata bore another daughter, named Mary. H. C. was delighted and, to judge by all available evidence, treated the children with warmth and affection. Then, when he was forty-five years old, in November 1876, the last of his progeny, Charles Ware McComas, came into the world. Named for Juniata's younger brother, little Charley soon was described by a family acquaintance as "a rosy-cheeked boy who became the idol of his father."[61] Owing perhaps to the painful memory of the lost Frederick, as well as the angelic look of young Charles, both parents unashamedly doted upon their new son. Ada and Mary were devoted to him, too.

In the years when his family was growing, H. C. McComas became active in politics. During the first half of the 1870s, he allowed his name twice to be placed on the Democratic ticket for associate justice of the Kansas supreme court. He lost on both occasions, mainly, it was claimed, because of his party affiliation.[62] Had he run as a Republican, Kansas then being virtually a one-party state, he would have been a shoo-in. If he had reached the court, it is doubtful that he ever would have gone to New Mexico.

In 1876, shortly before Charley's birth, the partners McComas and McKeighan moved their law firm and their families to St. Louis. Not a clue can be found as to why this major upheaval was undertaken. One can assume that the relocation was for business purposes, but perhaps H. C.'s disappointment over his failure in politics also had something to do with it. Or there may have been some entirely different reason, of which we have no inkling. In any case, the move brought the McComases one step closer to their eventual meeting with an Indian war party.

❧ Chapter Two ❧

Apaches

The intricate web of circumstances in their early backgrounds that led the members of the McComas family to be traveling on the Lordsburg Road that fateful day in 1883 furnishes only half of the equation necessary to explain the tragic events that befell them. The other half of the story, required for full comprehension, must be pulled from a close examination of Apache history and culture. For the Apaches, traveling the same road as the McComases and primed for murder, did not appear suddenly out of a vacuum. While their encounter with the white family in a buckboard was purely accidental, what brought them to that convergence and what they did to Hamilton, Juniata, and Charley McComas must be interpreted in terms of the Apaches' recent historical experience and their own cultural code of conduct.

It is a truism of American history that few white men ever really understood the workings of the Indian mind or the motivations behind Indian behavior. By the same token, Indians equally were unable to figure out and deal with the new rulers of their lands. From such mutual misunderstanding sprang the litany of sorrowful episodes that so bloodied the annals of frontier expansion.

There exists an unfortunate tendency today to engage in sentimental reflection and selective indignation, imagining that the noble Indian was living peacefully in his small Garden of Eden when bumped from paradise by acquisitive and immoral intruders with pale faces. The truth of the matter is that native life was hard, brutish, and dangerous in the extreme and that, more often than not, war was the centerpiece of tribal life. In the matter of savagery, there is enough guilt for all sides to have their full share.

In the history of the American Southwest, the Apache people occupy a special place. In part, that can be traced to a succession of spectacular leaders who fought their way into the historical record—men like Cochise, Geronimo, Juh, Mangas Coloradas, Nana, Victorio, and perhaps even the lesser figure, Chato, who was responsible for the deaths of the McComases. Several of these leaders were still active in the 1880s, when some Apaches remained as the nation's last native holdouts against subjugation by the U.S. Army. That bringing up the rear in the business of surrender has lent to the name *Apache* a further glint of glamour.

Just how and when the Apaches entered the Southwest is even now a subject of speculation, although it can be said with fair certainty that they came from the north and are distantly related to Athabascan-speaking peoples of western Canada. Most scholars now hold that their arrival in the desert country occurred possibly no earlier than a hundred years or so before the coming of the Spaniards in the sixteenth century. Popular belief has long held that the word *Apache* derived from a Zuni Pueblo term meaning "enemy."

Originally, two divisions of the Apacheans, the Lipan and the Kiowa Apache, dwelled on the Southern Plains and followed the buffalo-hunting way of life. On their sunset flank roamed the Mescaleros and Jicarillas of eastern New Mexico, the latter engaging in marginal farming to supplement hunting and raiding. To the west of the Rio Grande reigned the incomparable Chiricahuas, their range stretching through the desert sierras of southwestern New Mexico, southeastern Arizona, and the upper reaches of the Mexican provinces of Chihuahua and Sonora. Beyond the Chiricahuas, to the north-west, could be found the Western Apaches, divided into five major groups.

During the more than three centuries of the colonial era, all of the Apache divisions caused problems for the Spaniards, although some were more trouble-some than others. In the latter category were the fearsome Mescalero and the equally terrifying Chiricahua of southwestern New Mexico, whom Spanish chroniclers were in the habit of calling Gileños, because their camps were concentrated along the upper Gila River. For generations, these Indians rav-aged Hispanic settlements and herds with impunity.

As a result of that prolonged period of conflict, anthropologists now say that an Apache raiding complex crystallized to become a fixed and ever-expanding aspect of the native economy.[1] Initially Apacheans had survived by hunting, gathering, and occasionally farming. But when they discovered in the seventeenth century that herds of cattle, horses, and sheep were easy to steal from the Spaniards and the settled Pueblo Indians, they began to turn more toward raiding, while their traditional subsistence activities declined in importance. In time the raid emerged as a legitimate tribal industry, one that involved ritual and the training of youth for its proper fulfillment.[2]

By the 1860s, Apaches west of the Rio Grande were living largely by theft, hitting American caravans and Mexican mule pack trains. As an Indian informant related, years after the fact: "One party after another went out. They went on raids because they were in need. Whoever is in want of food and necessities goes."[3] According to Jason Betzinez, a cousin of Geronimo, "Our warriors were not satisfied to live in peace. They were always planning new raids."[4] That activity not only furnished booty, but also allowed warriors to gain status and indulge a deep-seated thirst for war. Some of the men, during their last free years, were said to have become obsessed with raiding.

This doleful practice, such an integral part of the Apache life-way, was the source of much of the woe that ultimately befell the tribe. But other cultural traits, or habits, also contributed. One of these was their reliance upon the so-called "revenge factor." All Apaches felt a strong obligation to respond with fierce reprisals for all injuries, real and imagined.

James Kaywaykla, a Chiricahua who lived through the final wars with the white man, told an interviewer in the 1950s that "it was our obligation to retaliate for the wrongs inflicted upon us" and that the Apaches were "taught that revenge is obligatory."[5] One of his fellow aging warriors, Asa Daklugie, phrased it even more succinctly: "Revenge was part of our philosophy."[6] When Apache raids sometimes resulted in the loss of warriors or even leaders, the surviving families would call for the launching of revenge parties. And the same call was heard when victims of Apache attacks retaliated by destroying their camps. Simply put, perpetual raiding and revenge-taking meant that tribal life was most precarious, and the odds were good that any given Apache man, woman, or child would come to a violent end at the hands of one of a host of enemies.

A corollary to the seeking of vengeance was the principle, recognized under Apache law, that, when another member of a tribe offended or a Mexican or American did so, then all persons of that group were held responsible and could be indiscriminately harmed or killed. After the peerless Chiricahua leader Cochise had a serious altercation with a bungling Lt. George N. Bascom at Arizona's Apache Pass in 1861, he wreaked horrible vengeance upon the first innocent Americans who happened to fall into his clutches.

Assigning collective guilt was almost a universal practice among Indians—and, for that matter, among non-Indians as well. American settlers new to the frontier tended to lump all Indians together and to look upon every one of them as a potential threat. Military officers who had gained some experience in border warfare usually knew enough to single out the tribe responsible for specific crimes, but normally they were unsuccessful in going beyond that to identify and arrest particular tribal members. Holding all members of a group accountable for the actions of a few became standard practice. It was an easy, if unfair, rule of thumb, and everybody resorted to it.

The bitterest enmity of all existed between Apaches and Mexicans. Each group had a long list of grievances against the other that had accumulated over centuries, and the list fueled the spirit of revenge. Apache losses in the prolonged feud are unknown, except as they were reflected in the steadily shrinking numbers of the tribal population. A former warrior, when well along in years, told historian Eve Ball that he had seen hundreds of people killed. But he added reflectively, "We did not have the mania for statistics that White Eyes do, and did not count the dead."[7]

With the counting of Mexican casualties, we are on a bit firmer ground, but not by much. Early reports of these vary widely, yet here again precision is seldom attainable. Scholars, for example, have pieced together fragmentary sources and from them concluded that about four thousand Spanish settlers were killed by the Apaches between 1748 and 1770.[8] Figures given thereafter were erratic and subject to exaggeration. Nevertheless, since losses consistently were tabulated in the thousands, the actual number, whatever it may have been, has to be regarded as truly staggering. Toward the end, Gen. George Crook estimated a rough total of one thousand deaths caused by the Apaches in Mexico and the United States between 1872 and early 1883. The figure was mentioned in his report to the U.S. secretary of the interior, which was dated March 26, 1883—that is, just two days before the slaughter of Judge and Mrs. McComas.[9]

At some point, the long-suffering Mexicans declared no-holds-barred war against all Apachedom. For them the whole matter was reduced to a simple formula: kill or be killed. The hundreds of ranches, hamlets, and towns which had been ravished and lay deserted across northern Chihuahua and Sonora furnished abundant proof that Indian war was merciless. That led governors of those two states, in the latter half of the 1830s, to take the extreme measure of offering bounties for Apache scalps—one hundred pesos for a warrior's hair, fifty pesos for a woman's, and twenty-five pesos for a child's. Those were silver pesos, then equivalent to an American dollar.[10]

The shady craft of bounty hunting attracted all sorts of undesirable elements and promoted especially vicious and treacherous behavior. Traps and ambushes, for instance, were commonplace. Jason Betzinez relates that, about the year 1850, a large part of his own Warm Springs band of eastern Chiricahuas was lured into a Mexican town with promises of free alcoholic drinks. Once they were good and drunk, the citizens massacred them and took their scalps to collect the bounties. In Betzinez's words, "The Apache could always be baited, by means of intoxicating liquor, to enter any trap. Even the enticing smell of *aguardiente* [brandy] dulled his native caution."[11] This particular episode, he maintains, was the one that established his band's undying hatred for Mexicans.

In the final hostilities, during the 1870s and 1880s, it was standard practice for soldiers of Mexico to return to their barracks after a campaign unencumbered with Apache prisoners. Any that had been taken in skirmishes or battles were summarily executed on the road. The troops knew to expect treatment in kind, should they be captured by the Indians. John Rope, a White Mountain Apache army scout, once recounted how Geronimo seized twelve Mexicans, including three women, working on a ranch in southern Arizona. He tied them up, kept them around camp overnight, and then calmly killed them all.[12]

Savagery, not the gentlemanly articles of war, governed the conflict along the southwestern border. Even some of the American press came to believe, with the Mexicans, that it was best not to bring in Apache captives. The McComases' hometown newspaper, the *Fort Scott Monitor*, in reporting their murders by Apaches, proclaimed in bold type: "IF CAPTURED, NO PRISONERS WILL BE TURNED IN!"[13] And its companion paper, the *Evening Herald*, informed readers: "The Mexican government has issued orders to take no [Apache] prisoners, but to kill all indiscriminately, so far as this particular band is concerned. Our Interior Department seems also inclined to take the same course."[14]

Hostilities between Americans and Apaches can be traced back as early as 1826, when the Southwest still formed part of the Republic of Mexico. In that year, a small party of mountain men was trapping in the country that straddles today's Arizona–New Mexico state line. Suddenly the group was surrounded by a band of Apaches, who at first "made all sorts of manifestations of friendship." After consuming a feast prepared for them, the Indians took their leave. But on the way out, one of them shot an arrow into a white man's horse, and a brisk fight erupted. The trappers fled, barely escaping with their lives and losing all their equipment and furs. Upon arriving destitute in Taos, a mountain-man headquarters, they spread the word that Apaches were a perfidious and dangerous people who should be avoided.[15]

That perception grew and was reinforced as the years passed. Based on a widening circle of experience, white men became convinced that the Apache personified duplicity, treachery, and blood-curdling cruelty. They did so, however, without tallying the injustices the Indians had suffered and their many legitimate grievances.

It was simple to ignore those things when the Apaches, in their revenge quest, annihilated human beings by the dozens, often in a manner too horrible to be described in detail by newspapers. As an army scout in Arizona summed up the situation: "Those were rough days and fierce resentments. Now recalling all the crimes of the Indians, which were black enough, one cannot but cast up in their behalf the long column of wrongs they suffered at the hands of the whites."[16] Such liberality of attitude, unfortunately, was fairly rare among outsiders who staked some kind of claim in Apache land.

Of the several divisions of the tribe, the Chiricahuas stood out as the most aggressive, recalcitrant, and least willing to give up predatory raids for a peaceful, sedentary existence. It was they who, in the twilight of their ferocity, were to snuff out the lives of the McComas couple.

Scholars are accustomed to dividing the Chiricahuas into three subdivisions. The Eastern Chiricahuas occupied the southwestern quarter of New Mexico, from the Rio Grande to the Arizona line and even a short distance beyond that boundary. In their own language, they called themselves the Cihene (or Chihinne), meaning "Red People," because of the custom of painting a red band of clay across their faces.[17]

The Cihene were further divided into two groups. The easternmost group (called Mimbres or Mimbreño Apaches) was composed of the Warm Springs band, centered at Ojo Caliente near the Rio Grande; and the Coppermine band, who lived in the vicinity of the Santa Rita copper pits, on the southern flank of the Mimbres Mountains. The other half of the Eastern Chiricahuas went by the name of Mogollon Apaches, because they inhabited the Mogollon Mountains on the western rim of New Mexico.

Apache informants have maintained steadfastly that the white man's scholarship is confused and that his designated groupings differ from those recognized by the Indians. James Kaywaykla of the Warm Springs band, for instance, insisted that the Mogollons, although closely associated with his people, were a completely distinct group.[18] Indeed, he and others represented them as a separate subtribe of the Apaches. Geronimo, born a Mogollon (or Bedonkohé in his language), concurred and in his dictated autobiography spoke of the Mimbres Apaches as allies but not as close kinsmen.[19] With regard to classification and identification, professors and Indians have come up with separate systems, it seems.

The second major subdivision of the Chiricahuas was known to the Apaches as the Chokonen. Whites referred to them as the Central Chiricahua, the True Chiricahua, or sometimes as the Cochise Chiricahua, after their renowned chief. Apaches claim these were the only real Chiricahuas and that lumping neighboring groups with them is an error. Be that as it may, the Central Chiricahua homeland sprawled over southeastern Arizona and extended marginally into New Mexico and the Republic of Mexico.

Earliest known photograph of Geronimo, taken in 1884 by A. Frank Randall, while the Indian chief was still hostile. Courtesy National Archives

Finally, the third subdivision was the southern Chiricahua (or, in Apache, the Nednhi, probably meaning "enemy people"). This group's range was centered in Mexico's Sierra Madre Mountains, along the Chihuahua-Sonora border. Therefore, they sometimes were spoken of as the Sierra Madre Apaches. On occasion, however, they also were called the Bronco Apaches. The latter name, according to Jason Betzinez, derived from the fact that the Nednhi population was made up primarily of outlaws recruited from other bands, some renegade Navajos and Mexicans, and a few whites captured as children and raised to be Apache. Betzinez tells us that his own Warm Springs band looked upon the Nednhis or Broncos as "true wild men, whose mode of life was . . . devoted entirely to warfare and raiding the settlements."[20] Their leader Juh (pronounced Whoa) is remembered for his unbridled ferocity.[21]

Taken together, these three subdivisions perceived by whites to be Chiricahuas roamed a vast tract of territory, perhaps exceeding one hundred thousand square miles. Whatever their formal tribal relationship, in fact they maintained close blood ties, intermarrying frequently and mutually supporting one another in conflicts with Mexicans and Americans.

In the turmoil of the 1870s and early 1880s, as family units increasingly were broken up by war, individuals and fragmented families appear to have shifted fairly freely among the subdivisions and bands. Geronimo, for example, lived for a time with the Southern Chiricahuas in their Sierra Madre stronghold, afterward married a Central Chiricahua woman, and then spent some of his later years in residence with the Warm Springs band of the Eastern Chiricahua.[22] Chief Chato's raiding party that attacked the McComas buckboard contained, as near as we can tell, warriors from all three divisions of the Chiricahua. By that date, 1883, the few hostile bands left were composed of an assortment of refugees from various wings of the tribe who had escaped confinement on reservations and eluded army pursuers.

To grasp something of the motives and behavior patterns shared by all Chiricahuas, one must take into account that they arrogantly considered themselves to be superior to other people, even other Apaches. In the native language, the Apache used the word *Indeh,* meaning "The People," as the name for the tribe. It carried the connotation of being "superior to all other humans" and was an expression of the ethnocentrism common to most American Indian groups.[23]

The Chiricahuas thus were far from unique in thinking of their own status as exalted. It was just that they took the attitude to extremes. What they prized most was proficiency in raiding, an activity that required war skills and physical endurance, along with cunning and a specialized intelligence. Chiricahuas seemed to think that other Indians lacked these traits or at least possessed them to a less developed extent than the Chiricahuas did.

Geronimo is reputed once to have stigmatized Western Apaches, the subtribe whose territory bordered that of his own people, as "brainless ones." If the story is true, it might be interpreted as evidence of Geronimo's own superiority complex.[24] The swaggering and haughtiness of Chiricahuas did not go unnoticed by the remaining Apaches, who harbored resentment and even furnished scouts to the army to track down their insolent kinsmen. Their aloofness and imperious disdain for others more than likely contributed to the Chiricahuas' hard fall in the end.

Gen. Nelson A. Miles, the man who accepted the final Apache surrender in 1886, stated in his personal memoirs that "the Chiricahuas were the worst, wildest and strongest of all." And he added knowingly that "in some respects they really were superior."[25] He did not necessarily mean that in a positive way, however.

In one particular, Miles may have borrowed the phrasing of his immediate predecessor, Gen. George Crook, who was a good deal more familiar with the Apaches and their ways. In a report sent back to Washington, D.C., Crook declared emphatically that the Chiricahuas were "the worst band of Indians in America."[26] He was in a position to know, having campaigned against most of the principal tribes west of the Mississippi. Being "the worst band," of course, was a superlative in itself and one the Chiricahuas heartily approved, since it confirmed their belief in their own superiority.

Army men who fought them in the Arizona and New Mexico territories generally agreed that the Chiricahuas reigned unchallenged as the greatest guerrilla fighters the world has ever seen. Courage, resourcefulness, daring, agility, hardihood, and recklessness were the qualities regularly attributed to them. As to their physical prowess, one of Crook's young aides, Lt. Britton Davis, affirmed that they were "the most perfect specimens of the racing type of athlete . . . thin arms and legs, sinewed as though with steel cords . . . chests broad, deep and full." And he added, "They moved along the trail with a smooth, effortless stride as tireless as a machine."[27]

Warriors under pressure could cover fifty to seventy-five miles a day on foot. They would dogtrot for hours and then "rest" by walking.[28] On horseback, too, Chiricahuas were able to travel upward of seventy-five miles in a day. That was the daily average Chato achieved in his 1883 raid. Such speed, whether mounted or on foot, was truly astounding—far beyond the capacity of white men. Moreover, Apaches typically sought out trails in the rugged

Gen. George Crook, during his later years, in hunting costume.
Courtesy National Archives

high country, because soldiers could not easily follow and because of the greater availability of water. Lieutenant Davis admitted that "the thought of attempting to catch one of them in the mountains gave me a queer feeling of helplessness."[29] He was not the only soldier who felt that way.

Col. Richard I. Dodge, from first-hand experience with the Apaches, concluded that their craggy homeland, almost inaccessible to whites, was the chief obstacle to defeating them.[30] Agreeing, General Miles thought that their desert and mountain strongholds were the natural allies of the Chiricahua, who, in his words, could find water "where a white man would die of thirst." An intimate knowledge of the landscape and its resources, according to another Crook aide, Capt. John G. Bourke, gave to the Apache one more point of superiority: "His perfect ability to take care of himself at all times and under all circumstances."[31] That, above all else, made the Chiricahua fighting man particularly formidable.

In the Apache scheme of raiding and warfare, the aim usually was to hit the enemy hard, seize booty, and escape with as few casualties as possible. For the Chiricahuas, that was a common-sense strategy, inasmuch as their total population was only about three thousand (estimated in 1850), so they could ill-afford heavy losses.[32] Stand-up fighting in formal battles was something they worked hard to avoid. Rather they preferred the carefully laid ambush that gave them the choice of terrain and the element of surprise.

Being masters at ambushing, they entertained a healthy fear of falling into a trap themselves. To guard against that, war parties moved swiftly, both night and day, and roaming scouts were kept far ahead and in the rear. If vigilance failed and the party experienced an attack, warriors scattered like quail and disappeared, leaving virtually no trail for pursuers. The party would reassemble at a distant rendezvous site, which always was predesignated by Apaches when traveling in enemy country.

Leadership of a raiding party might be assumed by a recognized chief, but an ordinary man, too, might simply announce his intention to head an expedition and call for volunteers. A reputation for courage and success, along with shamanistic powers, assisted in recruitment. The leader exercised authoritarian control only when hostilities threatened, and even then he couldn't order any man to fight. On the march, the individualistic warriors often journeyed at their own pace, so the party might become scattered over a long section of trail.[33]

An unusual feature of the Apache raiding complex was that women participated in many of the forays. Some were wives who accompanied the group to perform camp chores and care for the wounded. But in some instances women actually were warriors who fought alongside the men and served as messengers. The most celebrated female in this category was Lozen, an exceptional fighter who belonged to the Warm Springs band of the Eastern Chiricahua. Such women enjoyed high status in the tribe and were excused from domestic tasks while on a raid.[34]

One or more females may have been in Chato's force when it claimed the McComases. Present also were several warrior apprentices—adolescent boys who were receiving instruction in both the physical and ceremonial aspects of raiding. Their conduct, while in training, was surrounded by taboos and ritual. They wore a sacred war cap, for instance, were allowed to drink water only through a hollow reed, and used a wooden wand with lightning designs to scratch themselves. On the raid, novices had to speak in a special "warpath language."[35] Any infraction or failure on their part might jeopardize the success and safety of the expedition. In camp, apprentices assumed the role of servants, collecting firewood, building the campfire, and cooking for the men. If women were along, they engaged in such work under their direction. Each boy was attached to an older man who taught him how to speak and act on the war trail, how to stand guard properly, and how to care for the warriors' horses.

Allan Houser, whose father Sam Haozous was an apprentice on Chato's raid, recalled hearing that boys on the warpath carried the food, water, and extra ammunition. Specifically, he remembered his father saying that, as a novice, he had lugged gunpowder for the muzzleloaders.[36] Up through the 1850s, the Chiricahuas still relied primarily upon native armaments—lances and bows and arrows. By the next decade they had begun to acquire single-shot Springfields, and in the early 1880s they were well supplied through theft with the latest Winchester and Marlin repeating rifles. Ammunition for those guns was unobtainable in Mexico, so Chiricahuas in the Sierra Madre had to sweep north of the border to get it. That was Chato's mission, in fact, on his spectacular raid. When they were short on modern cartridges, the Apaches fell back on old black powder muskets stolen from Mexicans.[37]

In March 1883, while Chato cut his bloody swath across southern Arizona and New Mexico in quest of ammunition, Geronimo led another Chiricahua war party deep into Sonora after loot and livestock. The boy novice attached to him on that occasion was his second cousin, Jason Betzinez, who years afterward candidly related a curious incident that happened along the way. On an isolated road, the Chiricahuas overpowered a Mexican pack train that included mules loaded with dry goods and whiskey. The captured booty was taken about three miles beyond, where the Indians went into camp.

"Many of the older men now proceeded to get drunk," related Jason. He explained that, as a result, the apprentices had to go out and stand sentry duty during the night, since they felt that otherwise the camp would remain unguarded, owing to the drunkenness of their mentors. "Whenever the Apache can get whiskey he loses all caution and restraint," was how Jason summed up the matter. On another occasion, he referred to liquor as the great curse of his people, one that repeatedly brought them to ruin, because "they never seemed to learn from tragic experience."[38]

In describing native characteristics and practices related to war that have a bearing upon the McComas case, it is impossible to avoid mentioning Apache cruelty. It was that habit of behavior, more than any other, which inflamed the public, inspired fear, and ultimately led to heavy-handed retribution against the Chiricahuas and even to calls for their extermination. People closest to the scene of action in the nineteenth century, perhaps understandably, were unable to regard the savagery of frontier warfare with anything but outrage and disgust. Even today, although for wholly different reasons, objectivity is difficult to come by.

It is indisputable that, at the time of hostilities, the Apaches had an unparalleled reputation for ferocity. "Tigers" was a word commonly applied to the tribe collectively and to its individual leaders.

Historian Jacob P. Dunn, Jr., writing in 1886, defined the Apaches as being the most "treacherous, cruel, and inhuman savages . . . who have committed atrocities that devils alone would seem capable of."[39] Newspapers and popular literature of the day were filled with lurid accounts of the many ways captives of the Apaches died under torture. In his memoirs, General Miles deleted the details, saying that they "were simply too horrible and shocking to write out in words."[40] He was referring specifically to the Chiricahuas.

Apologists of a later day would attempt to explain away native torture as being "justified and sanctified by their religious beliefs."[41] But Colonel Dodge declared that abuse of captives had nothing to do with religion. The Indian inflicted torture, he said, "because he likes it."[42] That may not have been true in every instance, but some of the Chiricahua Apaches at least seemed to take pride in excelling in the matter of brutality. Asa Daklugie, son of Juh, boasted, "I'm Nednhi (Southern Chiricahua), and we were the worst of the lot. . . . We had the Sioux beat [for cruelty]."[43] What the white man viewed as reprehensible, Chiricahuas took as another point in favor of their superiority.

That Apaches derived pleasure from inflicting pain, as Dodge suggests, seems to be supported by the references to their torture of animals. Miles made note of it, mentioning the keen delight they took in mistreating a bird, mouse, or any living thing.[44] Army scout Frederick Burnham, while in Arizona's Tonto Basin, observed Apache youngsters playing in front of their beargrass wickiups while women ground corn. "The children," he lamented, "had captured some young turtle doves from a nest and were intent on sticking large thorns into the birds eyes, much to the amusement of the women."[45] When war leader Chato killed a horse for food, he did so in an unnecessarily brutal manner. At least that was the vivid recollection of fellow tribesmen years after his death.[46]

If tales of animal abuse angered foes of the Apaches, reports of their torture and killing of babies inflamed public wrath and inspired hatred and loathing. Territorial newspaper accounts of captured infants having been tossed on a prickly pear or impaled on a steel hook and left to die aroused something very near hysteria in the frontier settlements.[47] Even allowing for the gross exaggerations to which the journalists were prone, the reality was horrible enough.

In his late years, Geronimo reputedly expressed the greatest regret for having killed small children, a sentiment at least partially echoed by the unre-constructed Daklugie. He confessed, "It was terrible to see little children killed. I do not like to talk of it. There were times when I hated Geronimo for that."[48] In fact, a desire for revenge, as much as any ingrained taste for cruelty, may have prompted child slaying by warriors who had lost women and children of their own in battles with American and Mexican soldiers.

What the white man saw as inhuman cruelty, the Chiricahuas, we can be certain, saw in an entirely different light. That conclusion is derived in part from the fact that, as a people, they were as unsparing of themselves as they were of others. Army men, observing them at close quarters in the field and on the reservation, were appalled at their self-destructive conduct. Any one of the salaried Apache scouts would go into the mountains to hunt down a hostile member of his own tribe and kill him, even though the victim might be a blood relative. Remarked a government worker: "A fancied wrong or an injury to their pride would start them killing one another even in the presence of their enemies."[49]

While in army service, a Chiricahua named Dutchy is supposed to have gone in pursuit of a lone renegade, his own father. A week later, he returned with his sire's head in a sack, which he dumped at the feet of the Indian agent at San Carlos. Although the story cannot be fully confirmed, it was widely told and believed in southern Arizona. Several years after that alleged inci-dent, Dutchy fled the reservation and is known to have been a party to Chato's 1883 raid.[50]

In his ethnographic study of the Chiricahua, Morris Opler relates an epi-sode that occurred in the early reservation period. A young Chiricahua man was on guard duty when a Western Apache crept up, shot him in the back, and then cut off his head. The Chiricahuas were enraged and went after the killer. He had fled, but they found his wife and children at his wickiup and slew them, leaving their bodies on the ground. For an angered Apache, the exacting of revenge seemed to have no limits.[51]

Forms of Apache punishment, considered excessively cruel by outsiders, were accepted as standard practice, in conformity with cultural norms, by na-tive tribesmen. Pvt. Sylvester W. Matson, stationed at Fort Webster, New Mexico, near the Santa Rita copper mines, provides an example. According to his diary, in the summer of 1852 the eminent Mimbreño chief, Mangas Coloradas visited the fort, wearing the gaudy uniform of a Mexican artillery officer he had killed.

"Mangus [*sic*] speaks Spanish well," Matson wrote. "He possesses supreme power over the Apache people and thinks a great deal of himself." The chief brought forth one of his subjects to exhibit before the soldiers. Noted Matson: "This one had his nose cut off and pieces of both his ears sliced off, permanently disfiguring him. Mangus told our officer he had done this to perpetually disgrace him because the man had killed a Mexican [and] taken his horse and rifle, without permission from Mangus."[52] Cutting off the nose was the usual punishment inflicted on unfaithful wives, among the Apache as well as other tribes.

Jason Betzinez always claimed that one of the Chiricahuas' most serious faults was their "fondness for fighting among themselves." That and bitter jealousies between rival chiefs, he testified, kept the social pot constantly boiling. The fighting proved, contrary to what whites imagined, that "all was not harmony in the Apache tribe."[53]

At bottom, much of Chiricahua behavior and many customs of the culture which white men found repugnant probably can be traced to the tribe's struggle for survival in a hostile environment and to its undue emphasis on war, raiding, and revenge-seeking. That is by no means the full answer, however. Comanches, for example, shared those same traits and were no laggards in the area of cruelty. Yet the tempo and mood of their way of life were entirely different.

Herman Lehmann, a boy captive who lived with both tribes and was qualified to make a comparison, phrased it thus: "As a rule the Comanches are a fun-loving people and enjoy a good laugh, while the Apaches are morose and prefer to laugh only when someone is hurt or has had some calamity befall him."[54] So far as can be determined, no person of the nineteenth century ever depicted an Apache as fun-loving.

The negative image of the Apaches delineated to this point is the one held by citizens of the Southwest, who knew them largely as fiends and tigers in war. Some astute military men and government employees who got to know the tribe on a more intimate level, however, soon discovered that the story had another side and that the Apaches had their own case to make. This alternative viewpoint became more evident after the wars were over and the several tribal divisions (excepting the Chiricahuas, who were exiled to Florida and later to Alabama and Oklahoma) quickly settled into peaceful reservation life. Gradually, then, one began to hear that Apaches were moral, family-loving, honest, truthful, and generous, and that they even had a sense of humor.

Nevertheless, to southwesterners who lived through the great raid of 1883, in which the McComases and two dozen others lost their lives, a characterization of the Apaches that used those adjectives would have sounded like pure fiction.

General Crook, a man not given to excusing Apache crimes, tried to put matters in perspective. A correspondent for the *Los Angeles Times* quoted him as saying that, as the Apache was "ignorant of the rules of civilized warfare . . . it is therefore unjust to punish him for violations of a code of war which he has never learned, and which he can with difficulty understand."[55] That was a view based on reason, but reasonableness remained in tragically short supply during the turbulent decades of the Apache wars. Crook learned that very thing in the wake of Chato's raid, when the public heaped blame and abuse upon him and the army for failing to control the Indians.

The Chiricahuas' own tribal history in the years immediately prior to 1883, as much as their cultural traditions and habits of conduct, contributed to the circumstances that lay behind the gory foray made by Chato. Throughout most of the 1850s, these Indians maintained fairly amiable relations with Americans, principally because, in that early period, so few had penetrated their country. Indeed, in 1858 Dr. Michael Steck of the Indian Bureau met Cochise at Apache Pass and persuaded him to grant safe passage for the Overland stagecoaches, then operating between El Paso and San Diego.

Hostile incidents did occur, however, caused mainly by forty-niners traveling the Gila Trail to California and by miners beginning to prowl the mountains in the heart of Chiricahua country. But repeated Apache raids directed at the largely Mexican communities of Tucson and Tubac and at encampments of the Papagos, who were allied with the Americans, played a part in pushing matters toward full scale hostilities.

The Bascom affair of February 1861 ignited the war. Cochise rode into Apache Pass to parley with a troop of soldiers under Lt. George Bascom. He and six of his people entered a tent and were told by the lieutenant that they must return a boy recently captured in a raid on a Tubac ranch. When Cochise denied knowledge of the captive, he and his men were seized as hostages. The chief slashed the tent wall with his knife and escaped, but his warriors, left behind, later were hanged.[56]

The border country erupted in a blood bath. Within sixty days, some 150 whites had fallen victim to the vengeance of Cochise. As the Civil War opened and soldiers were withdrawn eastward, the Apaches gained in confidence and daring. White settlement grew, but at a terrible cost in casualties. Following the regarrisoning of forts after Appomattox, the military regained the offensive, and Chiricahua strength and numbers gradually diminished. By 1872, Cochise had accepted confinement of his Chokonen, the Central Chiricahuas, on a sprawling reservation in southeastern Arizona, within the county that now bears his name.

At the same time, the Western Apaches were crowded onto two large reservations north of the Chiricahuas, at Fort Apache and San Carlos. The Eastern Chiricahuas earlier had become reconciled to accepting a smaller reservation at Ojo Caliente, in central New Mexico. Cochise died in the Dragoon Mountains during the summer of 1874, and shortly afterward the federal government closed his reservation and transferred the Indians to San Carlos. It was part of an ill-conceived plan by the Indian Bureau to concentrate the majority of the Chiricahuas and Western Apaches at one location, to facilitate their administration. The Ojo Caliente reserve also was ordered abandoned and its residents removed to San Carlos.

Located on the Gila River in eastern Arizona, San Carlos was incapable of accommodating the large numbers of Apaches suddenly dumped within its boundaries. A place of death—so one Chiricahua described it. And he added, "There was nothing but cactus, rattlesnakes, heat, rocks and insects. No game; no edible plants."[57] Quite a few of Cochise's warriors had skipped below the Mexican boundary rather than come here, and over the next several years other parties, finding conditions intolerable, bolted and returned to the warpath.

Among the leaders in these last Apache disturbances were Nana and Victorio of the Warm Springs band. Claiming to have been goaded into guerrilla warfare, they became recognized, in the words of one army officer, as "the shrewdest and most successful Apache warriors that ever ravished the frontier."[58] Victorio, or "Old Vic," as he usually was called by whites, is credited with having, on his last wide-ranging campaign (1879–80), killed one thousand men, women, and children and destroyed more than one million dollars' worth of property. He and seventy-eight members of his band perished in October 1880 upon being trapped by Mexican soldiers at Tres Castillos, Chihuahua.[59]

The previous January, Juh had brought his band of Southern Chiricahuas and the remnant of Cochise's fighting men north out of Mexico to surrender and be settled at San Carlos. Constantly being hounded, the shortage of food, and a desire to be with friends and relatives prompted them to take that course. With the subsequent destruction of Victorio and his raiders, a brief calm settled over Apachería.

Not unexpectedly, the peace was short-lived. A White Mountain Apache medicine man soon started a religious revival, involving frenzied dancing and communication with spirits of dead warriors. When soldiers sought to arrest him and his followers on Cibecue Creek north of San Carlos, in late August 1881, a serious fight broke out, and the native prophet was killed. Although the incident occurred on the Fort Apache Reservation, the army, fearing that the unrest would spread, rushed large bodies of soldiers to neighboring San Carlos.[60]

The presence of the troops unnerved the excitable Chiricahuas, most of whom had no involvement in the Cibecue affair. After a squad of soldiers arrived to collar a subchief named Bonito and six of his men, several tribal leaders became so alarmed that they gathered a party of seventy-four, including women and children, and slipped away in the night, headed for Mexico. Led by the indomitable Juh and including such fierce fighters as Geronimo, Natchez (or Naiche, son of Cochise), Bonito, and Chato, this band, before it reached the border, clashed several times with pursuers, slew eighteen whites, and made away with a herd of cattle for food.[61]

Juh's flight, coming in the wake of the violence at Cibecue, caused consternation all across the Southwest. The public had assumed that the Apache troubles were over, but as the bloody details of the latest killings filled the newspapers, that fond hope appeared dashed. And no one believed that the fugitive Chiricahuas would stay put in their Mexican sanctuary. Sooner or later they would recross the border, and with that grim prospect in the offing, not a single person within range of their guns could feel secure.

Oddly, that included the majority of the seven hundred Chiricahuas still in residence at San Carlos. Many of them, having realized the futility of resistance, doggedly were attempting to accommodate themselves to the realities of a changed world. That was the aim of Loco, now chief of the much-reduced Warm Springs band. It is believed that, when Juh and Geronimo broke out, they tried to persuade Loco to escape with them, but he resisted their blandishments. They, however, indicated their intention to return and get the Warm Springs people, even if it meant kidnapping them.[62]

The army learned of that threat and fielded several troops of cavalry to patrol the border. Nevertheless, in April 1882, the renegades eluded them and slipped into San Carlos, where, eyewitness reports say, they forced Loco and his band at gunpoint to join them on the warpath. Among those spirited away were the boy Jason Betzinez, his mother, and his sister. "Our safety depended on keeping quiet," he recounted long after the event. "We were filled with gloom and despair. What had we done to be treated so cruelly by members of our own race?"[63]

The worst cruelty, however, was reserved for whites unfortunate enough to be in the way of the retreating cavalcade of Indians. A growing litany of atrocities caused the telegraph wires to hum. A news bulletin from Tucson, picked up by the national press, told of one massacre at the ranch of George H. Stevens. The only survivor, a nine-year-old boy, had seen six workmen butchered, his father tortured to death, and his mother and two small brothers die when their brains were beaten out with stones. The boy was saved only by the intercession of an Apache woman. "Horror is depicted upon his every feature," intoned the news story.[64]

Even though the country was swarming with army patrols and citizen posses hurrying to intercept them, the fugitives paused to hold a girl's puberty rite. "Since this is one of the most important events in a woman's life the ceremony is never neglected," commented Betzinez, "not even at a time such as this."[65] The ritual usually required four days, but in the current emergency it was telescoped and completed in a few hours. In this we perhaps are offered a clue as to why the Broncos, the wild ones from the Sierra Madre, risked so much to abduct fellow Apaches from San Carlos. They needed a minimum population to maintain the structures of their small nomadic society, particularly its religious forms. If a mountain exile was their destiny, then they wanted to spend it living properly as Apaches.

The fast-moving Chiricahuas swept east from San Carlos, up the Gila River, and then moved into the Stein's Peak range, where they fought a sharp engagement at Horseshoe Canyon with forces from the command of New Mexico's Lt. Col. George Alexander Forsyth. From there, they turned south across the San Simon Valley, made a lightning strike at the mining camp of Galeyville, Arizona, and clashed one more time with U.S. soldiers, before disappearing across the Mexican border. All in all, it had been a nearly miraculous escapade, a mission that no one but a band of determined Apaches possibly could have accomplished.

The nation was stunned by these events, for it now was clear that the Chiricahua problem, far from being settled as formerly thought, actually had entered a new and more dangerous phase. The government therefore took two decisive steps intended to meet the crisis head-on. First, it reassigned Gen. George Crook to command the Department of Arizona. During his first term in the area, in 1871–75, he had compiled an outstanding record as a man who could deal firmly and effectively with the Apaches. Those who served under him said that he "thought like an Indian." Of equal significance, he treated Indians honestly; some tribesmen gave him the nickname "The Chief Who Would Not Lie." Upon returning to the Southwest, Crook seemed to have become the lion of the hour.[66]

The second step taken by the government was the signing of an accord with Mexico, "providing for the reciprocal crossing of the international boundary line by the troops of the respective [nations] in pursuit of savage Indians." In so doing, soldiers were required to avoid settled areas; to notify civil and military officials of their entry, ahead of time if possible; and to cross the border only when in hot pursuit of raiders who recently had committed depredations. That Mexico, with its long-standing skepticism concerning American intentions, would enter into such an agreement was a measure of its strong desire to end the Apache menace once and for all.[67]

Although, as a line, the Mexican border was utterly invisible, the marauding Chiricahuas long had been aware of its presence and of its power to shield them from armies on either side who were trying to chase them down. As Juh and Geronimo, with the hapless Loco in tow, crossed that unseen boundary in flight from San Carlos and disappeared into their old Sierra Madre refuge, they had no way of knowing that the defensive barrier soon would be dissolved by mutual consent of their American and Mexican enemies.

Within a year, General Crook would invade Mexico and come pelting after the Chiricahuas in their mountain lair. His aim was to secure their surrender and at the same time to obtain the release of a little boy, Charley McComas, whose captivity had stirred the nation. Only one of those goals was he able to achieve.

Chapter Three

Silver City

St. Louis in 1876 was a bustling, cosmopolitan city of more than a half-million people. In the years before the Civil War, it had catered to the Indian trade and the commerce in furs, earning the nickname "Gateway to the West." But by the time the McComases arrived, the city had cast off its frontier image, emerging as a manufacturing center and a communication and transportation hub. It had its own cotton exchange and the world's largest cotton compress warehouse. New stockyards and packinghouses were flourishing. Mercantile firms in all branches of trade brought in and exported tons of goods through the busy Mississippi River port on the eastern edge of downtown.

City boosters proclaimed that St. Louis residents possessed that "push, vigor, and enterprise characteristic of America." And they confidently announced that theirs was destined "to be the only great city of the Mississippi Valley." Several of the more enthusiastic municipal fathers dared to predict that St. Louis one day would emerge as a chief commercial entrepôt of the world. Clearly, the business mood was more than just upbeat; it was downright euphoric. The whole city bubbled with a spirit of optimism.[1]

Was it that general climate, offering opportunity and the prospect of material reward, that brought the attorneys Hamilton C. McComas and John McKeighan to St. Louis? Surely that had to be part of it, although other motives as well must have figured in their thinking. For H. C., it was the beginning of a four-year residency—a period, like earlier ones, about which we have precious few details.

The move was made in early fall, and not long afterward, in November, little Charley was born. McComas and McKeighan opened new law chambers, found clients, and soon were engaged in both civil and criminal trials. A fellow attorney would say later that Hamilton C. McComas had "few equals as a jury lawyer."[2]

H. C. installed his family in a house at 2803 Cass Avenue, and they were still there at the time of the U.S. Census in 1880. His two older boys were not listed as members of the household, so they may have been away at boarding school. Very quickly after reaching St. Louis, Juniata transferred her membership from the Fort Scott church to Reverend Goodell's Pilgrim Congregational Church, located at the corner of Washington and Ewing avenues. The McComases seem to have settled into their new life comfortably, perhaps with the expectation that they would spend the remainder of their days in quiet ease beside the Mississippi.

The four years in St. Louis were not to be altogether uneventful, however, mainly because H. C. became afflicted once more with the itch to enter politics. As a person with respectable credentials, he moved among power brokers, and some of them may have been responsible for persuading him to seek the Democratic nomination for the post of chief justice of Missouri. He won that nomination handily, but, as had happened in Kansas, in the general election he lost to the Republican candidate.[3] If he made his mark in life, it now became evident to him, it would not be as a holder of high political office.

Sometime about the midpoint of his St. Louis residency, McComas became interested, as an investor and speculator, in mining properties in the New Mexico Territory. In fact, gold and silver fever was rampant among the city's prosperous professional class, whose members, as small- and medium-sized holders of capital, avidly sought out any enterprise that promised large returns. In the late 1870s, western mining, particularly in the territories of New Mexico and Arizona, looked like an attractive area for investment.

That corner of the country long had been known to contain mineral riches. However, exploration and development were delayed by two serious problems. The first was hostile Indians (mainly Apaches), and the second was the absence of the modern transportation needed in order to bring in heavy equipment and to export ores. But the Indians at this time were rapidly being subdued and confined to reservations by the U.S. Army. And rails at long last were advancing toward the Southwest, from Kansas in the east and California in the west. The day was swiftly approaching, therefore, when the desert country would be made to yield its natural treasure, and a significant number of St. Louis investors hurried to position themselves to share in the profits.

One of those was McComas's fellow attorney back in Illinois, Gen. John Boyle (the title was a relic of his term as adjutant general of Kentucky volunteers in the Civil War). Boyle and family settled in St. Louis during the spring of 1875, and he reentered the practice of law.[4] Nevertheless, it is clear that his real interest lay elsewhere.

The uncle, Gen. Jeremiah T. Boyle, who had spent the last years of his life amassing a personal fortune through speculation in land and railroads, was dead now, but nephew John Boyle was eager to follow in his footsteps and build a little financial empire of his own. St. Louis, filled with excited talk about western mining booms, seemed a good place to start.

It may well be that John's attention was drawn to the Southwest initially by Col. William G. Boyle, a native of Londonderry, Ireland. As a youth, William had immigrated to California during the Gold Rush; later he operated a quartz mill in Virginia City, Nevada, and by the 1870s he was actively engaged in mineral discovery and development throughout southern Arizona and adjacent sections of New Mexico. Indeed, by 1877, the colonel was identified in the press as "the great Arizona mining engineer," and to him was attributed much of the success achieved by new mines in the vicinity of Tucson.[5] How he came by his military title is unknown, but he won election as a Fellow of both the Chemical Society and the Geological Society of London, so he clearly was an individual of some substance.[6] Soon he began to represent investors from the eastern United States, England, and Belgium.

In the conduct of his far-flung mining business, William G. Boyle shuttled constantly by stagecoach across lower New Mexico and Arizona, from Mesilla in the Rio Grande Valley to Silver City to Tucson.[7] During trips east, New Orleans and St. Louis were apt to be included in his itinerary. At the latter city, Gen. John Boyle appears to have provided him with introductions to men who had money to invest.

Since the two Boyles shared a last name, it is easy to assume that somehow they were related, probably as distant cousins. On that point, no firm information has come to light. What we are able to say with certainty is that the pair, in May 1879, organized the Shakespeare Gold and Silver Mining and Milling Company, with head offices in downtown St. Louis. Directors elected Gen. John Boyle as president and treasurer, and Col. William G. Boyle as manager.[8]

Was Hamilton C. McComas one of those directors, or at the very least a stockholder? Since the business records of the company are believed to be lost, the question cannot be answered. But the chances are good that he was involved in some capacity in the launching of the new enterprise. The following spring, when he departed for his first visit to New Mexico, he was charged, among other things, with representing the interests of the Shakespeare Mining and Milling Company. That leads us to believe that the influence of John Boyle may well have played a key role in luring H. C. into the mining game originally and steering the course of his life toward the New Mexico Territory.[9]

On that maiden trip, however, McComas represented more than just the interests of the Boyles. Press reports speak of his going to the Southwest at the behest of a powerful St. Louis mining syndicate headed by B. Gratz Brown, a Kentucky-born lawyer and journalist, radical abolitionist during the Civil War, and one of the founders of Missouri's Republican party.[10] As far as the records show, to this point H. C. had never set foot inside a working mine, nor did he have any background in geology. Obviously he was selected to represent the syndicate in legal matters.[11]

In mid-March 1880, the first of two parties of St. Louis investors and promoters departed by train for the mining camp of Shakespeare, New Mexico, in the far southwestern corner of the territory. One of its members was Hamilton C. McComas. The second party left on March 28 and, according to newspaper reports, included the two Boyles and "other capitalists."[12]

Both groups would have traveled on the Atchison, Topeka and Santa Fe Railway, which at that time was busily laying track south from Santa Fe down the Rio Grande Valley toward El Paso. When the St. Louis men reached the rails' end at a point just above Albuquerque, they had to transfer to a stagecoach for the rest of their journey.

The regular coach descended to the lower territory by way of the old colonial Camino Real. At Mesilla, near Las Cruces, westbound travelers changed to the overland stages that twice weekly crossed the dangerous arid plains of southern New Mexico, stopping at Fort Cummings and Shakespeare en route to Tucson and San Diego.

Victorio had been ravishing the countryside in recent months, but at the time the Missouri capitalists passed through, he was regrouping and resting at a mountain lair sixty miles inside Mexico. Later that summer, however, one of his war parties struck the white man's stagecoach sixteen miles west of Fort Cummings, butchering the driver and two passengers.[13] The lurid stories McComas and his companions would have heard on this trip must have given him his first inkling of the nature of the Apache menace.

Shakespeare, the destination of the St. Louis parties, lay nestled in some foothills at the northern end of the Pyramid Mountains, a low, knobby range that was heavily mineralized. The town site, some eighteen miles east of the

Arizona line, looked out upon an arm of the Animas Valley and beyond that to the purple wall of the Burro Mountains. Representatives of William C. Ralston, a West Coast financier, mining promoter, and founder of the Bank of California, had come into the area in 1870 and, at a stage stop called Grant (after Ulysses S. Grant), had staked silver claims and formed the New Mexico Mining Company. The new boom camp at Grant was renamed Ralston City; and stock in the company, worth upward of five hundred thousand pounds, was peddled in London.[14]

William C. Ralston's personal empire collapsed in 1875, and he drowned in San Francisco Bay, a probable suicide. His namesake town in the Pyramid foothills withered away, so that when Col. William G. Boyle happened by in 1879, while out scouting for promising mine properties, it had only a handful of residents. After a brief survey of the district, Boyle decided that there was plenty of silver left in the hills, and he began buying up old claims. For promotional purposes, he changed the name of Ralston City to Shakespeare, the colonel being an avid fan of England's greatest author. Main Street was renamed Avon Avenue, and the principal hotel became the Stratford. Boyle then hurried to St. Louis to raise money and see to the organization of the Shakespeare Gold and Silver Mining and Milling Company.

The Boyles and their associates came to New Mexico in the spring of 1880 to make a close inspection of the company's mining claims and to ascertain what would be required for promotion and development. Unfortunately, as they approached their destination, Col. William G. Boyle was stricken on the road with a serious illness. He left his party at Shakespeare and evidently continued on by stage to Casa Grande, Arizona, north of Tucson, which then was the railhead of the eastward-building Southern Pacific.

From that point, he proceeded by train to San Francisco, where the press published his obituary on April 22, noting: "Col. Boyle was interested in the mining camp of Shakespeare and was on his way there accompanied by General Boyle of St. Louis and other capitalists when he was attacked by the fatal malady of which he died. Dropsy was the immediate cause of death, incurred by exposure to the high altitudes of New Mexico."[15]

News of the colonel's passing was slow in reaching southwestern New Mexico, but when it did, after May 1, it must have caused dismay among his friends. He had been a mere forty-two years of age and energetic, seemingly with a long career still ahead of him. Company president John Boyle, we believe, now assumed the additional duties of manager.[16]

From his arrival in the mining country, H. C. McComas had been active. The tasks required of him by the Shakespeare Mining and Milling Company were fairly limited, leaving him time to roam far afield scouting investment properties for B. Gratz Brown and the St. Louis syndicate, or even for himself. His first impressions of the country were highly favorable. Despite the aridity and vast, empty distances, he found the stark landscape appealing. With the railroad approaching and prospectors swarming through the hills, he hardly could have missed the signs that the entire district was poised on the edge of an economic boom. It was an exciting time, and southwestern New Mexico was a beguiling place to be during the spring of 1880.

On April 16, McComas addressed a letter from Shakespeare to his youngest daughter, Mary, back in St. Louis. He opened with: "My sweet little girl, As I am resting and as I wrote to Ada once since I have been out here, I thought I would write to you today. Well I just came back last night. I was over in a country called Arizona, west of here. I rode on a big stage." H. C. described the strange country of his visit, in simple terms a seven-year-old could understand—the dry hills and plains where, for ten months at a stretch, no rain might fall; the ugly, thorny plants called *cactus;* the fierce heat of day and the bone-chilling cold of night.

To reach the location of mining claims that interested him, he had left the stagecoach and climbed aboard a saddle mule. Some of his trails, through rock-ribbed mountains, were so rough that he was obliged to dismount and lead his animal. "I get very lonesome out here at night," H. C. confided to Mary. "Sometimes I sleep on the ground. I have my old overcoat for a pillow and a blanket to cover me. If I wake up I can see the stars shining on me and everything is still."

He closed with these tender words: "Be a good girl, my little daughter, and do not forget how much I love you. From your pa, H. C. McComas."[17] That letter, with three others, Mary would preserve to the end of her life, as small mementos of a father who tragically was taken from her in her childhood.

One other brief statement in the letter requires comment. McComas had remarked in passing, "I am well now." Upon leaving Missouri several weeks earlier, his health, according to our sources, had been failing badly. Inconveniently, there is no mention of the nature of his ailment.[18] St. Louis, and the Mississippi Valley generally, were plagued with dysentery, malaria, diphtheria, cholera, and pulmonary diseases, especially tuberculosis. Physicians, with limited means of cure at their disposal, had grown accustomed to sending patients on western excursions in the hope that these trips might produce relief or even a complete recovery.[19]

Had H. C.'s doctor in St. Louis suggested something of the sort? If so, did that recommendation influence his decision to go to the Southwest and combine health-seeking with business? The record is silent on that point. But what we *can* say is that, almost as soon as he reached New Mexico, the dry desert air commenced to work its magic. Somewhat to his surprise, his health improved rapidly. He had been in the territory only a matter of days when he wrote to Mary that he was "well now." Undoubtedly he overstated the case to ease a child's worry, but plainly he was on the mend. At a later time, when he decided to take up permanent residence in New Mexico, McComas gave as one of the reasons the physical benefits of the climate.[20]

On this, his initial survey tour of the region, H. C. purchased interest in a mine in partnership with his younger brother, Rufus French McComas. As a young man, according to his descendants, Rufus had left Cabell County, West Virginia, and gone west to the plains with Stephen B. Elkins. Settling at Nebraska City, Nebraska, eventually Rufus became a successful banker.[21] Likely it was through Elkins that Rufus first developed a connection with New Mexico.

Stephen B. Elkins was raised at Westport, Missouri, one of the towns at the head of the old Santa Fe Trail. He attended a Masonic school in nearby Lexington and there met another student, Thomas B. Catron, with whom he formed a lifelong friendship. After service in the Union Army during the first half of the Civil War, Elkins left for New Mexico, to be followed two years later by Catron. Both men, in close association, practiced law, helped form the Republican party in the territory, acquired title to huge land grants originally issued by the Spanish and Mexican governments, and invested heavily in new mines just being discovered. They also became key figures in the notorious Santa Fe Ring, a powerful clique that attempted to control New Mexico's political and economic life.[22]

In the 1870s, Elkins and Catron each acquired mining claims in the vicinity of Ralston (the future Shakespeare).[23] Was it mere coincidence that H. C. McComas became financially involved in the same mineral district just a few years later, or did his brother Rufus's former link with Elkins play some role in drawing him to the area? The definitive answer continues to elude us.

Nevertheless, we are now presented with three different things that, individually or collectively, might have aroused H. C.'s original interest in New Mexico and persuaded him to cast his fateful lot with the future of the territory. First was his association with Gen. John Boyle and other St. Louis capitalists, who were firmly committed to the development of mining in southwestern New Mexico. Second was his health problem (a lung ailment is the best guess), which he might have hoped would be alleviated during a sojourn in the desert. And finally, if Rufus had remained in contact with his friend

Stephen Elkins, he could have acquired inside information that led him and his brother H. C. to make their first purchase of a mine. All of this is patched together from the scantiest of sources, but the suggested picture of the judge's actions and motives at this time seems consistent with the few solid facts that can be established.

His survey tour brought McComas during the last week of April to Socorro, a nondescript New Mexican town on the Rio Grande, eighty miles below Albuquerque. The stark mountains immediately to the west were known to contain abundant ores, a fact he would have learned earlier in the month when he passed through town by stagecoach, on his way to Shakespeare. From Socorro H. C. wrote a second letter to his littlest daughter.[24]

April 23, 1880

My Dear Mary,

You will get by this mail or the next, a silver grey fox-skin which I killed upon the Chiricahua Mountains in Arizona. I shot him, skinned him, dressed his hide with alum and salt, and sent his hide to you. Spread it on the floor by your bed so when you get up in the morning you can put your feet on it.

With a thousand kisses,

Your loving father,

H. C. McComas

It seems fairly certain that, by the time Judge McComas appeared in Socorro, he had undergone something of a transformation, having shifted from the role of an attorney representing the interests of others to that of a mining promoter and developer in his own right. In April, he was still feeling his way and learning, but all the while he kept moving toward the day when he would begin raising capital, forming partnerships, selling ownership rights in working properties (as a middleman searching out buyers), and bonding mines to finance their operation. He found such activity exciting, unfolding as it did against the backdrop of a picturesque landscape. And then there existed the alluring promise of spectacular profits.[25]

McComas's movements around the territory during the next month cannot be traced, although we have reason to believe he may have paid a brief visit to the capital at Santa Fe, the business hub of the region. By the final week of May, at the very latest, he had returned to southwestern New Mexico, for the surveyor and lawyer Oscar W. Williams saw him in Shakespeare at that time.

Williams claimed that he was introduced to Judge McComas by Adolphus B. Preston, a native of Carthage, Illinois, who was manager of some mines in the Carrisalillo Hills down near the Mexican border. Preston, according to

Williams, had become McComas's "field man in matters of mines and prospecting."[26] His statement merely confirms that H. C. had branched out to become an independent operator and in so doing wisely had engaged the services of a man with practical knowledge of the mining industry.

Whether McComas retained a formal connection with Gen. John Boyle and the Shakespeare Gold and Silver Mining and Milling Company is not altogether clear. Williams, in his memoirs, revealed that Boyle, "about fifty years old, a man of quiet manner and pleasant ways," liked to hang around the Shakespeare camp playing whist or cribbage. But on the Fourth of July, 1880, Williams and the general, after enjoying a meal of Gila River trout, climbed in a buggy and left Shakespeare for Silver City, which lay some forty-eight miles to the northeast, beyond the Burro Mountains.

"The General drove a spanking team of Kentucky horses," according to Williams, "and by bedtime we were housed in John Parks' home at the old Knight's Ranch in a room marked by portholes. These holes had been used more than once, we were told, in defense against Indians." The road thus far had crossed the open flats of the Animas Valley and then approached the west face of the Burros, heading for steep-walled Thompson Canyon.

At the edge of the mountains, the road led a short distance to Knight's Ranch, where travelers could count on a safe and comfortable refuge for the night. Early the next morning, the pair resumed their journey and by noon were in Silver City. They had covered the very same route that H. C. and Juniata McComas would follow, in reverse, less than three years later when they rode to their deaths.[27]

Silver City! "The treasure vault of New Mexico," it was being called by 1880. The seat of huge Grant County, the town site lay nestled in a natural bowl off the southern flank of the Pinos Altos Range, an extension of the sprawling Mogollon Mountains. As the most significant metal-mining district in the territory, the surrounding country fairly hummed with activity. On every hand, the inquiring visitor could find mine tunnels, vertical shafts, and open pits. The ore bodies, veins, and placer deposits produced silver, gold, copper, zinc, iron, and lead. "No where in the Southwest," chortled a Las Cruces newspaper, "can so striking an example of energy and enterprise be found as in Silver City."[28]

Scarcely ten years old when H. C. McComas arrived on the scene, Silver City was situated in the heart of an area that long had attracted miners. As early as 1800, still within the colonial period, men speaking Spanish had ventured up from the south, discovered the famed Santa Rita copper deposits (fifteen miles east of the future Silver City), and over the years developed an enormous open-pit mine. Primitive ore crushers and smelters, built on site, had made possible the production of heavy bars of raw copper, which had been loaded on the backs of mules and burros. The pack trains transported the metal four hundred miles south to the royal mint at Chihuahua City, where it was converted into coin of the realm.

Perhaps because the land swarmed with hostile Apaches, the Spaniards tended to stick close to Santa Rita and a triangular adobe fort they built there. Their quick excursions into the countryside to hunt and to collect firewood afforded little opportunity for prospecting, so they missed finding the rich deposits of gold and silver that rested within a day's ride. The privilege of unlocking New Mexico's hidden bonanza would be left to others.

In 1860, the discovery of placer gold ten miles west of the copper mine sparked an initial boomlet. By that time, southwestern New Mexico, along with southern Arizona, had passed from the Republic of Mexico into the hands of the United States, by way of the 1854 Gadsden Purchase. Three prospectors, recently arrived from California, located the gold on Bear Creek, which flowed between the Pinos Altos Mountains and the Diablo Range. Other miners poured in, and the town of Pinos Altos (Tall Pines) was born.

From the outset, Mimbres Apaches did their best to drive out the white interlopers, who muddied the streams and tore up the hillsides with their picks and shovels. Early on September 22, 1861, some four hundred Indians unleashed a furious attack on the community but were beaten off. Nevertheless, the miners suffered casualties, including the death of their leader, Thomas Marston. Many, unwilling to live in constant peril, abandoned the district.[29]

Interest revived in 1866, with discovery of valuable gold-bearing quartz. The Apache menace notwithstanding, legions of prospectors and adventurers from afar descended upon little Pinos Altos.[30] Numbers of Chinese even showed up, intending to mine, but they soon found that it was more profitable to wash and cook for the men already there.[31] Then, in 1868, Grant County was formed, encompassing a vast expanse of desert and mountains in the southwestern quarter of the territory. Pinos Altos became the first county seat.

In the late sixties, John Bullard, his brother, and several other miners moved a few miles downcountry to a little valley known as La Cienega de San Vicente (the Marsh of St. Vincent), where grass and water were plentiful and where they set about farming. We gather that they had been crowded out of the Pinos Altos district and had come to the conclusion that agriculture and not mining would determine the county's future. It turned out that they were quite wrong.

During the spring of 1870, the first silver strike at Ralston City (Shakespeare) occurred. Being curious, Bullard and several companions saddled up and rode over the Burro Mountains to have a look. They were gold men. Upon viewing the fresh Ralston ore, John Bullard expressed surprise and is alleged to have exclaimed, "Boys, if this is what silver looks like, we have plenty of it at home."[32] And indeed they did, right in their own backyards.

The residents of the Marsh of St. Vincent hurriedly formed the Bullard Mining Company, staked their first claim (called the Legal Tender), and brought in ore that assayed one hundred ounces of silver per ton. A rush followed, and a town sprouted at the upper end of the pocket-sized valley. Miners assembled at the newly built livery stable and voted whether to call the community San Vicente, following tradition, or to go with something that had a prosperous ring to it. In the end they chose the name Silver City. It proved appropriate enough, as mineral strikes in the vicinity multiplied rapidly. During their first century of activity, the district and county would produce more than a billion dollars worth of metals, much of that in silver.[33]

The founders of Silver City, unlike the early residents of most mining towns and camps of the Old West, were on the whole an honest, hard-working, and dedicated lot; among them were men of breeding, who rejected boundary quarrels and claim jumping.[34] In marked contrast, the prospector class generally was heavily weighted, to use the pungent phraseology of the day, with "mining riffraff."

Both Arizona and New Mexico at this time suffered from an oversupply of "some of the most precious scoundrels in the whole world," many of them chased out of California by vigilantes.[35] Like flies drawn to fresh hanging meat, they gravitated to the mining districts of the Southwest. There they became a plague upon honest white men and especially upon the vulnerable Indians, who increasingly were being confined to bleak but sometimes mineral-rich reservations. The rabble, a large element among the prospectors, played a major role in fanning the flames of war with the Apaches.

The Bullard brothers and their friends, not being rabble themselves, were able to get Silver City launched on a proper footing, so that from the start the town enjoyed a reputation for being respectable and progressive. By decade's end, it could boast a full range of businesses, hotels, banks, newspapers, churches, fraternal organizations, professional offices of lawyers, doctors, and surveyors, and one of the first public schools in the territory (established in 1882). The town also hastily shed its frontier appearance.

When Eugene F. Ware came out from Fort Scott in 1883, after the slaying of his sister and brother-in-law, he observed with some surprise that "Silver City is one of the best . . . and most distinctly American cities here in the

Southwest."[36] Except on its fringes, the adobe structures and rude log cabins of the earliest days largely had given way to handsome red brick commercial and residential buildings with gabled roofs, wooden porches, and assorted architectural details in the Greek Revival style. A local sawmill furnished the lumber, a deposit of suitable clay near the town limits provided raw material for a brickyard, and Spaulding's Iron Clad Tin Shop offered builders roofing, spouting, and sheet-iron work, freighted in by wagon from the railhead.[37]

In 1871 Silver City captured the county seat, taking it away from a declining Pinos Altos. Despite its bright prospects, however, Silver City was forced to struggle for a dozen years with the problems posed by a shortage of capital to develop mining and milling and by the lack of access to a railroad. The "prospector phase," in which metals were discovered and claims located, was the initial step in advancing the mining economy. But the men involved in unlocking the secrets of the hills generally possessed neither the money nor the organizational skills to move ahead with full-scale development. Therefore they usually sold their interests to men from St. Louis, Boston, and other eastern cities, or from the West Coast. Such successors represented the "investment phase," when, in an atmosphere of fevered speculation, capital was raised, companies were formed, stock was issued, and heavy equipment first was introduced to speed excavation and processing of ore. It was near the beginning of this second phase that Hamilton C. McComas first saw Silver City and recognized opportunity beckoning.

Not long before General Boyle and Oscar W. Williams made their buggy ride from Shakespeare over the Burros to Silver City, McComas preceded them. On May 22, he took up lodgings at the Exchange Hotel on the corner of Hudson and Spring streets. Over the next two years, this would remain his address whenever he was in town. The comfortable Exchange was run by a German innkeeper named Louie Timmer; hence the hotel commonly was referred to as the Timmer House. The two-story building was faced with red brick, its tall windows were crowned with carved pediments, and its shingled mansard roof was painted in imitation of slate.[38] The management brashly advertised that it was "the most stately edifice in New Mexico" and billed itself as "the Delmonico of the West."[39]

The good meals, a bar stocked with the finest liquor and cigars, and a convenient location within walking distance of the bank, stores, and stagecoach and telegraph offices—all these undoubtedly appealed to McComas. In addition, the adjacent Stock Exchange Corral offered the rental of a buckboard and team for those occasions when he needed to drive into the country-

Timmer House (formerly the Exchange Hotel), Silver City, New Mexico.
From author's collection

side to visit mining properties. The energetic town, the hotel, and the healthy pulse of the business atmosphere proved very much to his liking.

In reality, at least two other hotels challenged the supremacy of the Exchange—the Southern, a block up Hudson Street; and the Tremont House, over on Main, which styled itself "the leading hotel of the Southwest" and claimed to be the largest in the territory. In fact, the latter establishment may have enjoyed an edge in prestige, as is indicated by the fact that, when New Mexico's Gov. Lew Wallace, accompanied by an entourage of army officers, traveled down from Santa Fe to investigate the local Indian situation, he registered at the Tremont House.[40] That event occurred on July 19, 1880.

Wallace, a native of Indiana, now is best remembered as author of the popular novel *Ben Hur*. His tenure as territorial governor (1878–81), however, received high praise, mainly for his handling of the Victorio outbreak and the putting down of the vicious Lincoln County War, in which Billy the Kid was the chief celebrity. The governor also invested in mining ventures and, while moving about on official business, kept his eye peeled for profitable openings in that line. Subsequent to his 1880 excursion to southwestern New Mexico, for example, he acquired several mines in the Stein's Peak range west of Silver City.[41]

A brief reference in the governor's autobiography identifies Judge H. C. McComas as "a warm personal friend" of Wallace and his family.[42] How and under what circumstances their friendship began has not been determined, but we reasonably can conjecture that its origin dated back either to the period when H. C. lived in Monticello, Illinois, or to the Civil War, when both men were Union officers. In any case, H. C. was in Silver City on July 13 (he mailed another letter to his daughter Mary on that day), and, being well aware by this time of Governor Wallace's impending visit, he assuredly would have arranged his schedule so as to be on hand to greet him.[43] As a newcomer in town, and one angling to find a niche for himself, he must have realized what a boost it would be to his reputation if he were seen hobnobbing with Lew Wallace.

If that is, in fact, what happened, it would help to explain why, on July 24, H. C. was listed in a news story as one of fifteen members selected to serve on a citizens' committee to deal with Apache hostilities. Specifically, the group undertook "to procure evidence showing the extent of Indian depredations and to gather evidence as to the number of persons killed or wounded and the value of property stolen or destroyed by Indians in southern New Mexico."[44] It also discussed at its first meeting the desirability of communicating with other southern counties, notably Socorro, Doña Ana, and Lincoln, in order to take united action in petitioning Congress for relief.

Both the formation of the committee and its agenda obviously were consequences of the governor's official trip to Silver City. He might have recommended his old friend, H. C. McComas, for membership, or the town fathers, observing that the judge was so well connected, could have decided on their own that he would embellish their committee and bolster any appeal made to Washington. Given McComas's disastrous encounter with Apaches scarcely three years later, it is surely a stunning irony that the first bit of public business to engage his attention in New Mexico concerned those very people, about whom he knew absolutely nothing.

From H. C.'s choice of Silver City as a prospective new home and his participation, early on, as a member of a citizens' committee on Indian matters, we can discern the continuation of a pattern identified earlier—the tendency to swim in a small pond. In his residency first at Monticello, then at Fort Scott, and finally at Silver City, he could rapidly emerge as a big fish. In the first two places he had been regarded as a pillar of the community. St. Louis, the big city, had been another matter. Despite good political and business connections, he appears to have remained on the fringe of the municipal power structure. The turn in his fortunes that led him to the New Mexico Territory furnished him with a new pond, one whose dimensions allowed him to flourish.

As mentioned, an added attraction was the improvement in his failing health. During his first few weeks in the desert, he had noticed a change for the better. But in writing to little Mary from Silver City on July 13, he indicated that he might have suffered a temporary relapse. The letter was sent to the Ware farm, outside Fort Scott, where his wife and children were spending at least part of the summer while he was away in New Mexico.[45] The letter reads in part:

Silver City, N.M.

July 13th 1880

Dear Mary: I wrote a letter to Ada and she has not answered it. I have written several letters to your ma which she has not answered. I thought tonight I would write to you as we are (you and me) twin rose-buds upon one stem. I am a pretty looking rose-bud. Don't you think so?

What are you doing at Grandma's? Do you feed the chickens? And throw in an ear of corn to those little black pigs? . . . Do any of Grandma's cows give buttermilk? . . .

I am not very well. I hope this letter will find you all well and that you, Ada, and Charley will all have a good time. . . .

If I come down there, you and Ada & Charley must promise not to come to my bed in the morning and tickle my feet. If you do—I'll pull your noses. Give my love to Ada and Charley. Tell that boy he must quit sucking his thumb. Now come kiss me good night, my dear sweet daughter,

from your pa,

H. C. McComas

In the absence of any other concrete record, it is difficult to assess his admission to Mary that he was "not very well." Oscar W. Williams, in his memoirs, refers to Judge McComas during this period as "deadening physically but still wise and ripe in the charms of intellect and experience."[46] That would suggest that H. C.'s sickly condition was obvious to his friends. Nevertheless, in the months that followed, his infirmities in no way seem to have slowed him down. Either he began to feel better, or, if not, he simply decided to ignore pain and weakness while building a new life in Silver City.

With the town poised to become the center of New Mexico's burgeoning mining industry, McComas hurried to stake his own claim to a share of the anticipated profits. The full extent of his involvement has to be left to guesswork, since only a few of his business papers have been found. We know, for example, that in October 1880 he was the chief figure in the formation of at least two mining companies, the Leroy Silver Mining Company and the New Mexico & Arizona Mining and Reduction Company. On the sale of shares for each one, the stock certificates carried the signature of H. C. McComas as president.[47]

Initially, he had focused on claims in the Pyramid Mountains above Shakespeare, but soon his interest shifted southeastward to the Carrisalillo Hills, where his field man, Adolphus Preston, had worked. Some time during the summer, Williams saw him headed there with a promoter named Hyatt and several prospective investors, possibly from St. Louis, since the country then was full of such individuals.

By the following year, 1881, H. C. acquired a promising property called the Arizona Mine, located in the Victorio Mountains about forty miles south of Silver City. Through 1881 and into 1882, he spent a good deal of time there, hoping to see the venture pay. The *Grant County Herald,* for instance, in its edition of June 26, 1881, announced that the judge had returned to Silver City from the Victorio district, where he had been "pushing work on his Arizona Mine."[48] The only ore that came out of the Victorio area in that period was lead; but McComas, like everyone else, was intent upon finding gold and silver. In fact, abundant traces of both the richer metals were in evidence. However, they were not extracted in profitable amounts until long after H. C.'s death.[49]

As he became more and more immersed in his New Mexico business affairs, McComas was forced to shuttle back and forth between the territory and his family and home in St. Louis. The return from his first trip out west occurred about the middle of October 1880. He had been absent more than six months. If the letters to daughter Mary can be accepted as accurate reflections of his mood, then he had missed his wife and children dreadfully.

It is conceivable that H. C.'s long stay in the Southwest had placed something of a strain upon his marriage. Could his lament in the letter of July 13— that he had written several times to Juniata from New Mexico without receiving an answer—be indicative of that? Perhaps the explanation is simpler: the dutiful wife indeed had responded, but with the uncertainty of the mails in those days, the letters never caught up with her itinerant husband.

Not long after his return to Missouri, McComas and an associate, Thomas L. Smith, crossed the Mississippi to East St. Louis, Illinois, where they filed incorporation papers for the New Mexico & Arizona Mining and Reduction Company. Earlier that same month, on October 8, while he was still in New

Mexico, H. C. had incorporated his Leroy Silver Mining Company under the laws of that territory.[50]

The Illinois incorporation remains puzzling. It could be that, having formerly practiced law in that state, McComas was aware of some business advantage to be gained by having his new company headquartered there. Or maybe numbers of his officers and board members resided on the Illinois side of the river. Long afterward, Oscar W. Williams recollected that H. C. had left a distinguished legal career in East St. Louis to relocate in Silver City.[51] His memory doubtless was faulty, because, other than the incorporation of his mining company in the Illinois city, McComas lived and worked strictly in Missouri's St. Louis—or so our few scattered references make us believe.

Over the next two years, H. C. came and went from St. Louis on an irregular schedule. During summers when he was away, Juniata took the children out to Fort Scott and to the nearby farm belonging to her parents and her brother Eugene. McComas made reference to that in the letter quoted above, as he did in the last piece of correspondence to Mary which has been preserved. That final letter contains no biographical details of value, but it is given here in full to covey something of the sentiments of a doting father.[52]

Victorio Mining Camp

Deming New Mexico

January 20th 1882

My Dear Rosebud: I have never had a letter from you since you were down in Kansas shooing Grandma's chickens. I wrote a letter to Ada "nose" but she is too busy skipping around the corner to write to her pa. I am afraid she is getting "too utterly utter." As for Old Man Dodo—He can't write. He is too old and feeble. Now my only chance to hear from you all is for you to write. What do you say?

> *Are now a man's chances slim*
> *Who expects to get a letter from "Jim"*
> *When she comes home from school*
> *And whirls around on the piano stool.*

I want to see you and Ada and Charley all very much. I want you all to come sit on my lap. From your old no account pa.

Very truly———

H. C. McComas

One thing that facilitated H. C.'s travels was the completion in early 1881 of direct rail service between Missouri and southwestern New Mexico. On

March 8 of that year, track gangs of the AT&SF and the Southern Pacific came together at Deming, a newly founded railroad community about sixty-five miles due east of Shakespeare. In a colorful ceremony, officials of both lines met and drove a silver spike, marking completion of the second transcontinental railway. The very next week, the first through train for California left Kansas City.

The Southern Pacific, laying track eastward from the Arizona border, skirted the northern end of the Pyramid Mountains to take advantage of the level terrain in the Animas Valley. But that course left the little boom camp of Shakespeare isolated, more than two miles from the line. Like Deming, Lordsburg suddenly sprouted beside the tracks and bloomed as the depot and shipping point for miners and ranchers within a fifty-mile radius. As Lordsburg grew, Shakespeare, just up the road, declined correspondingly.

Passengers from St. Louis and Kansas City whose destination was Silver City now could detrain at either Deming or Lordsburg and catch a stagecoach for an easy ride northward and completion of their journey. Small, independently owned stage lines sprang up to provide this service, giving access to the scattered mining camps as well. We have to believe that H. C. felt grateful for this giant improvement in transportation.

The completion of the railroad through this corner of New Mexico had two noticeable effects. First, as anticipated, it encouraged even more vigorous exploration for new mines and stimulated rampant speculation. Lower-grade ores suddenly were in demand, since heavy machinery for their extraction now could be imported at low cost. And the poorer ores became profitable to ship, owing to the cheap rates and rapid delivery provided by the rail companies.

Following on the heels of McComas and the Boyles, midwestern and eastern investors, dressed in bowler hats and bat-wing collars and looking for quick and easy riches, descended in swarms. Even before the silver spike was driven, a newspaper in Silver City declared exuberantly: "Our hotels are full to overflowing. Every incoming coach is crowded with passengers. The Tremont House and the Exchange abound with strangers."[53] A tremendous feeling of excitement filled the air, and people genuinely believed that wealth and success were theirs for the taking.

The other effect of the railroad's arrival was not quite so obvious but nonetheless was important. The huge locomotives chugging across the yucca-studded flats of the Animas Valley were symbols of progress. As instruments of change, they heralded the dawning of the modern era in the American Southwest. Some people mistakenly concluded that the advent of rails automatically spelled the close of the violent frontier and its replacement by a settled, orderly existence.

In fact, the tumultuous spirit and the dangerous atmosphere of the Old West was to live on for another generation in the remote nooks and crannies of New Mexico and Arizona. But developers, investors, and town boosters on the scene preferred to downplay, or even to conceal, that reality, in the interest of accelerating the march of progress and lining their own wallets.

Yes, the train had come to the desert, and the telegraph, too. New towns had been staked out next to the shiny rails, and the population was mushrooming. Still, one very obvious piece of business remained, an untidy problem inconveniently left over from the dark days of the pioneer period. That problem was the Chiricahua Apaches.

Chapter Four

Prelude to Disaster

"The great and all absorbing question which fills the minds and occupies the thoughts of our people, old and young, is the Indian—the everlasting Apache, where they will turn up next and who will be their next victims." These sanguinary words appeared on the front page of Silver City's leading newspaper on September 3, 1881.[1] And they accurately reflected the mood and fears of territorial citizens.

By this date, there existed more than sixty farms divided between the Mimbres Valley to the east of town and the Gila Valley to the west. Ranching too was flourishing, large herds of cattle, horses, and sheep having been driven in from Texas and Arizona to stock the ranges. And, as already indicated, the hills in every direction were alive with prospectors and miners. All these activities necessarily led to a scattering of the population and left individuals and families vulnerable to Indian attack.

Cowboy and hunter James H. Cook, who entered the region in the early eighties, recalled that everywhere he rode he saw proof of the high toll taken by the death-dealing Apaches: "Whole skeletons of white men bearing the marks of bullets, knives, arrows, and skulls crushed by blows from stones . . . [offered] mute testimony to these deeds of bloodshed and human suffering."[2]

Cook testified that once, when traveling through the Mogollon Mountains above Silver City, he ran across in a canyon the bones of one unfortunate fellow who had met a roaming war party. It was obvious that he had made a desperate but futile stand, and in the end he scratched a few words with his knife on the cliff face. Jim Cook found the rusty blade, but the writing, whether a name or a message, no longer could be deciphered. "A thigh bone badly smashed by a bullet, and a partially rusted iron arrow point lying among the bones, as if it had been imbedded in his body, told a little story of the thrilling scene which had been enacted there."[3]

The pioneer always had relied upon an ability to shoot straight and a steel nerve as his first lines of defense. Newcomers to the frontier, in particular, tended to overestimate their stock of both and realized their mistake only when it was too late—upon confronting that superb and reckless fighting machine, the Indian warrior. Like the nameless victim whom Cook found in the Mogollon canyon, many of them perished horribly, their bones left to bleach under the southwestern sun.

The U.S. Army furnished a second line of defense. For Silver City, that meant Fort Bayard, located ten miles to the east astride a small stream at the base of the Santa Rita Mountains. Established in 1866 by troops of the 125th U.S. Colored Infantry, the post was named for Brig. Gen. George D. Bayard, who died of wounds at the Battle of Fredericksburg during the Civil War. By 1880, Bayard was garrisoned by more than 350 officers, enlisted men, civilian employees, and Indian scouts. In campaigns, its troops cooperated with patrols and expeditions from Fort Cummings, down near Deming; and with posts in Arizona, such as Fort Bowie in Apache Pass and Forts Thomas, Grant, and Apache on or near the reservations.[4]

While American military defenses may have looked impressive on paper or charted on a map, in reality, they were only marginally effective. The reason swiftly could be discerned by anyone traveling through the enormous, arid, corrugated domain of the Apaches. Trying to defend such a land with small numbers of soldiers, operating out of widely separated forts, was an all but impossible task. "One regiment of troops cannot accomplish the difficult feat," pleaded a beleaguered Arizona resident, "so let us have a score or more of regiments."[5] Despite repeated cries for the beefing up of army manpower in the war zones of the Southwest, Congress gripped its purse strings tightly and looked for other, less expensive solutions to the problem.

In its dealings with the Indians, the army, besides being hamstrung by a shortage of soldiers, had to follow policies that had been shaped by politicians or by bureaucrats in the Indian Bureau, whose agendas were notorious for their wrongheadedness. An outraged journalist in Silver City condemned the paralysis that resulted, attributing it to "the criminal imbecility that has controlled and still controls our Indian policy."[6]

Not surprisingly, the citizenry, periodically terrorized by new raids or general outbreaks from San Carlos, leveled blame at what was close at hand. As one officer put it: "Upon the Army descended a storm of reproach, even abuse."[7] The territorial press was unsparing in its use of invective, frequently referring to the troopers sneeringly as "our brave defenders," with the quotation marks added so that no reader would mistake the words as praise.

Strangely, however, at the first sign of Indian hostilities, the public never hesitated to put in a call for military protection. And on those rare occasions when the overburdened soldiers actually achieved some measure of success, the fickle citizens were apt to do an about-face and deliver extravagant applause. But within a few days or weeks, the pendulum would swing again, and the men in uniform had to accept their lumps once more. Captain Bourke said of his commanding officer, General Crook, that he ignored and made no reply to the "scurrilous attempts at defamation [that were meant] to do him injury."[8] Notwithstanding, the heavy and persistent barrage of complaints had a damaging effect on army morale.

The truth was that Crook and some of his brightest junior officers had, within limits, an understanding, admiration, and sympathy for the Indians' cause. That in itself was enough to earn them the enmity of American civilians who routinely disparaged the motives and actions of soldiers. The general, indeed, drove his critics to fury by uttering such statements as this: "Greed and avarice on the part of whites—in other words, the almighty dollar—is at the bottom of nine-tenths of all our Indian troubles."[9]

In 1866 Congress had authorized the enrollment of conquered tribesmen as scouts, to be used in tracking down their own brethren who were still hostile. Bourke claimed that General Crook was "the only officer of our army who fully recognized the incalculable value of a native contingent," and in that statement he was not far from the truth.[10] When first posted to Arizona in the early seventies, Crook had organized a company of Apache scouts, and upon his return in 1882 to pursue Chiricahua renegades, he formed five additional companies.

Scarcely any white man could chase an Apache through his own country and catch him. But another Apache could do it, or, as Crook quaintly put the matter, "To polish a diamond, there's nothing like its own dust."[11] Indians who enlisted for a six-month period did so for their own reasons. Many simply wanted to escape the boredom of reservation life by turning their energies to what they did best—tracking and fighting. Others seem to have had personal grudges to settle or simply envied the hostiles who still were free.

Whatever their motives, the native scouts proved highly useful to the army, and without their services border warfare would have dragged on much longer than it did. In the end, the scouts paid a heavy price, being ostracized as traitors by their own kind and betrayed by the government they had helped.

General Crook saw the utility of the Apache scouts as one means to compensate for the small numbers and ineffectiveness of his own troops. But that was something his civilian detractors failed to appreciate. According to them, Crook's "pets" often secretly were in league with the renegades, supplying them with information and smuggling guns and ammunition. Some, they charged, had been on the warpath just before enlistment and were using membership in the scouting companies only as a sanctuary. At least in isolated cases, all that was true. Yet, on balance, the scouts were an asset and earned their keep.[12] That would become apparent in 1883, when they played a key role in hunting down the killers of Hamilton and Juniata McComas.

Putting little faith in the army to protect them, territorial residents were quick to jump to their own defense, at times with disastrous results, owing to monumental ineptitude. Thomas Cruse, a green second lieutenant, arrived in southwestern New Mexico in 1879 and reported in his memoirs a representative incident that came to his attention.

In November of that year, Victorio's marauders struck the booming camp of Hillsboro on the east slope of the Black Range, killing two or three miners. The excitement of the moment and indulgence in liquor caused townsfolk to toss saddles on their horses and gallop forth, one or two at a time, hell-bent on punishing the offenders. Their boast was that they would perform the job that the Regular Army seemed unable to do.

The wily Victorio saw them coming, separated and vulnerable. He ambushed and killed every one, about twenty men, and reaped a harvest in captured firearms and ammunition. When Lieutenant Cruse marched over the route a short time later, he observed the graves, placed where each man had fallen, scattered along a four-mile section of the trail. In his common-sense judgment, if as few as five or six of the pursuers had bunched up, dismounted, and fought, "it is highly probable that the Indians would never have got them."[13]

Such helter-skelter vigilantism was not that uncommon during the Apache wars. Frightened men, over drinks, hatched elaborate plans to capture the hostiles, but, according to a civilian employee at San Carlos, most of them never got outside the saloons.[14] Lt. Britton Davis derisively referred to such individuals as "barroom Indian fighters."[15]

On the other hand, in the aftermath of Apache attacks, town dwellers and rural folk not infrequently banded together, found a natural leader, and either mounted a respectable defense or fielded an expedition of pursuit that yielded tangible results. Sometimes they went even farther, organizing companies of home guards or rangers. These were paramilitary units sanctioned by the territorial government, their members serving without pay. When in need of arms, they could apply to the adjutant general of the territory. Some of the bodies, such as the Shakespeare Guards and the Duncan [Arizona] Rangers, performed admirably and earned praise for their services; whereas others, like the Tombstone Rangers, functioned as little more than an unruly mob.

In an emergency, when the public order was threatened, the governor had the authority to raise volunteer companies of militia, to serve six-month terms and be supplied and receive transportation at public expense. The officers and men, while on duty, were granted pay equivalent to regular United States troops.[16] Some of the independent companies, among them the Shakespeare Guards, applied for militia status and were accepted.

Emma M. Muir, who knew many of them as a girl, said that "those old Shakespeare Guards [were] men of education and background and high in courage, determination and devotion to others."[17] During Loco's flight from San Carlos in 1882 and again during Chato's raid the following year, the guards rode into the eye of each storm and acquitted themselves with distinction. At the time of the latter episode, the unit applied to Santa Fe for an extra stand of one hundred arms, to be used by homefolk for protection while the men were away trying to rescue Charley McComas.[18]

The denizens of Silver City, from the founding of their community, had to reckon with the Indian threat, although strangely it was not until 1885 that they got around to mustering their own company of militia. An early loss, the killing of town father John Bullard, shocked residents and had much to do with crystallizing public opinion against the Apaches.[19]

That event happened in February 1871. An all-night dance downtown had drawn the majority of the population. Taking advantage of the diversion, an Apache raiding party slipped into the heart of Silver City and stealthily made off with several prized horses. The theft, when discovered a few hours later, produced enormous anger and chagrin. John Bullard assumed leadership of a hastily formed posse and gave chase. The trail led around the north end of the Burros, across the Gila River, and into Arizona. At last the Silver City men overtook the horse thieves, and a fight erupted. As Bullard approached a fallen warrior, the Apache suddenly rose up and fired at him point blank. The bullet entered his chest, killing him instantly.

Although the whites won the skirmish, they paid a heavy price in the death of their leader. Bullard's body was carried home for burial, becoming one of the first to be placed in Silver City's pioneer cemetery. A full-dress honor guard came from Fort Bayard for the ceremonies, and he was eulogized

in flowery terms: "It is seldom that a frontier is called upon to mourn so ir-
reparable a loss. No one was more popular, none more universally loved by all
his comrades—steady and cool as a rock, daring almost to a fault, trusted as
the very soul of honor. John Bullard has given another valuable life to pave the
way for civilization."[20]

The sentimental idea that the defeat of barbarism and the advancement
of civilization required the spilling of the noble blood of martyrs was a popular one in nineteenth-century America. Silver City in the seventies and eighties, it seemed, furnished more than its share of candidates to wear the crown
of martyrdom. Among them was an influential young lawyer, John P. Risque,
whose death from a Chiricahua bullet occurred a decade after Bullard's slaying. The Risque incident also foreshadowed the larger tragedy of the Mc-
Comases, which followed soon afterward.

John Risque was another St. Louis man, brilliant and energetic. After
taking a law degree at Washington's Georgetown University, he returned to
his home city to practice. About 1872, he went to Santa Fe and formed a partnership with attorney Thomas F. Conway, who had come out to the territory
from St. Louis in the latter half of the 1860s. Conway was an old friend and
former classmate of the politicians and speculators, Tom Catron and Steve
Elkins. Two years later, in 1874, the firm of Conway and Risque decided to
open a branch office in Silver City; and John, as the junior partner, moved
there to take charge.[21]

As the fortunes of the new mining town soared, so did those of the youthful
and clever Mr. Risque. By 1879, he brought from St. Louis an attractive bride
and installed her in an adobe house on West Kelly Street, and the couple soon
had two children to enliven their hours.[22] With enthusiasm, John Risque threw
himself into the civic and business life of Silver City. He played an active role
in the Odd Fellows and Masonic lodges and in Democratic party politics. The
local paper proclaimed on July 3, 1880, that he had been named a director of
the new Bank of Southern New Mexico. Just a month before, citizens had
held a mass meeting to adopt resolutions condemning the army for not con-
trolling the Apaches. Risque signed the document as secretary of the proceedings.[23] And, in addition to his law practice, he began dabbling in mining
speculation, like practically every other man of substance in that precinct of
the territory.

In early 1882, John Risque became a party to a headline-grabbing legal
case that was tried in the territorial court at Silver City. It involved overlap-
ping claims to two mines, the Oasis and the Last Chance, located at Leitendorf
(also known as Pyramid City) in the mountains about six miles southeast of

Shakespeare. The Last Chance owners found signs of a major silver lode, a discovery that aroused the cupidity of the neighboring claimants and led to litigation over boundaries.

The Oasis faction hired Amos Green, a former practitioner at the St. Louis bar, as its senior attorney, and John P. Risque as his junior. The Last Chance people, the defendants in the case, engaged as their legal representatives Judge Hamilton C. McComas and John D. Bail, an old-timer well known in the territory. Oscar W. Williams, who by this date had become Silver City's postmaster, observed that "in the public eye Judge McComas was the star figure for the defendants."[24] Indeed, he and his associate won the lawsuit handily.

Although McComas and Risque faced each other in this particular case, it seems highly probable that, outside the courtroom, they maintained a friendly relationship. Both were from St. Louis and were Democratic party stalwarts; anyway, the legal community in Silver City was, understandably, small and intimate. Strangely, their careers in New Mexico had several similarities, the most conspicuous being their untimely deaths at the hands of Apache pillagers.

In early spring of 1882, John Risque developed an interest in some gold-mining prospects in the vicinity of Clifton, Arizona. That area was known primarily for its copper deposits having been promoted and worked as early as 1872. At that time the land was inside a reserve for the White Mountain Apaches, and a clique of mine investors and corrupt politicians, by adroit maneuvering, managed to have the Clifton district "segregated." That is, it was removed from Indian control, without consideration for the Indians' rights, and thrown open to prospecting.[25]

Clifton, located some sixty miles northwest of Silver City and about fifteen miles inside the Arizona boundary, was a rough-and-tumble mining camp, widely regarded as a haven for outlaws. Clifton and Silver City maintained strong ties to one another, being connected by regular stage service from an early date, and Clifton during the seventies shipping its ore by freight wagon through Silver City on its way eastward to the railhead. Even after the Southern Pacific arrived and a high percentage of Clifton traffic was diverted south to Lordsburg on the mainline, the faces of Silver City businessmen and promoters remained much in evidence. A group of them, including John Risque, showed up in the third week of April 1882.

Unluckily, that was at the very time of the flight of Loco and his Warm Springs band of Eastern Chiricahuas from San Carlos. As mentioned earlier, some of Juh's Broncos from the Sierra Madre, led by Geronimo, Chato, Chihuahua, and Naiche, had slipped past military patrols on the border and appeared suddenly in Loco's camp, where they forced his people to return with them to Mexico. To avoid interception, the renegades made a swing to the east, in the direction of New Mexico.

Jason Betzinez, then a mere boy in the Apache exodus, vividly recalled years afterward the terror and hardship of that experience. As his people moved hastily up the Gila Valley, bands of warriors split off to sweep the countryside for horses and mules. They were needed as mounts for the women and children. According to Betzinez's account, one of those bands veered northward, ascending the Rio San Francisco, a tributary of the Gila. The trail pointed straight toward Clifton.[26]

As they went, the Indians butchered everyone careless enough to fall into their hands, taking time when the moment allowed to commit some unspeakable acts of torture and mutilation. Several ranchers, who received a warning, were able to move their families, employees, and horse herds out of harm's way. Others were not so fortunate.

Heaviest fatalities were among roaming prospectors and travelers on the road who were surprised in a chance meeting with the Apache horse thieves. Among the latter was Felix Knox, a notorious gambler from Globe, who was driving his family to their ranch on the Gila. When he spotted the painted warriors, he sent his loved ones racing away, while he stayed behind and gave his life so they could escape. When the story was reported, Arizonans dismissed his unsavory reputation and acclaimed him as one of their own heroes.[27]

Although the Indians were cutting the telegraph lines, word still reached Clifton of the breakout from San Carlos. Then news arrived that a wagon train owned by the freighting firm of O. K. Smythe & Babcock had been attacked four miles outside town and five teamsters massacred. The Shakespeare Guards were mustered in the crisis, and a company of fifty volunteers began marching to the relief of Clifton and the Gila Valley settlers.

On Sunday morning, April 21, a small party of prominent gentlemen made ready to leave Clifton for the purpose of inspecting mine sites at Gold Gulch, which lay seven miles west of the community. Old-timers, who had been through Apache uprisings before, tried to dissuade them from so foolhardy an undertaking, without success. In addition to John P. Risque, the group was composed of Sam Eckles Magruder, Capt. John Slawson (a mining superintendent), H. L. Trescott, and a Captain Frink.

Every detail known of this ill-fated excursion smacks of gross negligence and towering ineptitude. Only "Jack" Magruder, for instance, was armed with a rifle. Risque, Slawson, and Trescott carried pistols, which were less than adequate for Indian warfare, and Captain Frink was totally unarmed. Moreover, as they entered the gulch, the men made no attempt to keep together. Risque and Trescott moved ahead of the rest on the trail, farther back Slawson rode in front of Magruder, and tagging behind at a distance was Frink.

Their first intimation of trouble came about noon, when they heard a scattering of gunfire somewhere up the gulch. The shots were from Apache rifles, and they ended the lives of two miners. Captain Slawson began anxiously scanning the rocky slopes, and a few minutes later he exclaimed, "Jack, there are your Indians!" They were the last words he ever spoke.

The men had ridden straight into an ambush. The bullets seemed to come flying from every direction. John Risque, in the lead on his saddle mule, was shot through the jaw and under the shoulder. His body tumbled to the ground. In the next instant, Trescott received a wound in the thigh, and, before he could cry out, a second shot killed him.

Farther back, Captain Slawson had been felled by the first volley, being struck at least twice. Miraculously, Magruder was not hit, and he frantically spurred his horse up the side of the gulch. He gained a few crucial minutes on his pursuers as the Apaches, estimated at twelve in number, paused long enough to round up the loose animals and strip the bodies of the dead. They removed Risque's coat and vest and took his watch, money, and ring. Then they mashed his face in with a rock.

Magruder managed to reach a mine not far away, where he found a pair of men at work, Tom Woods and W. H. Antrim, the stepfather of Billy the Kid. The three forted up near the mine entrance, and when the Indians arrived shooting, they easily drove them off. About 5:30 in the afternoon, with things quiet, they slipped away and reached Clifton by dark.

Shortly, the last member of the original party, Captain Frink, also came in. He had been so far in the rear that he was able to hide in the grass and escape. In all, eleven people died in the environs of Clifton during this single raid.[28]

The mutilated body of John Risque was recovered, sealed in a casket, and escorted by friends back to Silver City. Once there, it was placed in his Masonic lodge on Bullard Street to await services. A friend recalled, "One of my most vivid recollections . . . is that of listening to the sobs of Risque's young widow as the choir sang the beautiful church songs at the funeral."[29] Indeed, the *Daily New Mexican* at Santa Fe reported Mrs. Risque "to have suffered near collapse."[30]

The family chose to have the remains returned to St. Louis for burial. At first word of the tragedy, Mrs. Risque's mother came out from that city to be with her. Following the funeral, the bereaved wife, children, and mother-in-law, with an escort of friends, Masons, and Odd Fellows, accompanied the coffin down to the railroad station at Deming. Out of respect for the deceased, all the stores in Silver City were closed on that day.[31]

Of the fact that Risque's sudden death left his adopted community profoundly saddened and heightened the level of public anger against the Apaches, there cannot be the slightest doubt. How the incident may have affected Hamilton C. McComas is less certain. If he was in town at the time of the funeral, he would have attended the services and witnessed at first hand the grief of Mrs. Risque. Had he been away, he would have learned the circumstances upon his return. In either case, he ought to have been deeply moved, and at the same time he should have experienced a strengthening of his sense of caution and a new wariness whenever the Chiricahua Apaches were a concern.

In the year of Risque's passing, 1882, McComas made several significant changes in his professional and personal life. He began to pull back a bit from his single-minded concentration upon mining affairs. The reason may have been traceable to a souring of his largest venture, the Arizona Mine, into which he had been pouring a great deal of his energy and probably his money, too.

By early 1883, he had managed to divest himself of that burden, because, on January 11, the *Silver City Enterprise* was telling readers that the Arizona had been acquired by a St. Louis company headed by Joseph W. Branch, and that an outside expert, brought to the site, already was sampling ores. The paper described the mine as "only partially developed, but in a very unsatisfactory shape, being what miners term 'butchered.'" The poor condition of the property, in part, could have been attributable to H. C.'s inexperience and insufficient capital.

The court case involving the claimants of the Oasis and Last Chance mines, in which McComas was reputed to have turned in a glowing performance, marked the resumption of his public legal practice. He might have decided that, with his limited knowledge of the mining industry, he was better off staying clear of the promotion and development side of it and sticking with what he knew best—that is, the law. The Last Chance syndicate paid him the substantial fee of five thousand dollars for his successful defense of their interests and retained him as attorney after conclusion of the case.[32]

H. C., in conformity with his previous custom of seeking a partner, found one in Silver City: lawyer Andrew Sloan. On May 6, 1882 (the same week as the Risque funeral), the new firm of McComas & Sloan opened its office in the Corbin Building, at the corner of Bullard and Market streets.[33]

For reasons unknown, the business association of the two men lasted scarcely six months, but when the parting came, it seems to have been an amiable one. A notice appeared in the local press on January 11, 1883, stating: "The law firm of McComas & Sloan has been dissolved and Judge McComas and John M. Wright have joined hands. . . . Mr. Wright is a young man of talent and energy." And the paper added with a flourish: "The new firm will enjoy a legal practice second to none other in this section of the territory."[34]

Originally from Pemberton, New Jersey, John Wright had moved first to St. Louis and then to Silver City. He started his career as a schoolteacher and then drifted into the law. Whether his initial meeting with H. C. was in St. Louis or later in New Mexico is uncertain, but he was not a resident at Silver City very long before he became chummy with all the mining magnates from Missouri, Gen. John Boyle among them. His partnership with Judge McComas eased his entry into the inner circle, but before that relationship advanced very far, misfortune overtook the firm with the violent death of the senior member.[35]

In connection to H. C. McComas's legal career in New Mexico, a small but perplexing episode occurred that began in 1881 and continued over two years. In retrospect, it seems to have left a trace of tarnish upon his name. The affair had its genesis in a letter he wrote from New Mexico on May 25, 1881, addressed to Smith & Keating Implement Company, dealer in wagons and carriages at Kansas City.

Therein, H. C. declared that he was representing one James G. Crittenden of Grant County, New Mexico, and in his name was placing an order for a two-seater spring wagon, complete with whiffletree and neck yoke. He instructed the company to have the wagon knocked down, boxed, and shipped by railroad to Gage Station outside Deming. Mr. Crittenden wanted the vehicle "to go prospecting in." McComas closed his correspondence with this promise: "[The purchaser] will remit money at once on information that wagon has been shipped to him, or I will for him."

In due course, the wagon was sent, along with a bill for Crittenden. He eventually replied, saying that Judge McComas had made a trip back to Missouri and he had given him the money owed to Smith & Keating. Thereupon, a new bill was sent to H. C.'s St. Louis address, where he was staying while visiting his family.

McComas responded by letter, dated September 27, 1881, informing the company that Mr. Crittenden, in fact, had not placed money in his hands to pay for the wagon. "I owe him $100 on a mule trade," he explained, "and he may have taken it for granted that I would send that amount to you, but he never told me to." And H. C. closed with this pledge: "I will be in Kansas City in a day or two, say about October 5, and will call and pay you the account." He never appeared, nor were the creditors ever again able to get an answer from him.

A year later, with the bill still unpaid, Smith & Keating contacted G. Gordon Posey, a Silver City lawyer who had been referred to them, and attempted to engage him to settle the matter. After outlining the circumstances of the case, their letter declared: "Mr. McComas is a friend of our house & a gentleman, we thought, of his word. We want you to proceed to get the money quickly, as the debt is old. McComas has trifled with our good nature & we are tired of waiting."

They closed the instructions with these words: "We hardly think that you will be obliged to put this into suit. We are of the opinion that you can scare it out of him, for the debt is just. Will allow you ten percent on the account if collected."

While Posey accepted the case, any scaring he may have tried failed to resolve the problem. When the judge was massacred less than six months later, the bill from Smith & Keating remained unpaid. Subsequently, however, John Wright, as executor of the McComas estate, decided that the claim was just and paid the amount in full, plus interest that had accrued. Coincidentally, in settling the claim, G. Gordon Posey was assisted by Thomas Conway, the law partner of the late John Risque.[36]

This whole matter has been described at some length because it is practically the only incident occurring during the last years of H. C. McComas's life for which ample details are available, if we make an exception of the events surrounding his death. Since all other contemporary documents refer to him and his character in the most laudatory terms, his unwillingness to meet what was, after all, an inconsequential financial obligation appears baffling. The most reasonable explanation is that the judge, through some process of rationalization, managed to convince himself that he was not liable for the Smith & Keating debt. Whatever his thinking may have been, the failure to settle up cast a tiny cloud over his reputation.

A full two years after he had first set foot in the New Mexico Territory, H. C. McComas finally arranged to bring his family out from St. Louis to join him in Silver City. In March 1882, they rode the train as far as Deming and there took either the regular daily stage or a private buggy on the last lap of the journey to their new home. For Juniata, the two girls, and little Charley, now aged five, the drive over the spacious desert plain, dotted with exotic tree yuccas, toward the hazy mountains that sheltered Silver City had to have been filled with keen excitement and, quite probably, a bit of apprehension as well.

The land so unfamiliar and vast, with its mysterious air and hint of hidden dangers, inevitably frightened newcomers.

H. C. had negotiated with proprietor Louie Timmer for space to accommodate his entire family in the ornate Exchange Hotel. There the McComases would reside for the next seven months, while they adjusted to the novelty of life in a southwestern mining town.[37]

Juniata McComas, from all we know, was welcomed warmly into the bosom of the community. She probably repressed a smile when proud boosters triumphantly informed her that she now was living in the "Diamond City of the Hills," so called because it was like a rare gem among New Mexican municipalities.[38] To Juniata's eyes, the gemlike qualities of Silver City would have been dimmed somewhat by the effects of its lingering rough edges.

For example, as one citizen publicly complained, the streets and sidewalks were deplorable. All the thoroughfares were made of dirt, which turned into impossible quagmires after winter snows and during summer rains. The board sidewalks in front of buildings were either irregular or nonexistent, and there were no street lamps at all to light the nightly passage of pedestrians and

An overview of Silver City at the time of the McComases' residency. Courtesy Silver City Museum, Silver City, New Mexico

vehicles. Untidy accumulations of garbage left in front yards and back lots prompted some recent arrivals to proclaim that "they would not like to risk living here in the summer, on account of the sanitary conditions of the city."[39]

On the other hand, while Silver City might come up short in providing the standard amenities, it managed to furnish others not often seen under frontier conditions. When the town was scarcely a year old, a social club known as the Silver City Lyceum had been founded with fifty charter members. The group's purpose was to open a reading room for entertainment and instruction. That noble effort was followed in 1880 by incorporation of the Silver City Library Association.

Several churches lent an air of respectability, among them the Methodist, said to be the first Protestant church established between Santa Fe and Yuma, Arizona. The smaller Methodist Episcopal, we think, was the one attended by the McComases, there being no Congregational church, which Juniata would have sought out. Furthermore, in 1882 Silver City built a two-story red brick school with a gabled roof, the very first independent public school in New Mexico, authorized by the territorial legislature. It stood on high ground west of downtown, and the McComas girls soon were enrolled.[40]

On December 15, 1882, H. C. McComas purchased a comfortable brick single-story house with white trim, on Hudson Street, a block north of the Exchange Hotel.[41] Was it intended as a Christmas present for his family? Although that cannot be determined, it is certain that the new residence symbolized the McComases' commitment to make Silver City their permanent home.

The official inventory of their household goods and furnishings, made shortly after the massacre, runs to nine closely worded, legal-size pages. Many of the things on the list seem to have been old family possessions, necessarily freighted from St. Louis at considerable cost. The document affords a revealing and quite personal glimpse of the interior of the McComas home.

The living room held the usual armchairs, tables with lamps, window curtains, and carpets, plus something rarely seen at that date in the territory—a piano and its stool. Framed pictures decorated the walls: one was a pastoral scene focusing on a covey of quail, another depicted statuary, and a third bore the title, "War and Peace." A finished cabinet stood in the connecting hall.

The master bedroom contained a white double bedstead, bureau, large looking glass, and wash stand. Juniata's Wilcox & Gibbs sewing machine, listed separately, may have been kept there also. In other rooms could be found a second double bedstead, evidently for the girls, and a smaller single bed that likely belonged to Charley. The kitchen was well supplied with the customary assortment of domestic utensils, including such items as glass goblets, ornamental pitchers and vases, a Majolica pickle dish, pepper box, coffee mill, and demijohn. Two oak water barrels rested on the floor, next to a wash bench, indicating that inside plumbing had not yet reached the house.

And books! Large numbers of books filled pine shelves in the front rooms. Beyond a ten-volume *Chambers' Cyclopedia*, the titles ran heavily to English literature (the complete works of Shakespeare, two volumes of Byron's poems, the poetry of Wordsworth and Tennyson, and so forth), European history, ancient classics, science, philosophy, and, of course, religion, since Juniata McComas, as mentioned earlier, was the reader in that marriage. Copies of *Dana's Geology* and *Mines of the West*, together with two dozen law books, obviously represented the judge's part of the family library.[42]

The picture these details convey is of an upper-middle-class family living in relative luxury, at a time and in a place where the majority of the people got by on bare necessities. Still, there were men wealthier than H. C. McComas then inhabiting Silver City—mine owners, bankers, and merchants who were building Victorian mansions and whose political influence stretched to Santa Fe and even to Washington. Incontestably, Judge McComas had become part of their circle, and probably it was by wire pulling that he emerged as head of the Grant County Commission (either by election or appointment) during December 1882, the same month in which he acquired the Hudson Street house.[43]

The move to their own lodgings and the settling in must have kept Juniata occupied for some time. From what is known of her habits, she ought to have been a diligent housekeeper. For reference, she kept among her books a copy of the instructional manual, *Woman, Wife and Mother*. And, it was undoubtedly she who, at some point, persuaded the wife of her husband's friend, Oscar W. Williams, to give the girls, Ada and Mary, music lessons. The living room piano, therefore, served as more than just an ornament.[44]

Not long after the McComases were reunited in Silver City, they established a strong friendship with the young photographer Harry W. Lucas and his wife. Lucas had blown into town about April 1, 1882, to work for Alfred S. Addis, who had a downtown photo shop and a gallery. Within three months, Lucas was able to buy out the shop, and the following year he acquired the gallery, prompting the press to note that in the way of photography, Lucas "has the field to himself."[45]

Harry Lucas's wife, whose maiden name was Sanborn, hailed from Iowa. The couple had married on March 27 and headed straight for Silver City, arriving just a few days after Juniata and the children.[46] The fact that both women were Iowans may have brought them together initially—that and their status as newcomers struggling to adapt to an unfamiliar environment and to find a niche for themselves in the social life of the community.

An idea of the depth of their relationship can be drawn from Mrs. Lucas's words, contained in a letter to Charles Ware, written immediately after the untimely death of his sister. "Mrs. McComas and I were very intimate friends, and she has been a true, dear sister to me ever since we both came to this country; and the judge has been like a father to me. I feel as though I had lost a home, and two of the truest friends one can have on this earth."[47]

Soon after the start of their association, the McComases and the Lucases began making regular excursions together into the countryside. These were outings for recreation, but they also provided Harry Lucas an opportunity to make photographs of the spectacular landscape. When he wasn't at work in his Silver City studio, taking portraits or developing prints, he was ranging far afield in search of customers in need of his photographic services. He made frequent trips to Clifton, Arizona, for instance, where he was said to be very popular and able to do "a bonanza business." There he captured what were described as elegant views of the scenery.[48]

Juniata found these short trips particularly enjoyable, and, in writing to her brothers Eugene and Charles at Fort Scott, she spoke of them with enthusiasm. Furthermore, she sometimes enclosed prints, given to her by Harry

McComas family, left, and two friends, on an outing shortly before the massacre.
From author's collection

Lucas, that showed the splendid beauty of the country she was learning to love.[49]

One remarkable photograph that has come down to us shows the Mc-Comas family and friends posing, rather stiffly, for a group portrait. They are seated upon a rock formation that existed somewhere within easy driving distance of Silver City. The formal clothes the subjects are wearing suggest that the occasion is a pleasant sightseeing tour after church on Sunday, perhaps including a picnic. The weather must have been mild, since the ladies are not dressed in heavy coats, suggesting a date sometime in the fall of 1882.

Judge McComas, with graying beard and a bowler hat on his head, sits tall and erect at the left of the group. Next to him is an impish-appearing Mary, her long hair resting on a lace collar. The child leaning against a boulder is thought to be the eldest daughter, Ada McComas, and the white-gloved woman at the center of the photograph is her mother, Juniata. The two females at the right are unidentified, but the younger, tightly corseted figure on Juniata's left may well be Mrs. Lucas. Conspicuously missing from this picture is son Charley McComas who may have been left at home that day.[50]

During the year that the McComas family lived in Silver City, the law firm that H. C. had established with his partner John M. Wright grew vigorously and prospered. One source predicted that the office of McComas & Wright "will soon be recognized as among the strongest legal teams in the territory."[51]

The chief reason for this success can be found in the partnership's early decision to specialize in cases related to the mining industry. H. C.'s former dabbling in mine development and promotion had not gotten him very far, but it did serve to educate him in field matters, so that when he turned back to the law, he had good grounding in the technical and scientific aspects of the work. That was demonstrated in the publicity given to his victory in the Last Chance Mine case.

The ascendancy of McComas & Wright, therefore, was rapid. Observed the *Silver City Enterprise* toward the end of February 1883: "They already enjoy a large practice, which is daily increasing and extending into every mining camp in southern New Mexico."[52]

The firm won a valuable plum when it was selected by the Pyramid Mining and Milling Company to take charge of its numerous suits then pending before the courts. Those suits, it was claimed, involved more capital than had been in litigation within the territory during the last few years.

The Pyramid operation, situated a half-dozen miles below Lordsburg and Shakespeare, was in the hands of St. Louis men, among them Amos Green, who were well known to H. C. Beyond doubt, it was through friendship and the use of influence that McComas managed to secure a position with the company for his oldest son David, now twenty-one. The young man came out from the East, found lodging at Lordsburg, and went to work at nearby Pyramid City, which, despite its exalted name, was little more than a primitive mining camp. His younger brother William at this time was living in Nebraska City, Nebraska, under the charge of his uncle Rufus McComas, a prominent banker there.[53]

H. C. was reported to have been at the Pyramid mines in February 1883, "looking after the affairs of the company."[54] He could have come down from his home by private conveyance or by taking the Silver City Fast Stage Line, whose four-horse coaches made the run to Lordsburg daily, except Sundays.[55] With the well-traveled stage road he was thoroughly familiar, having been over it numerous times in the past three years.

Probably McComas was looking forward to the completion of the Silver City, Deming and Pacific, a narrow-gauge railroad which at that very moment was laying ties and track northward from Deming. Upon its completion, he would be able to travel in comfort from Silver City on a roundabout route down to the Southern Pacific main line and thence westward on that track to Lordsburg.

For the time being, however, he was limited to the more traditional means of transportation. Upon winding up his business in the Pyramids, H. C. made a swing westward into Arizona's San Simon Valley and then steered a course toward home, arriving at Silver City late in the opening week of March.[56]

On this wide-ranging tour, there is no evidence that Judge McComas entertained any concern at all for his safety. Since the outbreak of the previous year, when Loco and his Warm Springs Apaches had decamped from San Carlos, the border country had remained unusually quiet. Troops of soldiers were patrolling the international boundary to prevent the hostiles from leaving Mexico and slipping back inside the territories, and an uneasy calm had settled upon the desert.

Once more within the security of his house on Hudson Street, Hamilton Calhoun McComas could have paused to reflect upon the good fortune that seemed to be flowing his way. His wife and children were busy and content. His newest law partner, the fourth in his career, was working out splendidly; and their business together promised large future rewards. As chairman of the board of the Grant County Commission, he possessed a post highly visible and well respected in the community. And to satisfy his ambition, or maybe from a desire to engage in more public service, the judge was running for a position on the city council, in the municipal elections scheduled for the following April 3. Yes, if he thought about it, his little mountain-ringed world must have looked positively rosy.

On March 7, Juniata McComas celebrated her thirty-seventh birthday. Family and friends gathered to give her a delightful little reception, an occasion never forgotten by those who were there, since, as things turned out, it was to be the final social event in which all the McComases participated.[57] Scarcely three weeks later, amid Apache war cries, their rosy world came to an abrupt end.

Chapter Five

The Raid

After Juh and Geronimo abducted Loco and his band from San Carlos in April 1882, fleeing south into the sheltering embrace of the Mexican sierras, a welcome quiet settled upon the country north of the international boundary. No one in either New Mexico or Arizona thought the peace would last very long, least of all Gen. George Crook, who was returned to the Southwest in September to begin preparing military forces for the anticipated next round of hostilities. Now though, he had in hand an added weapon, which provided the army a much-needed edge—the treaty with the neighboring republic, allowing "hot pursuit" across the border.

The Sierra Madre Apaches, meanwhile, were busy regrouping. As had happened north of the line, their theater of operations in Chihuahua and Sonora was steadily diminishing as ranching and mining expanded, some of it undertaken by immigrant Americans, and as agricultural settlements spread into the farthest valleys. However, the parallel ranges of mountains were so vast and formidable that the Indians had little trouble finding a secure haven. A pressing problem was that they could come up with no way of acquiring the necessities of life except through theft and murder—the very activities that had turned all men against them.

Just how many Apaches remained free in Mexico at this time is difficult to calculate. Jason Betzinez, who as a youngster was with them, declared that there had been several hundred men, women, and children, of whom seventy-five or eighty were "first line warriors."[1] A White Mountain Apache, riding with these Broncos, later informed Crook that, in addition to the men, there were "fifty big boys able to fight."[2] Reports place the total population of hostiles at perhaps five to six hundred.

The numbers, in fact, kept changing, as individuals or small groups slipped away to return to relatives and friends at San Carlos, while at the same time new recruits from the north, fed up with the hardships of reservation life, drifted in and attached themselves to the leader of their choice. Jason indicates that representatives of many Apache subtribes, and not just Chiricahuas, were present in the camps, along with a few renegade Navajos and some young Mexicans and Americans who had been captured as boys and now were married and fully assimilated into the tribe.[3]

Following the April 1882 return from Arizona, the Indians commenced to raid the Mexicans with a vengeance. From their mountain stronghold they sallied forth, robbing pack trains loaded with goods and seizing livestock. Everywhere they left the landscape littered with dead and mutilated bodies. When troops of soldiers, assigned to small towns and isolated haciendas, attempted to pursue the marauders, they usually fell victim to an ambuscade and sustained heavy casualties. Chihuahuans and Sonorans lived in a state of terror; and the governors of those states, unable to check the carnage, were overcome with despair.

The Apaches, however, experienced losses of their own—an irreplaceable warrior here, another one or two there. From May 1882 through the first quarter of 1883, they lost 150 women and children, either captured or slain. The most grievous incident for them in this period, which occurred at the town of Casas Grandes in northwestern Chihuahua, was largely of the Apaches' own doing.

During that summer, the band's leaders convened a council in their mountainous hideaway and decided to seek an armistice with the Mexicans at Casas Grandes on the plains below. The sole motive for this bizarre proposal was to obtain a supply of liquor, for which the Apaches had a fatal fondness. Geronimo spoke strongly in favor of the plan.

About one-third of the Broncos, led by Juh and Geronimo, descended to Casas Grandes and opened negotiations with the *alcalde* (mayor) and other community officials. An accord was soon reached, and the Mexicans smilingly proclaimed that old troubles were forgotten, peace reigned, and the Apaches could freely enter the plaza and engage in trade. What they traded for was mescal, a highly intoxicating beverage that flowed like water in the local cantinas. The fierce warriors imprudently embarked on a two-day drunk, which effectively defanged them.[4]

Before sunrise on the third day, their armed hosts entered the Indian camp just beyond the municipal walls and, finding many of the occupants lying in a stupor, launched a wholesale butchery. Chiricahuas on the perimeter were able to escape. Among them were Juh, Geronimo, and the boy Jason Betzinez, who credited his salvation to being a fast runner—"always a good accomplishment when you tangle with your true, everlasting friends, the Mexicans," he wrote acidly.[5]

That Geronimo could have been lured into such a trap seems incomprehensible today. Back in 1850, soldiers had killed his mother, first wife, and three children at nearby Janos, leaving him with a remorseless hatred for the people of that country. Both he and Juh considered Mexico a land of treachery. But that did not prevent them from succumbing to the alcalde's offer of friendship, a mistake that cost their followers dearly. Philosophized Betzinez: "Once again the Indians had fallen victim to their own weakness, the love of strong drink, which has been their ruin."[6]

The survivors made their way back to the main camp in the sierra. Subsequently, dissension arose among the leaders as to the best course to be followed. Loco and some of his people, less inclined toward raiding, earlier had withdrawn to a sanctuary deeper in the mountains. Now the main body of the Apaches split, with Juh taking the largest contingent and moving farther into the high country wilderness; while Geronimo, left with the bloodthirstiest firebrands, rode westward into Sonora to plunder and slay.

On this rampage, the Apache raiders penetrated a populous district, rich in mines and ranches, north of the Yaqui River. They made a broad, wobbly circle completely around the city of Ures, fought sharp engagements with government troops, and finally retreated northwestward, weighted down with booty.

Then Geronimo guided his band to an isolated spot some thirty miles from the outpost town of Fronteras. Here, where deer and firewood were plentiful and enemies could not track them, the Indians settled in to spend the heart of the winter. The idle time was passed in making preparations to resume their raiding at the first sign of spring. The beloved sixteen-shot repeater rifles got a thorough cleaning and a fresh coat of grease, new moccasins and shirts were sewn, and tough rawhide ropes braided. By mid-March 1883, the warriors old and young were chafing to be on the move again.

Three days' ride to the north in Silver City, New Mexico, Juniata McComas happily was making plans for her upcoming birthday reception, wholly unaware that events transpiring in the renegade camp down in Sonora would lead, inside two week's time, to her death and that of her husband. What set the whole tragic episode in motion was a council at which the Apaches formulated their strategy for the war season's first major operation.

Geronimo announced to the assembly that he would lead about fifty warriors back to the vicinity of Ures, where the earlier foray had been so profitable. His principal aim was to hit horse herds and remount the men, in addition to driving away livestock to be used as a reserve food supply for his people.

A smaller party was formed to carry out a second equally important mission—an "ammunition raid" over the border, into the land of the hated White Eyes. By now the Apaches, as noted, were largely dependent upon their American-made guns; and getting new shells, as their old supply became exhausted, was a recurring need that could not be ignored.

Asa Daklugie, son of Juh, told of the inception of this raid when he was interviewed by historian Eve Ball in the 1950s. According to him, a subchief named Chihuahua was the organizer and leader. That individual, by established custom, had the right to invite warriors to join his party at the war dance, following adjournment of the council. Daklugie claimed that Chato, "without waiting for Chief Chihuahua to call his name, arose and joined the dancers, thereby signifying his desire to become a member of the raiders."[7] Such insolence, in violation of tradition, was frowned upon, but nevertheless Chato gained admission to Chihuahua's ranks because he was brave and a respected fighter. For the same reason, another man called Tzoe (meaning Yellow Wolf or Coyote) who "crashed" the war dance also was accepted.

Daklugie was in his teens and far away in the hideout of his father Juh when all this occurred. However, as he informed Ball, he had known intimately nearly all the men who went to Arizona for ammunition, and from them he obtained his information. Virtually every other contemporary source, from both Indians and whites, places Chato and not Chihuahua at the head of this raiding party.[8]

The first Arizona newspaper accounts of the new Apache onslaught attributed it to renegades from Juh's band out of Old Mexico. So too did P. P. Wilcox, the Indian agent at San Carlos.[9] The public was not yet aware that Geronimo had emerged as leader of a separate faction of the Sierra Madre Chiricahuas, and that Juh no longer was the grand chief of them all. Some early, unsubstantiated reports placed Juh himself at the head of the raid, but before many days had passed, it was learned that an unheralded figure, a warrior named Chato, was in charge. It was this single episode, on which he was now embarked, that would catapult him into the history books.

In 1883 Chato had reached thirty years of age and stood in the prime of his fighting form. Running true to the Apache type, he was short and stocky,

Chief Chihuahua, who rode with Geronimo to raid in Mexico while Chato pillaged Arizona and New Mexico. Courtesy Arizona Historical Society, Tucson, Arizona

with a barrel chest and bull neck. His most memorable physical feature was a disfigured nose, which had won him the name Chato, a Spanish word signifying Flat Nose. The flattening had occurred when he was young and a mule kicked him full in the face.[10]

Prior to the raid, Chato seems to have done little that might have made him stand out. In the early eighties, he was attached to the remnant of Victorio's old band. Later, Apaches who were antagonistic toward him, which was the majority of the Chiricahuas, described him in those days as "arrogant, overbearing, quarrelsome, and cruel."[11] Daklugie insisted that he was motivated by ambition and envy, because he aspired to lead and, having no hereditary claim to the position of chieftain, usually was thwarted. However, Daklugie's hatred of Chato appears to have colored his judgment and testimony, so when he claims that Chihuahua rather than Chato captained the ammunition raid, his statement cannot be accepted.[12]

The exact circumstances that brought Chato into that important position are unknown. As was pointed out in an earlier chapter, any Apache man could field and lead a war party, provided he could recruit others willing to join in. Henry W. Daly, a civilian mule packer for the army's Quartermaster Department, once observed that, among the Chiricahuas, "each chief had his own following, and each was extremely jealous of the other."[13] Was there bad feeling at this time between Geronimo and the self-assertive upstart, Chato, that led them to part company and go raiding separately?

While that remains a highly plausible theory, not much can be found in the record to support it. Jason Betzinez, who, unlike Daklugie, actually was on the scene, makes no mention of hostility between Geronimo and Chato, although he could have had his own reasons for failing to refer to it. When the band split, with the larger segment raiding toward Ures and the smaller making for the United Sates, there is nothing in Jason's narrative to suggest other than an amiable parting. He does declare pointedly that Chief Chihuahua accompanied Geronimo as his second in command, and that the ammunition raid was proposed and led by Chato. That would seem to settle the matter of who was in charge of the party that met and massacred the McComases.[14]

Historical sources of the period are fairly consistent in establishing that a total of twenty-six warriors participated in Chato's raid. At least eight or so can be identified by name, and these were men of some note in Apache affairs. The inference that must be drawn is that Chato possessed sufficient strength and ability to attract worthy enlistments. Throughout the days they were on the trail, he in fact would prove his fitness as a war chief.

The second most important man in the party, Chato's main lieutenant, was a White Mountain Apache subchief called Bonito (sometimes spelled Benito). A son-in-law of Chihuahua, his name first surfaces in 1882 at the time of the breakout from San Carlos. He had a pointed chin, a downturned mouth, extra-sharp cheekbones, and a skewed left eye that gave him a particularly sinister look. His fierce reputation as a fighter made him acceptable to the Chiricahuas. Strong evidence exists that Bonito carried Charley McComas back into the Sierra Madre.[15]

Among Chato's body of warriors were found two distinguished individuals, either one of whom could have claimed a leadership role, had he been so inclined. One was Naiche (or Natchez), the youngest son of the late Cochise, and a grandson, through his mother, of the celebrated war chief Mangas Coloradas. The other celebrity was Mangus, son of Mangas Coloradas and uncle of Naiche.

Lt. Britton Davis, who knew both these men, explained their willingness to let others assume command. Naiche, although a fine warrior, was fond of the ladies, liked dancing and having a good time, and was not serious enough to shoulder responsibility. Mangus, for his part, simply was not aggressive enough, "on account of his pacific character," as Davis phrased it.[16] His pacifism must have been entirely relative, since, riding with Chato, he could not have helped spilling blood.

Another warrior of more than passing interest was the volatile Dutchy, so called because the soldiers thought he looked like a German. The incident in which he pursued and killed his own father and reputedly brought his head back to San Carlos in a sack already has been described. Mule packer Daly portrayed him as "a most incorrigible and vicious scoundrel."[17] But later, after the raid, when Dutchy had become an army scout, some of the officers saw him as witty and appreciated his skill in tracking hostiles.[18]

Tzoe, the man who in Daklugie's account crashed the war dance, would become, through a combination of circumstances, a key figure in this episode. Whites generally knew him by the nickname Peaches, owing to his very fair, rosy complexion. Davis wrote that he was "a handsome young fellow about twenty-three or twenty-four years of age."[19] Captain Bourke added that "he never knew what it was to be tired, cross, or out of humor . . . and his absolute veracity and fidelity in all his dealings [was] a notable feature in his character."[20]

Like Bonito, Peaches was not a Chiricahua but a White Mountain Apache. He was married to a Chiricahua woman, and, during the flight from San Carlos the previous year, he had gone with her and her people into Mexico. Before long, however, his wife had been slain in a fight with Mexican soldiers; and, although he remained with the Broncos through the winter, his allegiance to them seems never to have been more than lukewarm. By going on the ammunition raid to Arizona, he saw a chance to get news of his mother and other family members at the San Carlos agency. He was accompanied by another young man, a close friend whose Apache name was Beneactiney.[21]

As it happened, Beneactiney was the older cousin of Jason Betzinez, who described him with pride "as one of the bravest men of our band."[22] In his early twenties, Beneactiney was the eldest male remaining in the Betzinez family unit, which included only Jason, his mother, and his sister. The other men all were dead. Perhaps under the influence of Peaches, Beneactiney decided to cast his lot with Chato. Thus, at the division of the band, he bid his young cousin good-bye, since Jason was going with Geronimo as a warrior apprentice. Neither was aware of it at the time, but they would never meet again.

As related in an earlier chapter, one or more apprentices participated in Chato's foray. Among them was the boy later known as Sam Haozous, who lived into the 1950s. According to his daughter, he was about ten years old at the time—the youngest member of the war party.[23] The presence of women on this raiding expedition is more difficult to verify. As we have seen, warriors were in the habit of using apprentices and females while on campaign to build and tend fires, cook, care for their horses, and stand guard duty. As things evolved, Chato swept through Arizona and New Mexico with such uncanny swiftness that he never paused long enough to make a real camp.

Nevertheless, stray references lead us to believe that Apache women actually were involved. Evidently they did not start out with the war party but joined it later. It seems that a small group of women from San Carlos were headed south, by themselves, to visit relatives among the Broncos, when they chanced to fall in with Chato and his men. Eyewitnesses who observed one of the initial attacks made north of the border claimed to have seen ten "squaws" herding a band of horses and mules stolen by the marauders.[24] Anton Mazzanovich, an Austrian-born mule packer employed by the government, places at least one Indian woman on hand at the McComas massacre, but other sources dispute that.[25]

When Chato separated from Geronimo, about March 14, he guided his followers out of the wilds of the Sonoran mountains and into the valley of the upper San Pedro River, which flowed for some miles in a northerly direction before entering the United States. On a road near the headwaters of the river, the Indians ran into three men on horseback—two Mexicans and an American. They wasted no time in killing them and taking their arms. The next day, upon approaching the border, the warriors met a wagon containing five more men. Shots were exchanged, and two of the travelers were slain, while the other three escaped. Thus, even before leaving Sonora, Chato bore responsibility for five deaths.[26]

On March 21 the party crossed into Arizona and commenced the whirlwind raid that would leave a string of bloody corpses in its wake. By this one headline-grabbing episode, Chato also guaranteed the conspicuous engraving of his name in the annals of frontier warfare. At first news of his ascent from Sonora, the editor of the *Tucson Daily Star* lamented, "The annual invasion of the Apaches is again upon us." And he predicted somberly that "renewed hate would stir in every [citizen's] breast against the savage fiends who delight to glut in the blood of our people."[27] Over the ensuing week, newspapers across the land ran one story after another, following the progress of the Apache pillagers and outlining in horrifying detail the nature of their murderous deeds.

A young army officer at Fort Lowell near Tucson, Thomas Cruse, contended that the effect of this raid upon Arizonans was much greater than it should have been, mainly because months of quiet had lulled them into believing that Indian troubles were over. "New settlers and prospectors had crowded in," he explained, "and many of the newcomers had little conception of frontier conditions. They wanted to go wherever fancy dictated, in perfect freedom and safety."[28] In those days, relaxing vigilance along the border could prove fatal.

One man not deceived by the quiet was General Crook. From the moment of his return to the Southwest, he began preparing for the inevitable day when the Broncos would ride out of their Mexican lair and launch still another round of attacks upon Americans. In October 1882, he had ordered Capt. Emmet Crawford to take the field with three companies of loyal Apache scouts, about one hundred men in all; and, from a site known as Cloverdale in New Mexico's bootheel, to patrol the international boundary westward into Arizona.

During the long winter, Crawford kept up his surveillance, even dispatching three of the scouts sixty miles into Chihuahua in the hope of getting a line on the hostiles.[29] In establishing the patrol in this sector, Crook supposed that it offered the most likely route for an invasion. But, as it turned out, he guessed wrong, since Chato made his entry much farther west, in the vicinity of the San Pedro Valley.

In that happenstance, at least one carping journalist saw something sinister, not on the part of the general but rather on the part of the scouts. Noting that the hostiles had steered clear of the territory over which Crawford's companies were ranging, he asked rhetorically: "Does not this fact show that there must be an understanding between the renegades and the scouts, and that they know of each others whereabouts and avoid one another? It looks very much that way."[30] Civilians generally believed the scouts were playing a double game, but in this instance, anyway, no evidence can be found to support the journalist's suspicions.

As soon as he was notified that the long anticipated rampage had begun, Crook ordered out every available soldier from the forts in the lower half of his department.[31] Some went in direct pursuit of the war party, while others were hurried to strategic points on the border in an effort to make an interception when time came for the retreat into Mexico. The general also wired Lieutenant Davis, temporarily in charge at San Carlos, to watch the reservation boundaries closely, just in case any of the raiders should try to slip in to see their relatives.[32]

Davis received instructions, moreover, to warn the friendly Apaches against harboring the invading Broncos. But that proved to be the farthest thing from their minds, for, after being notified of the war party's approach, the clusters of women and children who congregated daily around the agency buildings disappeared. Said Davis: "The Indian villages took on the appearance of armed camps. Guns and ammunition we had never suspected the Indians of having were produced, and a number of armed San Carlos Apache voluntarily took up the task of outposts in the neighboring hills."[33]

The majority of reservation residents looked with alarm upon the advent of their trouble-making kin out of Mexico, fearing—rightly—that the white man's wrath would fall indiscriminately upon themselves and the offenders. Attentive to that concern, Indian agent Wilcox conducted a quick head check at San Carlos and issued a public statement saying that all of his Indians were present and accounted for and that the Chiricahuas committing depredations were members of Juh's band of renegades from the Sierra Madre.[34] Not all citizens believed him.

The speed with which Chato and his warriors tore through southeastern Arizona, and the distances between their killings, initially led many people to assume that more than one party had to be involved. About midway through the week-long raid, it was firmly established that all the mayhem could be attributed to a single band of raiders. Moving night and day, riding captured horses to death, and sleeping as their mounts jogged along, the Apaches demonstrated an astonishing mobility. From their entry into the United States on March 21 to their exit on March 29, they covered, in their zigzag course, somewhere between two and four hundred miles.

Chato's slaughter commenced toward sunset the first day after crossing the border. Leaving the San Pedro Valley, he angled northwestward in the direction of the Huachuca Mountains. In the outlying Canelo Hills, the raiders stumbled upon a charcoal camp. They found three workers felling trees and a fourth burning charcoal, a product much in demand at nearby mines. A hail of bullets quickly ended the lives of William Murray, Ged Owens, Joseph Woelfolk, and a man named Armstrong.[35]

A fifth man, P. R. Childs, the only armed member of the group, was a short distance away; when the shooting began, he dashed inside a tent. From behind a corral, thirty feet out, the Apaches called for him to surrender. When there was no response, they opened fire on the tent. Then, all being quiet, Beneactiney, followed by Peaches, rushed it. Childs started shooting and dropped Beneactiney in his tracks, the first and, as it turned out, the only fatality the party suffered on this raid. Peaches turned on his heels and sprinted to safety. Chastened by their loss, the Indians abandoned the attack and rode northward.[36]

Childs hastened to Fort Huachuca twelve miles away and sounded the alarm. Six hours after the assault, Capt. Daniel Madden with Company C, Sixth Cavalry, arrived at the charcoal camp and found the bodies where they had fallen. Word was sent to the nearest town, Charleston, a milling center, and also to Tombstone, nine miles beyond, summoning the county coroner.[37]

Evidently a sizable number of Charleston folk accompanied the coroner to the death scene. There they decapitated Beneactiney's corpse and carried the grisly trophy home. The head was boiled in a kettle, polished with wire brushes, and skewered upon a pole to be displayed for public viewing in the center of town. Further, community leaders took up a collection and purchased a fancy rifle, which they had engraved with the name of P. R. Childs. In gratitude, it was formally presented to Beneactiney's slayer.[38]

From the Huachucas, Chato steered a course that led north toward the next detached mountain range, the Whetstones. On the road they encountered a Mexican in a buckboard and took his life. In addition, they cut the telegraph line that ran from mining camps on the border to towns along the Southern Pacific Railroad.[39] By this date, the Apaches were fully aware of the danger posed by the "talking wire," which rapidly could communicate news of their movements. Not only did they interrupt service at every opportunity, but also they had learned how to false-splice the severed line with rawhide, so that the cut was not easily detected from below by repair crews.

On their second day in Arizona, the hostiles penetrated the Whetstones, where there were several more charcoal camps. They struck, however, not these camps but a train of fourteen heavily loaded pack mules and a supply wagon. The pack master, a Frenchman named Stephen Barthand, and his three Mexican drovers all were massacred. The Apaches, as was their custom, looted the train for blankets and arms, destroyed what was left, and drove away the mules.

On the afternoon of March 22, an excited Mexican reached the Total Wreck Mine, located some ten miles from the Whetstones, and reported that Apaches were in the mountains and had attacked Barthand's pack train. That was the first news the miners had of Indians in their vicinity. The next day, a heavily armed party ventured forth, recovered the bodies, and then went on to

Caly's charcoal camp about two miles south of the massacre site. All the workers there were found to be safe.

At the Total Wreck, the miners assembled on March 23 and, following an inquest, saw that the Barthand pack-train victims were "decently interred." Almost at once, word of additional killings began to arrive, including those of S. E. James of the Contention Mine and his companion, C. M. Thorndykeson, whose bodies were found beneath their mangled buggy on the San Pedro road. A press notice from a correspondent at the Total Wreck contained this cry: "How much longer are the men who are trying to develop this country to suffer from the hands of these red devils? When will the government do something to stop this wholesale murder?"[40] Over the week that followed, the phrase "red devils" was picked up and featured boldly in the headlines of territorial newspapers.

Leaving the Whetstone Mountains, the renegades moved back into the San Pedro Valley, which they descended about thirty-five miles before veering off toward the northeast in the direction of the Winchester range. At three o'clock in the afternoon on March 23, J. J. Howard was shoeing horses in his corral with a friend, M. C. James, when both men looked up and were startled to see seven mounted warriors regarding them from a few yards away.

Instantly, Howard grabbed his rifle and fired. One of the Apaches toppled to the ground, but the others picked him up, placed him on his horse, and then all dashed through some large boulders, making for hills a short distance away. Farther out, the white men observed ten additional warriors, together with ten women (the "squaws" who were alleged to have come from San Carlos). They were herding a band of stolen horses and mules, estimated to number from 100 to 125 animals. Howard threw another eight or ten shots at the retreating Indians, while James held his fire. As he explained it later, they thought the warriors might return and besiege them, so he saved his bullets.[41]

Chato, however, was in no mood to linger. Two miles from the corral fight, he and his fellows emerged upon a height known as Point of Mountain, at the southern end of the Winchesters. Looking down on the road that led a dozen miles southeast to the railroad town of Willcox, they beheld two men traveling along, one mounted on a burro and the other on a horse, driving another loose horse in front. With war whoops, the Apaches charged the startled pair, shooting one in the chest and the other in the stomach. The latter victim was still alive, and his assailants finished their merciless task by crushing his skull with stones. Then they rode into the gathering gloom of evening on Good Friday, 1883.[42]

The first press reports described the two bodies found at Point of Mountain to be those of prospectors and noted that no identification was found upon them. Someone suggested, however, that one of the deceased might be a brother of Judge Henry C. Dibble of Tombstone. And so that official was notified, with the result that, the day after the massacre, he drove to Willcox. There he identified the remains of his younger brother and also those of his companion, whose name was Bateman. Afterward, he arranged for their burial.

Being an individual of some standing, Judge Dibble promptly wrote an open letter addressed to President Chester A. Arthur in Washington, both lamenting his personal loss and issuing a call for justice, as he put it, "in the hope that I may bring the country to comprehend the fact that the government is either unwilling or too powerless to protect the lives of American citizens from massacre at the hands of a tribe of incorrigible savages." The judge's own recommendation was that the Chiricahuas be held accountable for their murders under the criminal laws of the territories, and, to guarantee public safety, they—men, women, and children—should be exiled to the Tortugas in the Caribbean or to one of the Aleutian Islands off the coast of Alaska.[43]

The Dibble letter to the president was published by papers across the country. Tucson's *Daily Star* gave it full coverage and commented that the judge's words no doubt would be read by thousands of Americans and would "do much to correct public opinion on Arizona's Apache troubles."[44] That comment referred to a widely-held perception among southwesterners that their fellow countrymen, who lived far removed from the realities of frontier warfare, were overly sympathetic to the Indians.

In fact, Indian rights organizations, in which certain Protestant churches had become quite strong, had been campaigning to improve treatment of the government's native wards. But public opinion as a whole, which was easily influenced by the shocking news stories of something like Chato's raid, remained largely unsympathetic. As details of the latest atrocities began to reach the East Coast, the *New York Herald,* for one, pulled no punches in an editorial that appeared under the title, "The Chiricahua Apaches." Its conclusion? "These wretches . . . deserve no mercy, and the people of southern Arizona are justified in demanding their extermination."[45] A journalist on the scene assented and in print added his own call for "a total extermination of the pest."[46]

In plain truth, demands that the Chiricahuas either be destroyed or wholly removed from the region were being loudly voiced by prominent spokesmen everywhere in Arizona and New Mexico. Extremists wanted not just Chato's offenders punished, but all their kinsmen on the San Carlos reservation as well. At the mining camp of Tombstone, a hotbed of vigilantism, irate citizens held a mass meeting, formed a volunteer company to wage war against all Apaches, and owners of the Contention, Grant Central, and Toughnut mines each subscribed one thousand dollars to the effort.[47] A rumor also was picked up and reported on the national news wire to the effect that some Arizonans had organized a secret society whose aim was to exterminate male Apaches at San Carlos and any others discovered roving north of the frontier.[48]

Such intemperate measures derived, at least in part, from citizen frustration over the army's inability to engage Chato and put a stop to his mad foray. No settler, rancher, or miner was unaware that, when the invaders committed their first murders at the charcoal camp, four troops of cavalry rested comfortably in their quarters a few miles away at Fort Huachuca. Nor were their fears allayed when they observed how slowly the military units moved over the blood-stained trail after they were ordered into the field from all points. As one critic expressed it sarcastically, "The soldiers will follow at a safe distance and Washington dispatches will teem with reports of the troops being in hot pursuit, and all that sort of balderdash."[49]

The reaction was a symptom of the long-standing antagonism on the part of territorial residents toward their government and the army, who jointly were blamed for coddling the Chiricahuas and then failing to pursue them aggressively when they went on the warpath. Tombstone's famed newspaper, *The Epitaph,* advised its readers that a hardy civilian force was mustering to march forth and protect the soldiers. "The uniformed fellows who spend their days in the laborious task of sucking sutler whiskey shall not be put in jeopardy," it sneered.[50]

The rival *Tombstone Republican* fired its own salvo, reporting that an army detachment had boarded the Southern Pacific at Benson, the day after Judge Dibble's brother was slain, with the intention of discovering the trail of the Apaches. "They rode some distance and then returned, seeing no signs of hostiles. A strange way, this, of fighting Indians, but then, the soldiers are safer in railroad cars than they would be on the plains," said the editor mockingly.[51] Clearly, in this crisis, the white population had lost its last shred of faith in the army.

Another Apache crisis, which had arisen simultaneously with the onset of Chato's raid, now filled the front pages and served further to unnerve residents along the border. Geronimo, with his much larger war party, was sweeping with cyclone force across Mexican Sonora, leaving death and destruction everywhere. "A reign of terror" was how provincial officials characterized the onslaught. Arizonans anxiously scanned the casualty lists appearing in the daily press, for many had relatives and friends employed on the ranches and in the mines of Mexico. In fact, significant numbers of Americans were counted among the fallen.[52]

A dispatch out of Sonora declared that "the present raid is the most destructive which has occurred in many years." And it added that the Apaches "operate in detached parties and kill all the Mexicans they come in contact with." Furthermore, "an immense number of horses have been taken and cattle and stock of all kinds wantonly killed."[53] Gen. José Guillermo Carbo, in the field with two thousand troops, reportedly had issued orders that, in retaliation, his own soldiers should take no prisoners, whether men, women, or children. The age-old blood feud between Apaches and Mexicans allowed no quarter.[54]

Business in northern and central Sonora was paralyzed, regular road and trail traffic dwindled, and rural peasants by the hundreds were said to be streaming toward the larger railroad towns in a frantic search for safety. Some of them disclosed that the hostiles were scattering and raiding during the day and then concentrating again in a single force at night, a standard Apache strategy in an incursion such as this.[55]

The refugees also recited tales of atrocities that were eagerly seized upon and circulated by the American press: two women suspended by their hands, who had their stomachs ripped open; the mangled body of a child found at the feet of its dead mother; and a family of ten, slain, with two infants grabbed by the feet and their brains dashed out on a rock.[56] The accuracy of these stories is impossible now to ascertain, but it can be noted that the killing of babies in this manner figures rather commonly in narratives of Indian warfare.

Jason Betzinez remains our only source for the Apache version of the Sonora raid. He said that Geronimo's warriors started out on foot, intending as their first order of business to capture horses and mount the entire party. They soon had, in addition, a large herd of spares. When a man's horse was about to drop from exhaustion, he could leap to the back of a fresh one without slackening pace, and thus the durable Chiricahuas were able to cover vast distances in record time, outrunning all pursuers. Chato at that very moment was using the same tactic in his wild ride across Arizona.

Betzinez remarks that, as Geronimo cut his deadly swath through Sonora, it became more difficult to find pack trains for looting, so the war party turned to attacking whole villages, which was not their usual practice. They continued, as well, to round up cattle and horses, killing what they could not drive away. Understandably, Betzinez was quite vague about the massacres perpetrated against civilians, making no mention of the routine torture of captives. At one point, he does declare circumspectly: "We attacked every village we came to, . . . but not killing very many people."[57] In a preliminary tallying of the Sonora casualties, the *San Francisco Chronicle* put the number of dead at ninety-three, of whom twenty-seven were Americans.[58]

North of the border, Chato's raid entered a second and slightly different phase following the cutting down of Judge Dibble's brother and his friend Bateman at Point of Mountain on Good Friday. That same night the Apaches hurried eastward by way of the Sulphur Springs Valley, crossed the Southern Pacific tracks two miles above Willcox, and, after making their way through the wide expanse of Railroad Pass, took refuge in the northern end of the Dos Cabezas Mountains. Peaches later testified that we "remained there all day [Saturday], watching for troops in pursuit."[59]

As the renegade band had become aware, the entire country was up in arms. Military patrols, although slow-moving, were becoming more numerous, units of militia and home guards had mobilized, and desperate messengers raced to distant ranches and remote line camps, urging occupants to flee for their lives. Some ranchers intercepted the wide Indian trail and followed it several miles into Railroad Pass. They described it as marked with blood all the way. That could have been the blood of the Apache who had been wounded at the corral fight in the Winchesters and who now might be bleeding from the saddle. Or perhaps the whites' remark was based upon their finding the bodies of horses and mules, which the warriors were killing when the animals gave out.[60]

During the daytime layover in the Dos Cabezas, Chato and Bonito appear to have held a powwow, for they now decided to send two of their men, Dutchy and a warrior named Kautli (or Kahthli), on a scouting mission to San Carlos. Specifically, the pair was instructed to make contact with one Merejildo Grijalva, an army scout who had been captured in Sonora as a boy and raised by the Apaches. From him they were to learn the state of affairs at the agency, particularly the attitude of the Indians there toward the renegades, and also how they might fare with the authorities, should they decided at some future date to return from Mexico and surrender.[61]

Dutchy and his companion were allotted five days to complete this errand, after which they were to rendezvous with the main party, as it retreated south toward the Mexican line. The two scouts actually succeeded in finding Grijalva, who gave them an altogether grim picture of their prospects. He did his best, it seems, to persuade both warriors to return at a later date and give up their arms. Dutchy, a month afterward, did just that.

At nightfall on March 24, Chato guided his band out of the Dos Cabezas and launched a fifty-mile dash under the cover of darkness across the flat expanse of the upper San Simon Valley, driving toward the northeast and the ranches and settlements of the Gila River. According to several reports, toward the end of this swift ride, the war party broke into smaller groups, each one aiming at a particular target in the well-populated countryside ahead. It would prove to be their last episode of bloodletting in Arizona.[62]

The killings in the environs of the Gila began on a springlike Easter Sunday and came almost without warning, so fast was the Apaches' entry into the new district. That same morning, almost sixty miles to the east in Silver City, we have every reason to believe that all five of the McComases attended services at the Methodist Episcopal church and listened to the Easter sermon of the Reverend H. Landsdown Gamble. The family had no way of knowing, of course, that this would be their last outing as a group, and that the minister shortly would be delivering a funeral oration for Hamilton and Juniata. On Sunday, the people of Silver City had not yet heard of Chato's arrival upon the Gila, and they still considered themselves safely out of the war zone. By week's end, all would know how mistaken they had been in this.

Following their nocturnal sprint over the San Simon Valley from the Dos Cabezas, at least some of the Apaches paused to water at Ash Spring, a familiar landmark on the approach to the Gila. Beyond that point, they fanned out to apprehend horses grazing on the open range and to attack mining camps, where chances seemed best for them to lay hands on arms and ammunition.

It was just after the crossing of the San Simon that Peaches took his leave and started for the reservation a short distance to the west. Jason Betzinez describes a dramatic little speech that Peaches delivered to his fellow warriors, in which he is supposed to have declared his unhappiness, owing to the recent death of his friend Beneactiney, and announced his determination to abandon the raid and seek out relatives at San Carlos. "The other Indians did not argue with Peaches," asserts Jason. "They gave him some things which would be useful to him when traveling alone. Then they said good-bye."[63]

Taken into custody a few days later, Peaches told General Crook a very different story. His version was this. He had been more a prisoner of the raiding party than a willing accomplice. In his words, "The Chiricahuas didn't guard me exactly, but they watched me suspiciously. I was never allowed to go off anywhere by myself. They made me work for them . . . cooking their food and things of that kind."

The main party, Peaches recounted, was traveling toward a place called Pueblo Viejo when a stray burro was found on the road and killed for food. Just beyond, the Apaches entered some hills, where they halted for the night, and sent two or three men scouting over their back trail to learn if anyone was pursuing them. Everyone else, being weary, soon went to sleep, and Peaches saw his chance to escape. Removing his moccasins, he crept away through the rocks, stepping gingerly so as to leave no tracks. He must have hidden within sight of the camp, because he was able to tell Crook, "When morning came, they hunted for me without success." Then he saw the party gather up its herd of stolen horses and disappear like so many dusky phantoms. Once they were gone, Peaches returned to the burro carcass, sliced off a chunk for rations, and then started for San Carlos afoot. His defection would play a key role in subsequent events.[64]

After this incident, one band of Chato's warriors forded the Gila River below the York and Purdy ranches, both of which lay on the valley road connecting Lordsburg and Clifton. These Apaches scooped up every horse in sight, then scurried east toward the New Mexico boundary and the Steeple Rock and Carlisle mining districts which lay just beyond.

Another wing of the party struck the Mayflower district, located eight miles or so in the mountains northwest of York's ranch. The miners were working in a placer gulch sixty to eighty yards from their cabins, when the cry of "Indians" was raised. The next thing they knew, the Apaches had gained possession of the main cabin, where all the rifles and pistols were kept. A short distance down the gulch, miners John C. Emerick, a native of Philadelphia, and his Texas partner, Walter P. Jones, heard the commotion and started for their arms. Within moments, both fell, pierced with bullets. The remaining miners scattered for cover. When some of them returned after the departure of the raiders, they discovered the dead men and the ruins of their camp. Growled one of them, "Flour sacks had been ripped open and scattered over the ground, beans thrown here and dried fruits there, and in short, everything the Indians did not carry away they cut to pieces."[65]

Pausing only long enough to pick up the bodies, the terrified workers fled down to York's ranch for protection. Along the way, they collected the corpse of another victim, Harlan P. Haynes, originally from Maine, who was well respected in those parts for having gunned down a troublesome outlaw, Bob Johnson, two years before.[66]

Arriving at York's, the refugees from the Mayflower mines had a sad task to perform: presenting to Mrs. York, a widow, the body of John Emerick, whom she had been scheduled to marry on the very next day. In 1881, she had seen her first husband killed, and now the Apaches had taken a second husband even before they could wed. Shortly, Mrs. York announced that out of fear she, with her six children, was leaving the ranch and going to join friends in Trinidad, Colorado.[67]

On the river seven miles south of York's ranch, some of the Chiricahuas surprised the occupants of Swain's (or Swing's) Stage Station. At the first rush, three whites were caught in the open and killed, and two more died when the building was charged. This attack took place at 8 A.M. on Tuesday, the morning after the slaying of Emerick, Jones, and Haynes.[68]

A few hours later, most of the Apaches crossed into New Mexico. In the vicinity of Richmond (today's Virden), nine people lost their lives, including two miners slain at Gold Gulch in the Steeple Rock district. By the close of day, the dispersed warriors had reassembled at a predetermined rendezvous near the head of the Animas Valley. As the sun slipped behind the western mountains, Chato plotted his next move.[69]

⚶ Chapter Six ⚶

The Massacre

On Monday, March 26, the day after Easter, Hamilton C. McComas received a telegram sent from Lordsburg by his son David. It indicated that H. C.'s professional services were needed by the Pyramid Mining and Milling Company and that he should come down as soon as possible.[1] The attorney had been in Pyramid City three weeks before, but whether this sudden summons pertained to some business unfinished from that visit or to an entirely new matter is unknown. In any case, that telegram set off the final chain of events that led the McComases to their personal tragedy.

The same evening, at home, H. C. discussed with his wife the upcoming trip. Although Juniata had been in Silver City a full year, she still had not traveled the scenic Lordsburg Road. Now, with the weather fair and the judge planning a leisurely drive, it seemed like the perfect opportunity. Rufus McComas would say later that she decided to go along "to enjoy the scenery, which is the most beautiful in that country."[2] So, what began strictly as a business journey now was enlarged to include a family outing. Charley would accompany his parents, but the girls were to be left behind.

Arrangements and preparations needed to be made, and work upon them started early the following morning (Tuesday). First, Hamilton and Juniata walked over to the residence of their good friends, photographer Harry Lucas and his wife. According to the recollection of Mrs. Lucas, "They asked me to go with my husband to their home and keep house for the children [Ada and Mary] till they should return. I told them I would and [Juniata] said, 'Oh, I am so glad, for now we can stay as long as we wish, for my children are in good hands.' And the Judge said, 'Yes, but we will probably not be gone more than a week.'"[3]

That done, H. C. went to the telegraph office and sent a wire to Lordsburg, announcing that he, together with wife and son, would arrive in that town the next evening about dark. Then he headed for the Stock Exchange Corral, across the street from the Timmer House, to rent a buckboard and team from the owner-manager, John Graham. Records show that H. C. engaged a rig for five days, at seven dollars per day, the sum to be paid upon his return. Graham had a delivery man who drove hired vehicles to a customer's door, by appointment. Thus, we suppose that H. C., instead of taking the buckboard with him, arranged to have it delivered in the early afternoon.[4]

Meanwhile, Juniata McComas was busily readying the household for Mrs. Lucas and instructing Ada and Mary in their duties during her absence. She also packed the family's clothes. These went into a large square willow basket or hamper, which was to ride in the back of the buckboard and double as a seat for Charley. Perhaps at the last minute, recalling how changeable was the New Mexico weather, Juniata decided to take "rubber waterproof over-garments."[5] And it would have been surprising if she had failed to provide some snack food and a bottle or canteen of water.

After lunch, the rented buckboard, with its handsome pair of horses, arrived and was tied up while the family loaded the hamper and other personal belongings. The vehicle was a two-seater, with a dashboard and a doubletree for proper hitching. Mr. Graham had included, as part of the package, a whip and a lap robe. Without doubt, he had wished Hamilton C. McComas, chairman of the Grant County Commission, a safe journey.

For protection, the judge carried a Winchester target rifle, a Colt pistol, and a belt of cartridges. On his person he wore a watch and chain, both of gold, which he had purchased for $200 from a St. Louis jeweler. In his pocket was $125 in cash, a sum sufficient in those days to cover a week's expenses for three.

Blue-eyed, yellow-haired Charley clambered into the rear of the buckboard and took his seat on the hamper. Now six and a half years old, he was big for his age, weighing seventy-five pounds and wearing a size 6-¾ hat.[6] Like any young boy, he would have been excited at the prospect of this trip.

Chances are good that the girls, Mrs. Lucas, and maybe even a neighbor or two were standing in front of the house to bid the group good-bye as H. C. climbed aboard, untied the reins, shook them, and set the horses in motion. As Ada and Mary watched their parents and little brother disappear down

Hudson Street, they had no way of knowing that they would never see them again. Probably their last view was of Charley, waving happily from his perch on the wicker basket.

Here a mystery presents itself, one so deep and perplexing that to this day no final answer can be offered. The puzzling question is this: What possibly could have possessed Judge Hamilton Calhoun McComas to take his loved ones riding on the open road, straight into the jaws of danger? How was it that a mature man, known for his wisdom, let himself make such a monumental miscalculation?

The observation of Lt. Thomas Cruse, already noted, may explain part of it: newcomers to the Southwest had little conception of the realities of frontier conditions and thus easily strayed into perilous situations.[7] But McComas had been on the scene for almost three years, and, while he had no personal experience with the Apaches, he certainly had been in a position to learn at second hand about the danger they posed. Colleague John P. Risque, slain near Clifton ten months earlier, furnished a grim warning of the price that might be paid for carelessness. And from his friend Oscar W. Williams, now working in the Silver City post office, H. C. ought to have gotten more indication of the seriousness of the Indian threat.

About that very thing, Williams would write many years later: "Day by day the mail sacks came in from one place and then another—empty, gashed and covered with the blood of some faithful guardian. I could note the march of the Apaches by those silent testimonies of their evil work."[8] From the first moment of his arrival in Silver City, McComas hardly could have escaped noticing that talk of Indian hostilities predominated on the streets and in the saloons. But much of it was tainted by high coloring or embellishment, having the character of wild rumor rather than faithful reporting.

To quote Williams again: "Many of the reports [about Indians] were not true and what was true was often much exaggerated, but even stripped of all distortion, the situation was most dangerous for the traveler."[9] Having a legal mind, trained to weigh evidence, Judge McComas might have paid more attention to the first part of that statement than he paid to the last part.

His familiarity with the Lordsburg Road, having driven it safely a number of times, undoubtedly lulled McComas into a false sense of security. Stagecoaches going in both directions used it daily, as did horsemen, so that the volume of traffic seemed to provide an added safeguard. Mrs. T. L. Smith of Lordsburg, a friend of the McComases, had gone by that route to Silver City with her husband the previous October. Upon learning of the deaths of the judge and his wife, she remarked to a journalist, "I've never heard of anyone being killed on the road between the two places. Travelers have frequently made the trip in safety in a two-horse conveyance and unaccompanied."[10]

News had reached Silver City that an Apache war party had stormed across the Mexican border into Arizona, having been published in the *Southwest Sentinel,* a local paper, as early as March 24—that is, on the Saturday prior to the McComases' Tuesday departure. The *Sentinel* issued a general warning, even while expressing the fear "that it might alarm a great many."[11] Several more days passed before it became known that the raiders were advancing toward New Mexico.

When H. C. drove his buckboard down Hudson Street and out of Silver City, he knew beyond question that Apaches were on the move somewhere to the west, but he must have figured they were too far away to pose a threat to himself and his family. Perhaps, too, he felt that, with his Winchester repeater and his Colt pistol, he could handle any encounter with a ragtag band of Indians. An old acquaintance in St. Louis, when he heard of the massacre a

A fully loaded stagecoach on Broadway at Bullard, downtown Silver City, New Mexico, 1882. Courtesy Museum of New Mexico, Neg. No. 11933

few days later, said in a newspaper interview, "Judge McComas was fearless, and perhaps this incaution and self-reliance brought him, his wife and child to their fate."[12] In attempting to understand how H. C. could walk headlong into catastrophe, that statement may clarify matters as well as any.

By coincidence, a mere ten minutes after the McComases started on their journey—in other words, at 2:10 P.M.—Capt. William A. Thompson left Fort Bayard at the head of two well-mounted companies of the 4th Cavalry. His orders were to march westward and cut off the hostile Apaches, whose raid had carried them inside the New Mexico Territory. Thompson was a seasoned hand, a native Marylander who had come up through the ranks in the Civil War, fought the Comanches in Texas, and earned promotion to captain in 1879.[13]

Now he led his men in formation through the streets of Silver City and out the other side, picking up a road that first ran west but within a few miles veered southwest toward the distant wall of the Burro Mountains. Initially Thompson must have followed the freshly minted tracks of the McComas buckboard. Before long, however, he turned off on a secondary road that took a more direct route into the Burros and eventually emerged on their west slope at Burro Springs.

Here was located a ranch belonging to the stepfather and mother of a local hunter and prospector, Julius Caesar Brock, then nineteen years of age. Earlier in the day, the youth had ridden south along the skirt of the mountains to warn isolated ranchers that Apaches were on the prowl, and he was not expected back until the next afternoon. From the parents, Captain Thompson, as he recorded in his official report, was unable "to obtain news of a definite nature regarding the whereabouts of the hostile Indians."[14]

The soldiers reached Burro Springs at 11:30 at night and bivouacked, having covered thirty-five miles since leaving the fort in the early afternoon. The captain was in something of a quandary as to which direction to go next. By now he probably was aware of the Apache raids in the Gila Valley the previous Sunday, and, as he thought about it, he decided that the Indians from that area probably would begin a withdrawal south through the attenuated spine of mountains that ran down the New Mexico–Arizona boundary toward Mexico. Hence, he resolved to have his men up and saddled by 5 A.M. the following morning. The troop would strike out, southwest, across the wide, salty flats of the Animas Valley, with the aim of intercepting the marauders somewhere in the vicinity of Horseshoe Canyon in the Stein Peak's Range. There Forsyth's forces had fought an engagement with the Chiricahua the year before, during Loco's flight from San Carlos.

Unbeknownst to Captain Thompson, a contingent of the Shakespeare Guards under Capt. James F. Black already had moved into the Stein's Peak Range, for the very purpose of blocking the Apaches' flight. The wily Chato realized that his swarms of enemies might be guarding that particular escape route, so, to outfox them, he elected to leave the Gila River and swing southeastward across the upper Animas Valley. Upon gaining the Burros, he could pick up an old Indian trail that wound through sheltering foothills along their western flank in the direction he wanted to go.[15]

As was their precautionary custom, the Indians crossed the open expanse of the valley under the cover of darkness and broke into small scattered groups to obscure their passage. Thus, while Thompson and his troopers were snoring peacefully in their blankets at Burro Springs, the Apaches were moving straight toward them.

In the predawn gloom of the following morning, as the sleepy soldiers started across the flats toward Stein's Peak, they must have cut one or more of the fresh trails just left by incoming segments of Chato's war party. But they failed to see the tracks, and Thompson rode away without the slightest inkling that Indians were all around him and he was headed directly out of the theater of action.[16]

A few hours after the cavalry's departure from Burro Springs, young Julius Caesar Brock, returning home, found the Apaches whom the army had missed. Further, his encounter became entwined with the fate of some people traveling the Lordsburg Road, a family named McComas. Until his death in 1952, Brock never tired of telling what happened to him on that unforgettable day.

✇ Once he had cleared Silver City, H. C. McComas made good time in his rented buckboard. After running west for several miles, the stage road turned south, forded Mangas Creek, and then ascended a long ridge in the direction of Burro Peak, the tallest mountain in the center of the range. The country, still garbed in winter brown, nevertheless was very beautiful. Tree yucca, oaks, and clumps of juniper dotted the landscape. Large bushy beargrass, looking like pampas grass, and varieties of thorny cactus lent an exotic note to the scene. The Burros, backlit by the slanting afternoon sun, presented a succession of enchanting views. Juniata must have been enthralled.

About twelve miles below Silver City, the Lordsburg Road passed through the mining camp of Paschal, at this date containing some three hundred people. The Valverde Copper Company had a fifty-ton smelter here, but the price of the metal recently had fallen, and the smelter no longer was operating at full capacity. The one hotel in town may have closed down because, when Paschal's

Deputy Sheriff H. E. Muse bumped into the McComases, he invited them to stay at his house overnight.

According to his recollection many years later, "Judge McComas wanted to stop, but his wife was a little afraid, so they went on."[17] If Juniata had become fearful by this point, it meant that the couple finally had learned of the Apache depredations the day before in the Gila Valley. Travelers they met on the road, or even the deputy sheriff himself, could have communicated the unsettling news. Muse's memory may have failed him, for, in view of what followed, it seems likely that Juniata would have been the one wishing to stop, while the judge expressed his determination to press forward as long as a bit of daylight remained.

Anyway, the McComases passed through Paschal and continued on their course for another five miles to a roadside hostelry called the Mountain Home, probably reaching it after dark. The place was a regular stop for stagecoaches and enjoyed an idyllic setting among scattered pines near the base of the rounded dome of the eight-thousand-foot Burro Peak. The frame building had a gabled roof and a porch with a white railing across the front.

Owner and operator of the Mountain Home was thirty-six-year-old J. M.

This 1908 newspaper photo is the only known picture of the Mountain Home, where the McComases spent their last night. A buckboard is parked next to the small building at left. Burro Mountain looms in the distance. Silver City Independent, *Sept. 15, 1908*

Dennis, a native of Vermont who had brought his family out to New Mexico by way of Colorado. He was mainly a lumberman, having purchased equipment for a sawmill after his arrival. The hostelry seems to have been a sideline, but one to which the New Englander and his wife gave serious attention. Not long before, they had placed a notice in the *Silver City Enterprise* advertising the good accommodations at the Mountain Home and touting it as "a pleasant place of resort with romantic scenery and pure water."[18]

The McComases, no doubt, were relieved to reach this secure haven and receive a hospitable reception and good dinner. The Dennis children, Eva (aged nine) and Herbert (aged six), must have welcomed little Charley eagerly as their playmate. Another guest at the table that evening was John A. Moore, the Grant County deputy assessor, who also was headed for Lordsburg on business. It is possible that he had run into the McComases at Paschal and that they had ridden together the last five miles to the Mountain Home.[19]

From all indications, the conversation following the meal was given over entirely to the raiding Apaches and to speculations as to whether they were close enough to pose a real hazard. Mrs. Dennis, in particular, was exceedingly alarmed at the prospect of the McComases resuming their journey, and she pleaded with them to wait a day or two, until the situation became clearer. To that, the judge replied that his legal business was too urgent for him to delay. He added that, in his opinion, the reports of Indian activity were greatly exaggerated. Juniata, although obviously frightened, expressed the intention of continuing with her husband. Before going to bed, H. C. sat by lamplight and wrote several pages of a campaign speech for the coming city council election.[20]

The team of horses, rested and fed, was harnessed to the buckboard the next morning; and, after breakfast, the McComas family climbed aboard, with Charley assuming his position on the hamper. Mrs. Dennis quite likely provided a lunch, and it is known that she again urged the judge to abandon the trip.

For some reason that has not been recorded, Moore, the assessor, did not ride out with the McComases when they left around nine o'clock. With all the talk about Apaches, he should have been eager to travel alongside the judge, under the theory that, in a pinch, two guns are better than one. The best guess is that the gentleman was having serious qualms about going ahead in the midst of an Indian scare. If that was the case, he must have wrestled with his fears and got them under control, for, forty-five minutes to an hour later, he saddled up and started after the McComases, probably expecting to catch up with them around midday.

The buckboard made good time, in the nature of three and a half miles an hour, for the road was mostly downhill, the McComases having crossed to the west slope of the Continental Divide. Around eleven o'clock, they came down a gentle grade into the upper reaches of Thompson Canyon, which at this point was fairly wide and open. The road now began to descend the canyon, staying in the center of the dry and sandy arroyo bed.

H. C. may have been experiencing mounting anxiety, because, just ahead, Thompson Canyon suddenly narrowed to become a steep-walled defile that twisted its way a mile or more through the westernmost ridge of the Burro Mountains. As he knew from previous trips over this same road, if any danger existed, it was apt to be encountered here.

As the family approached the eastern entrance of the pass, the north-bound stage from Lordsburg suddenly burst into view, spewing twin geysers

In the heart of Thompson Canyon, the original wagon road followed by the McComases went down the center of the sandy arroyo. 1994. Courtesy Barbara McBride, Santa Fe, New Mexico

of sand from its rear wheels. The mere sight of the coach must have caused H. C. to relax and given reassurance to a nervous Juniata. Since it had gotten through safely, the country behind it, they reasoned, must be free of renegades. Whether the stage driver reined in his team long enough to exchange a few words is something we do not know. At the very least, there would have been some waving as the two vehicles passed one another.[21]

Entering the confined stretch of Thompson Canyon, H. C. kept the laboring horses at a trot and scanned both sides of the road for any sign of trouble. Beside him, we can picture Juniata tight-lipped and pale, perhaps uttering a silent prayer. Before long, however, the buckboard emerged from the western exit of the canyon, and the land opened into low foothills with elder bushes and walnut trees scattered along the margins of the road. The McComases had traveled ten miles from the Mountain Home and still faced another seventeen miles to Lordsburg. But once past these outlying hills at the western base of the Burros, their route lay across the wide flats of the Animas Valley, and the mere prospect of reaching spacious country, where the threat of ambush disappeared, may have restored the couple's spirits.

That frame of mind, together with the sudden appearance of a large and inviting walnut tree growing on the right side of the road, prompted the family to stop for a picnic lunch. Besides, the jaded horses needed a rest after their hard pull through the sandy arroyo. The food was handed down and spread upon the ground beneath the shading canopy of overhanging branches. The judge's gold watch from St. Louis showed the time at a few minutes into the noon hour, the date being March 28, 1883, a Wednesday. The location of the tree and the meal stop was a bit less than a mile from the western mouth of Thompson Canyon, in Grant County of the New Mexico Territory.

Then, like a lightning bolt from hell, the Apaches appeared. In that instant, the serene world of Hamilton and Juniata McComas dimmed; during the ensuing few, horrible minutes, it ended forever. Every man is dependent upon circumstances. None is able to escape the law of cause and effect or the law of accident. In reflecting upon the life of Judge McComas, we can discern all along the way twists and turns, as well as personal decisions, that led inexorably to the deaths of the judge and his wife, beside a walnut tree in a remote nook of the far Southwest. It is apparent from the evidence that they stopped to picnic by the Lordsburg Road on the wrong day and precisely at the wrong time. Had they traveled the day before or the day following, or even if they had arrived at the tree an hour earlier or an hour later, they would have escaped their appalling fate.

The general consensus at the time was that the McComases succumbed to the Apaches by sheer accident. The ex-soldier and army packer, Anton Mazzanovich, put the matter thus: "That this unhappy encounter was purely by chance may be inferred from the fact that, had the Indians been waylaying the road in wait for victims, [they would have stationed themselves at] the canyon back in the mountains, [which] affords ideal places for ambuscades."[22] A news dispatch stated that the McComases perished because they just happened to halt right in the path of the Indians' escape route.[23]

The narrative of the ghastly drama that now unfolded has to be pieced together from a variety of conflicting and even questionable sources. As nearly as can be determined, however, the sequence of events was as follows. The war party, as usual, was straggling, with some scouts out front and an advance unit under Chato just a short distance behind. They must have approached from the northwest or west, because, when the McComases caught sight of the fearsome warriors, they hurried to their buckboard, jumped in, and turned the vehicle around in an attempt to flee back the way they had come, toward the Mountain Home.

The horses had barely lurched into motion when the judge was shot. We know this because his blood was found on the dashboard and floor of the rig. The wound was not mortal, and he either fell or leaped to the ground—probably the latter, since he was still clutching his Winchester rifle. Juniata grabbed the reins and attempted to whip the animals into a run. Her husband meanwhile picked himself up and, with blood gushing from his body, ran back toward the walnut tree, pumping cartridges and firing at their assailants as fast as he could. It was a noble but futile bid to sell his life dearly and hold the Apaches in check long enough for his wife and child to escape.

According to which account you read, Judge Hamilton C. McComas was struck by from four to seven bullets. One version summarized his wounds in this way:

> He had received one shot through the right wrist, shattering the bone completely; another through the fleshy part of the same arm below and near the elbow; another through both thighs entering from the right side and passing out at the left; another entering at the point of the left shoulder and passing clear through the body and out at the point of the right shoulder; another entering the back near the right shoulder blade and passing out near the pit of the stomach; another cutting the flesh slightly below his right breast; and still another cutting a gash in his left side.[24]

The judge died gamely by a clump of bushes at roadside. Near his outstretched arm was found an empty cartridge box; around the body were four empty shell casings. Three more casings lay along the path of his brief run. Did it finally dawn on McComas in those last few terrible seconds of his existence that he had committed a catastrophic blunder in venturing upon the Lordsburg Road, and that the error in judgment was costing him and his family their lives? We will never know, of course. The finality of his personal disaster was so complete that it yields no answers at all.

With the judge dead, the Apaches turned their attention to the wagon. Juniata managed to drive only three hundred yards farther up the road before a shot dropped the off-wheeler (the right horse), which collapsed in its traces and brought her flight to a sudden stop. She immediately leaped to the ground (the deep imprint of her shoes was observed the next day) and ran to the other side of the buckboard, evidently in hopes of grabbing up her son. A journalist, recreating the moment, lamented, "By then, the poor weak woman, utterly defenseless herself, was her child's only protector."[25]

As she frantically tried to reach Charley, a warrior rode up behind Juniata and delivered a powerful blow just above her right ear, crushing her skull with his rifle butt. Then he dismounted and administered two more blows with a smaller instrument, probably a pistol, to the back of her head to make sure she was dead. In the method of his killing, the pitiless assailant simply was being practical, for thereby he saved one of his precious bullets.

As no small footprints were discovered in the sand, it is believed that Charley McComas remained in the rear of the buckboard, from which he must have witnessed these traumatic events. He well may have been mute with shock. As already discussed, on a raid the Apaches murdered children, sometimes hideously, without the slightest compunction. But on occasion they would keep a young boy, if they thought he showed promise and could be raised as a warrior. By native custom, a child taken in war belonged to the person who captured him; but in this instance, with Chato's men ringing the disabled wagon, it was unclear which of them had first claim on the blonde youngster.[26]

In fact, two of the Indians began to quarrel over possession, and their disagreement became so heated that it appeared the matter might end in the boy's death. Luckily, Bonito, with another section of the war party, rode up about that time and intervened. He announced that he would settle the dispute by taking the child himself. And he swung Charley up behind him in the saddle, securing the lad with a piece of rope which Bonito tied to his own belt. Owing to his prowess and status as second in command of the raid, Bonito was able to have his way without being challenged.[27]

Once the McComas family had been dealt with, the Apaches turned to

Bonito, Chato's second-in-command on the 1883 foray. Courtesy National Archives

plundering their possessions. The chief prizes proved to be the judge's Winchester target rifle, Colt revolver, and cartridge belt, for it was in the quest of such objects that Chato's foray had been launched. In custody, a short time later, Peaches would inform General Crook that the warriors had left Mexico with the simple intention of killing everyone they met, whether the person was carrying guns or not.[28] That, and the revenge factor mentioned earlier, might explain why Juniata, although unarmed, was slain so senselessly.

The Indians cut loose the one surviving horse from the team, destroying the harness in the process, and added it to their herd of stolen stock. Then they rifled the corpses. The judge was stripped of all clothing, and the watch and cash were removed from his pockets. The nude body was left face down in the dirt, one arm outstretched. For a reason known only to Apaches, his personal papers, which ought to have included the speech he wrote the night before, were torn and twisted and laid upon his bare back.

Juniata's body, also stripped and reclining face downward, was left about ten feet from the buckboard. Her face rested on the left side, and the blood flowed in a pool about her head and soaked her disheveled hair. The shoes and stockings were cut from her feet and discarded in one direction, her corsets in another. The remainder of her apparel was carried away. She had been wearing a pair of large gold band bracelets and a diamond ring, and these were pulled roughly from her lifeless limbs by one of her attackers.[29]

Finally, the Apaches ransacked the buckboard, stealing virtually everything that could be transported, from the driving whip to the raincoats found in the wicker hamper. When the work of destruction and theft was complete, they rode away toward the southeast, probably as they had arrived, in straggling bunches. With them, perched behind Bonito, went a very frightened and stricken little boy. The Indians, as they had been from the first moment they entered Arizona, were in a pounding hurry. The entire episode beside the Lordsburg Road consumed no more than ten or twelve minutes. In that brief interval, the scene of a happy family at lunch was transformed into one of sickening desolation and death.

Although ultimately many questions arose, one was raised immediately by the first fragmentary reports of the massacre that described the McComas bodies as being mutilated and even scalped. White men automatically assumed that a massacre and scalping went together, whereas the Apaches, in reality, seldom engaged in the practice. Mutilation, on the other hand, was one of their specialties. Despite fairly quick press denials that this had been done to the McComases, residents of southwestern New Mexico for years persisted in saying that the couple had been mutilated, and the charge even crept into a few history books.[30]

The *Albuquerque Review* issued one of the earliest unequivocal statements: "The Apaches did not mutilate the bodies of Judge McComas and wife. Lack of time is the only reason assigned for this action on the part of those sons of Belial."[31] That is, the Indians were in too big a hurry to perform their customary rite of butchery upon the corpses.

The *Santa Fe Daily New Mexican* offered another reason: "There was no mutilation of the bodies, hence the conclusion that squaws are not with the marauders."[32] As often was noted in the record, Apache women usually (although not invariably) were the agents of torture and mutilation. Therefore, that explanation has plausibility.

More than six decades after the fact, Asa Daklugie gave the Apache version of the story. It originated with warriors who had been there. He asserted that the front guard under Chato had killed the man but did not mutilate him because he had exhibited great bravery in jumping from the wagon and attempting to hold them off so that his wife and child could escape. That was conduct understood perfectly by the raiders, since it is the way they themselves would have acted under similar circumstances. Of course, it would have been slight consolation to the judge, had he known that his courage was respected by his killers. In any event, later news stories declared emphatically that the murder victims were not mutilated.[33]

A more furtive question is less easily resolved—whether Juniata was violated sexually, either before or after death. An initial news dispatch wrongly indicated that she had been taken captive with Charley. In light of that report, the *Arizona Daily Star* speculated that Mrs. McComas "has no doubt been ravished by every brute in the band."[34]

Just as they anticipated scalping, whites expected that all their women who were captured by Indians would be raped. That gloomy presumption seemed to have had some basis in fact. Col. Richard Irving Dodge, who had wide experience with hostile tribes in the West, including Apaches, wrote shortly before the McComas incident that "no woman has, in the last thirty years, been taken prisoner by any wild Indians who did not . . . become a victim to the brutality of every one of the party of her captors." And he added that the female captive "belongs equally to each and all, so long as the party is out."[35]

Still, the colonel's generalization, while suggestive, provides no firm evidence of what might have been inflicted upon Juniata McComas. Buried in a few of the news releases is the remark that she had been "outraged," an obvious euphemism for "raped." The *Prescott (Arizona) Courier,* for instance, spoke of "the diabolical outrages committed upon the wife, previous to her death." For its part, the *Silver City Enterprise* couched the matter in words less blunt, even though the sinister meaning remained quite clear. "Ere death came to her," it said, "an awful fate met the poor wife."[36]

Only one contemporary account furnishes specifics, and it may not be entirely reliable. S. L. Sanders, a deputy under U.S. Marshal Alexander L. Morrison, made a statement about the McComas affair in 1890: "I had the opportunity to know the facts and I defy their impeachment." (Was he being forthright or defensive? The tone arouses the scholar's suspicion.) About the treatment of Mrs. McComas, he conveyed these details: "The person of this unfortunate lady was violated in the most brutal manner. . . . When her life was almost tortured out, they beat the back of her head until her brains oozed out, and then to exhibit still further proof of their inhumanity, they broke off branches of the elder bushes and thrust them deep into her body, as many as they could."[37] Others in a position to confirm Sander's testimony might have been inhibited from doing so by their sense of discretion.

Yet another looming question is this: who made the first discovery of the bodies following the massacre—the assessor John Moore or the youthful Julius Caesar Brock? Both arrived soon after the crime, took one look at the bloody tableau, and fled. Neither apparently was aware that someone else was in the vicinity.

From the Mountain Home, Moore had jogged along steadily, watching the tracks of the McComas buckboard grow fresher. Once through the steep canyon, he viewed the walnut tree in the distance; and, as he approached, an eerie feeling came over him that something was wrong. The vehicle was in sight, but it sat stalled in the road askew. Then, all at once, in a single glance, he saw the dead horse in its harness and nearby, on the ground, the nude white body of a man.

Instantly he checked his mount, and not a step closer did Mr. Moore venture. He knew with certainty what had occurred, and only a few minutes before his arrival. There he was alone, standing in the open—a prime candidate to be the Chiricahuas' next victim. Panic seized John Moore. He jerked his horse around, drummed heels against its ribs, and shot off at a fast gallop, back the way he had come.[38]

Brock is thought to have reached the scene approximately forty-five minutes after the tragedy, which would seem to place him there following the headlong departure of the assessor.[39] Early that morning he had delivered his warning message to Knight's Ranch, situated in the next canyon south of Thompson Canyon. Then, starting home, he followed the Indian trail stretching northwest along the foot of the Burros. Where the trail crossed the Lordsburg Road, a point he first reached about midmorning, he noticed a hawk resting high in the walnut tree and shot it.

Continuing toward Burro Springs, Brock began to see Indian signs and became nervous. So he took to a ridge on his right, believing that it afforded him more protection. Then he bumped into two mounted Apaches. Up went his rifle, but the warrior in front shouted, "Soldier! Soldier!" He pointed to a red scarf tied around his head. Government scouts customarily wore such a tag to identify themselves as friendlies rather than hostiles. The action caused Brock to hesitate and lower his gun.

It was a ruse, however, as he discovered when the Indian suddenly fired and the bullet whipped so close by his ear that he could feel it. The second warrior moved forward, and young Brock shot him in the shoulder, causing him to drop his rifle. Then the pair of Apaches, as the white man told it later, "busted out and ran like old billy hell down the mountain."[40]

Brock guessed, rightly, that they were scouts for the main war party which must be moving in his direction down below. Fearing an ambush ahead, he wheeled about and started to retrace his trail, so as to circle around the danger. From the ridge line, he evidently got a glimpse of the Indians or at least saw where they were by the dust cloud their horses kicked up. The party, traveling fast, rapidly melted into the distance. After waiting a bit to be sure they were gone, Brock descended and rejoined his original trail at the walnut tree where he had killed the hawk a couple of hours earlier.

There he found the McComases. During the past two years, the young man had met the judge on several occasions, and he recognized the body immediately. He also found Juniata's remains, which Moore had missed seeing. Under the tree, his keen eye took in the food spread upon the ground, making him the only observer to note that small detail which established that the family had paused for a picnic before the attack.

It crossed the mind then of Julius Caesar Brock that his thoughtless shooting of the hawk had led to grave consequences. In recounting events of that day, late in his own life, he confessed, "That shot may have been the cause of the McComas massacre for it told the Indians that somebody was there." At the moment, though, his first concern was for his own safety, and, fearing that stragglers from the war party might be lurking about, he hurried away. Late that afternoon, without further incident, he arrived back at Burro Springs.

Since Brock was the only one who got a look at the McComas assailants—well, two of them at least—his story, when told, aroused much public interest. When he mentioned that one of the Apaches wore a red headband, that sparked heated conjecture. Southwesterners long had been mistrustful of Crook's practice of arming and training reservation Indians and enrolling them as government scouts. They believed that the warriors acquired added military skills and inside knowledge of army procedures which they then could turn against the white man, should they decide later to desert to the renegades.[41]

Indeed, it subsequently was learned that four of the participants in the McComas attack had been employed as scouts at San Carlos within the previous year.[42] They would have known from first-hand experience how easily white civilians could be fooled by an Apache who donned a red headband to disguise his hostile intentions. The press, in fact, surmised that this very ploy might have been used to entrap the McComases.

According to one published report, "It is believed by those most competent to judge that the Indians were disguised as scouts; that they wore the customary red scarfs or handkerchiefs around their heads . . . so when McComas saw the red scarfs, he felt no alarm and allowed the Indians to come right up to him."[43] This may or may not have happened, but Rufus McComas tended to think it did. In a published interview, he remarked that prevailing opinion held that the Indians who slaughtered his brother and sister-in-law were wearing "red turbans on their heads . . . which accounts for their being able to get close enough to the Judge to kill him."[44] In hindsight, what seems certain is that the "red turbans" did not play a determining role, one way or the other, in the final tragic outcome of events.

☞ The first tidings of the McComas massacre were conveyed to others not by Julius Caesar Brock, but by John Moore. During his frantic ride back to the Mountain Home, he chanced to meet the stage from Silver City, making its daily run to Lordsburg. Upon the box was veteran driver Joe Baker, who listened in dismay as the assessor gasped out his story. Ignoring the danger to his coach, the brave Baker elected to proceed, and an hour or so later, he drove by the death scene. What he saw in those few moments left a vivid impression that would remain with him to the end of his days. In the late afternoon, he rolled into Lordsburg and announced the news.[45]

For some reason, John Moore did not make it back to the Mountain Home until midnight. In all probability, he had to stop, or perhaps he got lost when darkness fell and had to wait until a waning moon came up and floodlit his way. He paused only briefly to awaken the Dennis family and tell them what had happened. Then he rushed on to Paschal, the first place on the road where help could be obtained. J. M. Dennis and his wife were both shocked and frightened. Swiftly they packed their clothes, lifted their sleepy children into a wagon, and hurried toward Paschal after Moore. With Apaches sweeping through the Burros, their isolated hostelry was no place to be.[46]

Moore rode into Paschal about 2 A.M. and aroused the entire camp. Thomas S. Nickerson, the assistant superintendent of the Valverde Copper Company and the ranking man on the scene, took charge. Promptly he scribbled a message saying that "Judge McComas and his wife are doubtless killed by Apaches" but explaining that nothing was certain, as John Moore had seen only the body of a man, and that from a distance. Further, he was sending a wagon and men to the site to recover the remains. He closed by noting that Mr. Dennis and family had just come in safely.[47]

Nickerson put a courier on a fast horse, handed him the message, and sent him flying off to Silver City with instructions to warn miners and ranchers along the way. Then he called for volunteers. Fifteen stalwart citizens stepped forward, among them J. M. Dennis and the deputy sheriff, H. E. Muse. Besides the task of bringing in the body (or bodies), they were solemnly enjoined to go to the relief of Mrs. McComas and the child, should it be determined that they were still alive. Less than an hour after Moore brought his news, the company was on the road, spurring its horses toward Thompson Canyon.

Just before 6 A.M., the Paschal men approached the place of the massacre. Although the lower edge of the sky behind them was tinged with the pale light of dawn, here on the western flank of the Burros, the land remained under a mantle of night. Deputy Muse ranged ahead of the others and thus was the first to encounter the judge's wife. In 1928, he would recall, "I found Mrs. McComas on the ground with her hair about her face and clotted with blood. She was stripped of her clothing, and I took off my coat and covered her body before the rest reached us."[48]

Scarcely a day and a half earlier, the deputy had spoken to this woman on the road to Paschal. Now, in the predawn chill, out of respect and a sense of decency, he was surrendering his own garment to blanket her mortal remains. His touching gesture was of a kind not uncommon among rough frontiersmen.

Members of the party followed the wide trail of dried blood, clearly visible by moonlight, that stretched up the road beyond the buckboard. Their search brought them to the bullet-riddled body of Judge McComas, face first in the dust, his torn papers piled grotesquely upon his naked back. Carefully they placed him in the spring wagon sent by Mr. Nickerson, laying him next to his wife and covering both of them with a canvas.[49]

About then, another rescue company arrived from Lordsburg, also bringing a wagon. At noon on the previous day, just as the McComases were sitting down to their picnic under the walnut tree, Capt. James Black had returned home with his Shakespeare Guards after failing to find any hostiles in the Stein's Peak Range. Late that evening, telegrams sent from Lordsburg, telling of the McComas tragedy, reached both Shakespeare and Pyramid City. The captain reassembled his guards and prepared to sprint eastward, hoping to intercept the war party. At the same time, he detailed Bramble B. Ownby and George Parks (a former resident of Knight's Ranch, who was familiar with the Thompson Canyon area) to take several companions and go collect the McComas bodies.[50]

By the time the two parties united at the massacre site, dawn had come. The men fanned out and combed the country within a radius of one mile, looking for a trace of little Charley. Nothing! Bramble and Parks then set out to follow the Indian trail, even though it was cold, being more than eighteen hours old. The Paschal company started back with the loaded spring wagon.[51]

Before the men left the vicinity, some of them climbed a high point and observed on the opposite side of the Animas Valley an Apache smoke signal spiraling up from the rocky summit of Stein's Peak. They wondered whether it came from Indians who had been at the massacre and then had splintered off from the main band afterward. A better guess is that the signaling was the work of Dutchy and Kautli, trying to catch up with the war party after their mission to San Carlos and a meeting with Merejildo Grijalva. But no one really knows.[52]

At 2:30 in the afternoon on March 29, the spring wagon and its escort clattered into Paschal, to be met by the somber population of the whole camp. Mrs. Dennis and Mrs. Paschal R. Smith, wife of the mine owner, received the unenviable duty of preparing the bodies for the next stage of their trip. They washed off the blood, noting that the skin showed severe burns from having been exposed to the sun. And finally they clothed the corpses, both having arrived unclad beneath the canvas covering. This act of charity must have been highly painful for Mrs. Dennis, since the couple so recently had been guests at her table.[53]

Late that same afternoon, the remains of the McComases were delivered to the Derbyshire Brothers, Undertakers, in Silver City, where they were embalmed and placed in metallic caskets. Then they were removed to the family home on Hudson Street and left lying in state until relatives could arrive from the East. The grieving daughters, Ada and Mary, already had been moved to the Lucas house.

The calamity that befell Judge Hamilton C. McComas and his beloved wife was not that unusual in the annals of the American West. Families innumerable perished at the hands of Indians. What set their case somewhat outside the bounds of the ordinary was the lateness of the date: 1883. By then, most of the country was fully settled, and people at large assumed that frontier warfare was a closed chapter. The Chiricahua Apaches alone remained unwilling to concede that point.

A second thing that heightened interest in the tragic incident, of course, was the social and political prominence of the victims. Word of the massacre electrified the nation, becoming one of the chief news stories of the year. Americans wanted to know how such a shocking affair could have happened and what their government was doing about it. The return of the McComas bodies to Silver City merely ended the first phase of the episode. The dramatic second phase got under way without delay.

Chapter Seven

The Pursuit

From the walnut tree near the mouth of Thompson Canyon, where they had claimed the lives of Hamilton and Juniata McComas, Chato's band of warriors continued their descent toward Mexico. Driving their cumbersome herd of stolen livestock, they moved with all possible swiftness through the low, folded hills scattered along the sun-baked slope of the Burros. By evening, we believe, they came to the southern end of the range and in the gathering twilight looked out upon the broad and exposed Lordsburg flat.

In the distance they could see the dark points of the Pyramid Mountains, lying in their direction of travel. As the Apaches well knew, however, that route would take them close to Lordsburg, Shakespeare, and Pyramid City, populated by their well-armed and vengeful enemies. Did Chato and Bonito hold a hurried consultation to decide how to proceed? Or, in the typical Apache way, was there an unspoken agreement, an automatic understanding of what should be done?

Whatever the case, the war party chose to steer clear of the Pyramids and follow the wide level trough, studded with spiny yucca, that reached southward for many miles to the next far-off range, the Animas Mountains. That would carry them east of the Pyramids, but it also meant that, even though they rode all night, when sunrise came the next day, they still would be on the open alkali flats where the dust raised by their passage scarcely could be missed by soldiers or by miners' posses. There was no remedy for that, except to cover as many miles as possible while darkness hid the band's movements.[1]

Sometime during the night, Chato and his men crossed the Southern Pacific tracks between Lordsburg and a railroad siding and whistle stop called Separ, which lay twenty miles east of Lordsburg. In their hurry, they did not bother to stop and cut the telegraph line. Or perhaps they feared that, if the wire suddenly went dead, that would help to pinpoint their location.

A few hours earlier, over that very line, news of the McComas massacre, brought in by stage drive Joe Baker, had been flashed from Lordsburg to Deming. In the afternoon, Juniata's friend, Mrs. T. L. Smith, had caught the eastbound train at Lordsburg on her way to a visit in St. Louis. She had just pulled into the Deming station when the telegram arrived with the stunning word of the McComas murders. A few days later, still in shock, Mrs. Smith gave an interview to St. Louis journalists.[2]

Somewhere near the railroad tracks, the Indians lost four of the loose horses that were carrying packs of dried meat. The animals ambled westward and the next morning showed up in Shakespeare, much to the astonishment of residents who had spent a sleepless night anticipating an attack by the renegades.[3] By then the Apaches were many miles to the southeast, just entering the arid lakebed of the Aleman Valley, where the unshod hooves of their horses raised thick dust trails to float above the desert.

At noon on Thursday—that is, precisely twenty-four hours after the McComas massacre—ranch foreman Bob Anderson left the Eureka mining camp two dozen miles below Separ. He was driving a team of mules and a wagon loaded with supplies and ammunition for the home ranch that lay beyond the Animas Mountains. John Devine, a neighbor, rode beside him on the wagon seat.

The pair rumbled across the Aleman Valley (also called the Playas Valley), apparently unaware that they were following in the wake of an Apache raiding party. Soon they left the pancake floor and started up through a notch in the mountains that offered a natural pass to the country beyond. There they were ambushed by five Chiricahuas, some of Chato's stragglers.

A volley of shots from the Indian rifles opened the attack. One bullet hit Anderson in the left knee, and another struck Devine in the left hip. Both men jumped from the off side of the wagon in such haste that they left their firearms behind. As they raced for cover, Bob Anderson fell under a heavy fire.

Devine then ran back to the wagon to get his Winchester. As he grabbed it, a bullet zinged through his hat. The startled mules bolted and commenced a mad dash up the road, where they were quickly overtaken by the Indians. The wagonload of ranch supplies now diverted the Apaches' attention. They cut the mules out of their harness and began loading pillaged goods on their backs. Chief prizes were Anderson's rifle, a large quantity of ammunition, and eleven bottles of whiskey. After tossing a few more shots at Devine, the five assailants rode away in triumph.

At once John Devine went to his downed companion and found that Anderson was still alive, although dangerously wounded. Fearing return of the Indians, he piled up rocks to make a small fortification and stood guard till dusk. At night, leaving his gun, he set out walking to find help. With a painful wound of his own and unarmed, his chances of success seemed poor.

Indeed, the initial news stories reported that the two ranchers had been slain "by the very Apaches who killed Judge and Mrs. McComas." In the same dispatch, word appeared that the feeder stage operating between the Eureka Mine and Separ was missing and that all aboard were presumed lost.[4] Fortunately, both reports proved unfounded. The Separ coach turned up safe; while John Devine, at the end of his walk, fell in with rescuers who conveyed him and Anderson to Deming for medical attention. One admiring newspaperman wrote, "Devine showed remarkable presence of mind and bravery, and is lionized for those qualities and for his devotion to Anderson, who owes his escape to this gritty fellow."[5]

On the same afternoon that the McComases had left Silver City and Captain Thompson had left Fort Bayard, Lt. Col. George Alexander Forsyth (known to friends as Sandy) had marched out of Fort Cummings at the head of two companies of the 4th Cavalry. His orders were to rendezvous with Thompson and make a concerted attempt to block the escape of the rampaging Apaches.

From his earlier services on the Great Plains, Forsyth had garnered fame as an Indian campaigner. At the celebrated Battle of Beecher's Island in eastern Colorado (1868), he suffered three wounds; and in 1874, he accompanied George A. Custer on his expedition into the Black Hills. As commander of the 4th Cavalry in southern New Mexico, the colonel rode to intercept Geronimo, Juh, and Loco in their flight of April 1882. But when some of his troops were badly mauled at Horseshoe Canyon on the Arizona line and he himself failed to push the pursuit with the degree of aggressiveness the public deemed appropriate, Forsyth's reputation, locally at least, suffered.[6]

The hard-as-nails border folk demanded only one thing from the army—effective action. But to date, in the matter of Chato's raid, they had seen precious little of that. Nor were the first reports of Forsyth's movements of such a nature as to inspire confidence. On his first day out, according to the *Silver City Enterprise*, "his command got lost on the prairie, and having no guide, they wandered around helplessly for some time. This is fighting Indians with a vengeance." The paper then expressed the opinion that, had the troops actually come in contact with the marauding Apaches, they would, in all probability, have fallen victim to the merciless hostiles. "We shudder to think what might have been the consequence," it editorialized caustically.[7]

In this instance, anyway, the criticism proved misplaced, and in its next issue the *Enterprise* was obliged to print a retraction. It seems that a respected Grant County citizen and its first sheriff, Richard Hudson, had run into the soldiers at the time they were alleged to be lost, and he stoutly denied that they were any such thing. "Whoever informed you to that effect willfully and deliberately lied," he added. The newspaper sheepishly admitted that its source was mistaken and said that it had no desire to misrepresent Forsyth or any other officer of the army. Still, its original barbs were fully indicative of public sentiment.[8]

Lieutenant Colonel Forsyth's performance in chasing after the McComas murderers, as it developed, did absolutely nothing to restore his or the military's reputation. From Fort Cummings he had followed the now largely abandoned Overland Stage Road west, so he scarcely could have gotten lost. The command traveled through Tuesday afternoon and all that night, while Hamilton, Juniata, and Charley were sleeping serenely at the Mountain Home. About daybreak, Forsyth and his two companies trotted bone-weary into the old stage station at Cow Springs, which was now a ranch headquarters. They had covered fifty grueling miles in that single ride. As near as can be determined, the command spent the better part of the day napping and grazing its horses.

As the sun began to dip toward the crests of the western mountains, Forsyth got his men up, mounted, and moving, with the intention of making another night ride. Along the way, he passed another stage station, this one with the colorful name of Soldiers Farewell, and at some point he must have stopped and given his followers more rest. By late morning on Thursday, the colonel was on the Lordsburg flat not far below the Burros, when he ran into Bramble B. Ownby and George Parks.

Since earlier in the day, when they left the Paschal party at the massacre site, the pair had made good time following Chato's well-marked trail. Upon their sudden encounter with the soldiers, they were able to provide Forsyth with his first news of the deaths of the Grant County commissioner and his wife. George Parks, who had been personally acquainted with the McComases, offered his and Ownby's services as guides. And he called the officer's attention to a distinct dust cloud far southward, which he asserted was raised by the fleeing Indians. Their only chance to catch up with the raiders, he informed the colonel, was to hurry after them, make a night march, and hope to stage a daybreak surprise attack.

Incredibly, George Alexander Forsyth rejected out of hand this simple, commonsense strategy. He needed no bumptious civilian guides to tell him what to do, and, instead of turning south, he announced that he would go northwest to examine the massacre site. Nor did he give any reason for undertaking that pointless and time-wasting excursion.

Parks had a fiery temper, and when he heard this, he exploded. In front of the assembled troops, he dressed down the arrogant colonel, "sparing no invective that he thought suitable for the occasion." Bramble Ownby, relating the incident long afterward, declared with a chuckle, "It was the worst cussing I ever heard a man receive."[9]

Stubbornly, Forsyth struck out for the mouth of Thompson Canyon. Perhaps, going by the book, he wanted to confirm by personal observation that the trail the two civilians had been following really was that of the war party. When finally he saw it leading away from the blood-stained ground at the walnut tree, he was convinced. But only then did he face about and start his pursuit toward Mexico.

Late that same day (Thursday, March 29), Forsyth tardily reached the Southern Pacific tracks six miles east of Lordsburg, at the point where Chato and Bonito had crossed them during the previous night. There he went into camp, much to the relief of his tired men and horses. A few hours later, a special train under Army Quartermaster James Marshall pulled to a stop and began to unload Captain Thompson, his troops, and their mounts. They had boarded at Stein's Pass about three o'clock in the afternoon, after riding twenty miles down the mountains along the Arizona line without finding any Indians.[10]

Lieutenant Colonel Forsyth now had four companies of his own 4th Cavalry united under his command. At sunup on Friday, they commenced a rapid descent southward into New Mexico's bootheel. Their horses, fed and rested, carried them forty miles across the desert that day to a dry camp eight miles from Aleman Wells. Unbeknownst to the cavalry, the Apache marauders were laying over for the day, hidden in the cool heights of the Animas Mountains where they could watch the military column toiling across the sandy waste. The Indians no doubt also were enjoying the eleven bottles of whiskey plundered from Anderson's ranch wagon.[11]

Once darkness settled upon the land, Chato's raiders did what Apaches were accustomed to do when hotly pursued: they split and split again repeatedly, leaving only a bewildering skein of faint trails for their enemies to follow.

Captain Thompson, in his official report, noted that the Indian trail never again united, in the bootheel anyway, indicating that the warriors' rendezvous point was somewhere below the Mexican border.

No mention of it occurs in the military records, but a press release states that the Apaches committed one final killing before slipping across the international boundary. In the neighborhood of Antelope Springs, several of them encountered freighter L. G. Raymond, traveling with his wagon and team. They shot him, took his horse, and left the looted wagon standing in the road.[12] Chato's raid was over, although the chase continued for several more days.

In addition to the cavalry, another group of white men, the Shakespeare Guards, also was scouring the bootheel in an effort to check the Chiricahuas' flight. As already recounted, on Wednesday evening James Black and his men, following their western reconnaissance, had arrived back at Shakespeare just in time to receive initial word of the Thompson Canyon tragedy. Immediately preparations got under way to send the Guards out again. Their horses were worn out from the last scout, and Anton Mazzanovich, who was on the scene, says that "Captain Black had a hard job to mount his rangers, but finally rounded up enough animals for the men."[13]

That rounding up, and the laying in of supplies, took until noon the next day. Freighters were crowding the streets of Shakespeare and Lordsburg, afraid to venture outside town, and ranchmen were streaming in with their families. From these people Black may have commandeered fresh horses.[14]

James F. Black operated a saloon in Shakespeare. As a "weekend soldier," he had become commander of the local militia, owing to his leadership ability and reputation for bravery. But he had no experience as an Indian fighter, most of his activity in the field having dealt with the tracking down of outlaws. In the present emergency, however, he moved with the sure hand of an old campaigner. Upon departure, he commanded twenty-six men, including enrolled Guards and some added volunteers.[15]

Not long after their midday start, the company traveling east from Lordsburg came upon fresh tracks that crossed the Southern Pacific rails. "As we were told positively," related Black, "that the trail we saw had been made the day before by some stock driven by Mexicans, we took no further notice of it."[16] Exactly which passersby imparted such erroneous information the captain fails to say. But the mistake—for in fact the trail was Chato's—would cost him any chance he might have had to achieve the object of his pursuit.

Black then led his Guards east to Soldiers Farewell and on to Cow Springs, hoping to cut the war party's trail. He failed, of course, and upon reaching the latter place, it suddenly occurred to him that the tracks seen at the Southern Pacific crossing must have been made by the Apaches after all. By the time he got back to that place, an entire day had been lost. He also observed, by reading trail sign, that Forsyth's cavalry now was following the Indians, and that both groups were ahead of him.

One wonders why Captain Black did not break off his hunt at that point and leave it up to the four companies of soldiers to finish the job. The best answer is that, like most civilians, he had become skeptical of the army's ability to deal with the raiders. Furthermore, his men, although fatigued, were eager to continue the chase in hopes of exacting revenge. A number of them had known Judge McComas personally. So, after a quick side trip back to Lordsburg to acquire an additional three days' rations, the Guards on March 31 went pelting south toward the bootheel.

Remarkably, they covered forty-five miles that first day, reaching Aleman Wells just after sunset. Then, Captain Black wrote in his log, they "took the trail at daybreak and followed it about twenty miles to where the government troops had lost it, where it became very much scattered and difficult to find." What he did locate was the Chiricahua camp up in the Animas Mountains, at which site the Indians had rested, grazed their stock, and watched the worm-like line of Forsyth's column moving its way across the Playas Valley.

From scouting parties he sent out, the captain learned that most of the dispersed Apaches seemed to be moving down the east side of the mountains. But he decided to make a detour west of the range and visit Gray's Ranch in the Animas Valley, to secure grain for his failing horses. The dust-coated Shakespeare Guards rode into the ranch at 9 A.M. on April 1. They obtained not only their grain, but a small supply of flour and bacon as well. Within the hour, they were back in the saddle riding around the lower end of the Animas Mountains to pick up again the braid of faint trails that now was approaching the border.

Somehow Black and his Guards had managed to get ahead of the army troops. Toward the close of that same day, Lieutenant Colonel Forsyth and Captain Thompson rode into Gray's Ranch and arranged to camp there for the night. Although the pair would have been told of the visit of the Shakespeare men that morning, Thompson's report, our chief source on the army's movements, strangely makes no reference to it.

At the first sign of daylight on April 2, the cavalry set out to recross the Animas range. After a march of twenty-five miles, it reached Walnut Creek, flowing from the east slope of the mountains into the Playas Valley. Here

Forsyth went into camp, from which he dispatched his pack train northward to Aleman Wells to collect supplies he earlier had arranged to have delivered there. Evidently he was bracing for a plunge deep into Mexico, as allowed by the recent international treaty when soldiers were in "hot pursuit" of Apaches.[17]

During the wait, the colonel sent Captain Thompson and his Bayard Battalion to scout for Indian sign in the Alamo Hueco Mountains, situated in the extreme southwestern corner of the bootheel. Returning to the Walnut Creek camp on April 4, Thompson was surprised to find the command packing up, not for a run into Mexico but for a return northward. A courier had arrived bearing a dispatch from Gen. Ranald S. Mackenzie, the district commander at Santa Fe, ordering a withdrawal to Separ on the Southern Pacific. That directive had been issued after Mackenzie had received reports that other Apaches were moving from Sonora into Arizona and might pose a risk to settlers in southwestern New Mexico. The intelligence turned out to be false, and it resulted in the army's unnecessarily abandoning its pursuit of Chato.[18]

Meanwhile, the Shakespeare Guards were still hot on the trail, or on as much of it as they could find through some skillful and remarkable scouting. As they approached the United States boundary, the scattered tracks left by the Indian horses suddenly became quite fresh, showing that the white men were gaining rapidly. The unit trotted over the line in the vicinity of the Continental Divide and penetrated five miles into Mexican territory, where it halted at Lost Springs. Captain Black explained: "We camped there to await the expected arrival of the soldiers, hoping to procure provisions from them and accompany them farther into Mexico."[19] Perhaps in his mind also was the thought that, as volunteer militia, they might not have full legal sanction to be operating on foreign soil.

Curiously, after making such heroic exertions, the Guards now abandoned their quest. Black summed up the reason in a single unsatisfactory line in his official report: "The troops not arriving, we started the next morning, April 4th, on our return to Aleman Springs [that is, Wells] about fifty miles north."[20] The shortage of supplies and the failure of the cavalry to arrive could have provided sufficient motive for calling it quits, but there may have been more to it than that.

Once back in Shakespeare, the captain is supposed to have told another story, one that he declined to enter in the record. Toward the end of his expedition, he sent two scouts ranging down into the northernmost prong of the Sierra Madre. By luck, they found the raiders' camp in a deep canyon and got close enough to count sixty-two warriors and observe a large amount of plunder and a great many animals. When the Guards at Lost Springs learned of this discovery and heard that the Apaches outnumbered them more than two to one, "they feared to return and make an attack."[21] Hence, they promptly retreated back into the U.S.

One has reason to doubt that any of this actually occurred, except for the prompt withdrawal. The people of southwestern New Mexico had pinned large hopes on the Shakespeare Guards—that they might catch and punish the Chiricahuas and recover Charley McComas. Territorial newspapers kept saying that Black and his men were closing in, and that "a fight [could] be expected at any moment."[22] But as several days went by and nothing was heard from the company, concern mounted. Silver City's *Southwest Sentinel* declared, "Grave fears are entertained for their safety. They have either been ambushed and killed or are playing a desperate game."[23] A widely circulated press report stated the matter even more emphatically: "It is generally believed that the Shakespeare Guards have been annihilated."[24]

Thus, when the exhausted men suddenly rode into Shakespeare at 2 P.M. on April 6, there was a general feeling of relief. But there must have been some expressions of surprise as well, for Grant County's vaunted defenders had caught no Apaches, had fought no battle, and indeed had performed an about-face precisely when they seemed to be on the verge of engagement. Was the story of the sixty-two warriors in a canyon the fabrication of the scouts, or even of Captain Black, put forward to justify their retreat? We know with fair certainty that Chato's party by this point was composed of twenty-five men and boys. Of course, he could have been joined by another band that swelled his numbers, in which case the Guards' retirement would have been entirely warranted. Nevertheless, the unit's failure produced widespread disappointment.

The inability of Forsyth's troopers to achieve any success caused somewhat less consternation among the public, who had long since given up expecting positive results from the army. When the 4th Cavalry came limping into Separ on April 5, the day before the Guards' return, practically no notice was taken of them at all. In fact, as aggrieved citizens were quick to note, not a single member of the U.S. military ever caught so much as a glimpse of the hostile Apaches during the course of Chato's long and devastating foray.

Some historians have contended that the Indians on their raid actually reaped little in the way of arms and ammunition, so that their return to the Sierra Madre stronghold was anything but triumphant.[25] Close scrutiny of the record, however, will not sustain that conclusion. Peaches, for example, testified that when he abandoned the war party about halfway through its course, the warriors already had seized eighty-one guns and were acquiring ten to fifteen cartridges per victim.[26] The Apaches must have done that well or better during the final stage of their incursion, as they swept through the mining districts of eastern Arizona and into New Mexico. From Judge McComas, as we saw, they plundered two firearms and his cartridge belt. But their greatest windfall came with the capture of Bob Anderson's ranch wagon, which, besides the whiskey, reputedly carried an abundant supply of ammunition.

Jason Betzinez was in the stronghold, having just returned from Geronimo's pillaging swing through Sonora, when Chato and his followers arrived from the U.S. with their horde of guns and ammunition. If anyone showed displeasure over the quantity, he neglected to mention it. What Jason did chronicle was "the sad news that my cousin Beneactiney, who went with Chato and Bonito, had been killed." And he adds that Chief Chihuahua "came over

Peaches, the defector on Chato's raid and later the guide for General Crook on the Sierra Madre expedition, ca. 1885. Courtesy National Archives

and laid a hand on my shoulder, saying, 'Young man, don't grieve too much over this beloved relative of ours. He was a very brave warrior.' "[27]

At that moment, the Apaches had no inkling of what Chato's raid had stirred up or the degree to which the casualties they had inflicted, especially the deaths of the McComas couple, had infuriated the entire American nation. But very quickly they would learn, and the consequences would be ones they scarcely could have imagined.

When General Crook, in his headquarters at Whipple Barracks near Prescott, Arizona, first received notice of the advent of Chato's raiders, he fairly burned up the telegraph line sending troopers in pursuit, and also dispatching whole companies to take up stations along the border with Mexico, in an attempt to block the Apaches' escape when they had finished with their mischief. He was bound by necessity and public demand to go through those motions. However, as a seasoned Indian fighter who knew just how slippery such a marauding band could be, he seems to have held little hope that his men would succeed.

What the general had in mind was to seize this opportunity to launch a bold counterattack against the Chiricahuas in their Sierra Madre retreat. Chato's raid gave him the legal excuse to implement the "hot pursuit" provision in the recent treaty with Mexico, and he promptly sent a wire to Washington, asking for authorization to do just that. As well, he began lining up the military forces in neighboring territories.

On March 27, in the midst of the raid and the day before the McComas deaths, General Crook, with his staff officers and baggage, rode north, away from the action zone, to the little railway station of Ash Fork on the Atlantic & Pacific line. There they caught the eastbound train, which took them to Albuquerque. The party registered at the best hotel in town, the Armijo House. There they were joined by General Mackenzie, who came down from Santa Fe to confer with Crook and offer his support.[28]

A local reporter, coming to the Armijo House, was granted an interview with Crook, whom he found "taking a much needed rest upon his couch." The officer, while gracious, carefully evaded all questions that dealt with his plans in the present Apache emergency. Even so, the newspaperman was impressed and later wrote, "The people may rest satisfied that when General Crook and his able assistants get to work in earnest on the Indian question, things will hum."[29] But as news of the McComas massacre broke, others showed their impatience at the army's apparent tardiness in buckling down in earnest.

While in Albuquerque, Crook received Washington's reply to his earlier telegram. Granting him all that he sought, it read in part: "The General of the Army authorizes you, under existing orders, to destroy hostile Apaches, to pursue them regardless of department or national lines, and to proceed to such points as you deem advisable."[30] In other words, the general could march for Mexico or go anywhere else he wished in his campaign to bring the enemy to bay.

Pleased with this confirmation, Crook boarded a night train on the AT&SF for Deming, where he and his staff changed to the Southern Pacific and rode to Willcox, Arizona, a town he already had selected as the staging point for his proposed expedition to Sonora. General Mackenzie either accompanied him part of the way or followed a day or so later, because by April 7 he was reported to be in Lordsburg, evidently powwowing with Colonel Forsyth, who was just back from the bootheel.[31]

Upon his arrival in Willcox, General Crook had a very interesting development to deal with: Peaches had been captured! The accomplishment was credited to young Lt. Britton Davis. While other, more senior officers were in the field tracking Chato, Davis had been left in charge at the San Carlos Agency with a company of Indian scouts.

"The night of March 28," wrote he, "I was advised by telegram that hostiles had killed Judge McComas and his wife near Silver City. They were reported to have then headed west and might be expected to attack at some point of the Reservation within the next day." That the war party had turned west again was strictly misinformation, but Davis didn't know that and admitted, "The suspense was hard to bear in the face of threatened attack."[32]

About midnight on March 30, he had just retired when his door creaked open and the shadow of an Apache slipped noiselessly into the room. The lieutenant reached for a pistol on the bedside table and demanded the identity of the intruder. The familiar voice of one of his scouts replied in an excited whisper, "Chiricahua come."

That news brought Davis bouncing out of bed. He soon learned that an unknown number of the raiders had crept into a small camp of the White Mountain Apaches about a dozen miles from the agency. Rounding up some thirty of his scouts, he quickly set out by starlight. At daybreak, the officer entered the camp and apprehended one lone hostile, who proved to be not a Chiricahua but a White Mountain, known to the soldiers as Peaches.

Taking his captive back to the San Carlos Agency, Lieutenant Davis interrogated him, producing the first inside information on the leadership and makeup of the raiding party. After placing Peaches in irons for safekeeping, he fired off a telegram to Whipple Barracks, to be forwarded to General Crook.

Once Crook reached Willcox, on the evening of April 5, Davis sent him the valuable prisoner.[33]

The general was not long in recognizing the splendid piece of luck that had come his way. Peaches could not have been more accommodating, furnishing answers to the most detailed questions about his former companions and even agreeing to guide a military force back to the Chiricahuas' mountain hideaway. Crook considered his capture a turning point that might well guarantee success for the pending expedition into Mexico. Generously, he sent a warm letter of approval to Lieutenant Davis, commending him for his quick thinking and resolute action in this matter "of an especially delicate nature." The youthful officer must have glowed under the praise.[34]

As described earlier, Peaches recounted the circumstances of his "escape" from Chato's band, which according to him had occurred during the weekend prior to the McComas massacre, while the raiders were still in eastern Arizona. However, from the time of his supposed departure to the morning of his capture by Davis near San Carlos, on April 1, a full week would have elapsed. As the distance Peaches would have had to travel in that interval was only seventy miles, we are left to ponder what he might have been doing during this prolonged period.

An obvious but unprovable explanation is that in fact he did not leave the war party quite as early as he claimed and, indeed, did not do so until after its swing into New Mexico and the cutting down of the McComases at Thompson Canyon. Had he quit Chato immediately after that event and made straight for San Carlos, Peaches easily could have reached the White Mountain camp on the evening of March 31, in time for his capture the following morning by Lieutenant Davis.

It did not take the Apaches long to realize that the McComas slayings were something out of the ordinary and had particularly incensed the whites. Therefore, when questioned about the matter, they either would profess ignorance or manufacture some story to serve as a protective screen, on the theory that "a wise prisoner does not anger his warden." Up to his death in the 1950s, Sam Haozous, the warrior apprentice and last surviving member of the war party, cautioned his children not to speak to outsiders about the McComas affair until after he was gone.[35]

Did Peaches actually leave Chato's band in Arizona, as he claimed to Crook? Or did he leave later, after the Thompson Canyon tragedy, and disguise the truth to protect himself from possible reprisal? Colonel Forsyth, we know, assumed the latter. As soon as he heard of Peaches's capture, he telegraphed General Crook in Willcox and urged him to examine "the Indian who took part in the massacre of Judge and Mrs. McComas, . . . to try to find out what was done with little Charley McComas after he was carried off and whether he is still alive."[36]

On his march into the bootheel, Forsyth closely read the signs at the few places, such as watering holes, where the Indians had paused and dismounted. Failing to find any small footprints, he had come to the conclusion that the boy Charley had been killed soon after the butchering of his parents. But he wished Crook's prisoner, as a presumed eyewitness, to settle the uncertainty. Not surprisingly, Peaches never made a formal statement that linked him in any way with the massacre, and General Crook, who was said to believe that his captive "was honest and reported truthfully to him," may have avoided pushing the question.[37]

At Willcox, troops were congregating and supplies were arriving daily at trackside for the coming campaign. Six companies of the 3rd and 6th Cavalry Regiments under Maj. James Biddle and Capt. William E. Dougherty had assembled and, during the wait, conducted patrols to check out rumors that stray Apaches had been sighted in the surrounding mountains. The ranks of these regiments were beefed up by arrival of recruits from the Jefferson Barracks Cavalry Depot in St. Louis. A Missouri paper described them as "mostly young and bright fellows who are anxious to participate in an Indian campaign . . . and who wish to know something about the romance and reality of such things."[38]

Before he could depart for the field, General Crook was required to make two quick diplomatic trips, to apprise the governors of the Mexican states of Sonora and Chihuahua of his intention to enter their territory. On April 8, with a party of his officers and several ladies, he took the train south and then transferred to the new Sonora Railway, which brought him to Guaymas, where he conferred with the regional military commander, Gen. José Carbo. Entraining again on a special coach, Crook and his staff went next to the state capital at Hermosillo, where Gov. Don Felizardo Torres received them hospitably. In fact, he threw a state dinner for the visiting Americans, followed by a grand ball. The next morning (April 10) the two parties held a conference.[39]

Captain Bourke, a participant, informs us that the agreement hammered out required the American soldiers "to reach the boundary line no sooner than May 1, the object being to let the restless Chiricahuas quiet down as much as possible and relax their vigilance, while at the same time enabling the Mexican troops to get into position for effective cooperation."[40] The Sonoran governor was also worried about the large number of Apache scouts that would accompany the American expeditionary force. When they went out roaming the back country, how were his own soldiers to distinguish them from the hostiles? Crook promised to have the scouts wear conspicuous red headbands.[41]

Gratified with the smooth completion of the negotiations, General Crook loaded his party on a train and hurried back to Arizona. On April 13 he was off again, this time on the Southern Pacific to El Paso, where, after spending a miserable night in the flea-ridden Central Hotel, he caught the Mexican Central Railway for Chihuahua City. The generals and public officials there welcomed him as eagerly as had those in Sonora. Moreover, by enlisting a company of Yaquis to use in their next offensive against the Sierra Madre Broncos, they indicated that they were adopting Crook's policy of relying heavily upon Indian scouts.

The *El Paso Times* reported that the U.S. military delegation returned to that border city on the evening of April 16 and left early the next day for Willcox. "General Crook will take the field immediately after his arrival in Arizona. He is quite well pleased with his visit to Chihuahua," it said.[42] Indeed, the general felt entirely confident that he had lined up support properly—from Washington, from General Mackenzie at Albuquerque, and from the Mexican governors. For the rest, the actual operation was up to him, and now, a month after Chato had first sailed into Arizona wreaking havoc, Crook at last was ready to make a decisive move.

During the final week of April, he gave the signal to start; and his column of scouts, regular troopers, packers, and supply train of mules lurched into motion, amid a raging sandstorm. From Willcox, they trailed one hundred miles southeast to San Bernardino Springs, which was right on the international boundary in the lower corner of Arizona. At that point, the general halted to await May 1, the date stipulated for his entry into Mexico. His scouts used the pause to hold a frenzied all-night war dance. "They were in high feather and entered into the spirit of the occasion with full zest," remarked an officer—with some dismay, since the scouts were bent on tracking down their own people.[43]

George Crook determined to ride hard and fast into the mountains of eastern Sonora and, if possible, to drop upon the Chiricahuas when least expected. Peaches, serving as his guide, assured him that it was a feasible plan. High on the list of the general's priorities was the recovery of Charley McComas, should the lad still be alive. He could hardly have been unaware that the attention of the entire nation was focused upon the progress of his scrupulously prepared but slowly launched expedition.

It was perhaps inevitable, too, that the uproar over Chato's devilish foray should spark a new barrage of criticism leveled directly at the general. When he first appeared at Willcox, the *Arizona Daily Citizen* complained in an editorial, "General Crook has at last arrived in southeastern Arizona, where he should have been two weeks ago." And it expressed amazement that he had kept his headquarters so long at Whipple Barracks, when his presence was desperately needed in the lower Territory.

Specifically, with regard to the raid, the *Citizen* groused that Crook, well supplied with splendidly equipped men and hardy pack animals, "did nothing—absolutely nothing towards capturing the handful of renegade Apaches, or protecting the lives and property of our people. . . . Nor has he done anything to maintain his great reputation as an Indian fighter. Is it possible the general is resting upon his laurels?"

With the invasion of the enemy stronghold looming, however, the paper conceded that, despite past blunders and inefficiency, Crook now had everything he needed at his command. "We shall see if he is equal to the emergency," it declared sagely. In fact, virtually every resident on both sides of the border was hungering for a victory and hoped that the bearded old general would be able to deliver a decisive one.[44]

What ensued has been recounted fully in the history books—the daunting ride two hundred miles south into the deepest recesses of the Sierra Madre, an assault and capture of the main Chiricahua camp by the Apache scouts under Capt. Emmet Crawford, the gradual coming in and surrender of the leaders and warriors who had been absent on a new raid into Chihuahua, and the piecemeal return of the Bronco Chiricahuas to San Carlos. An elated Captain Bourke summed up the operation and lavished praise upon his commander with these words: "This was one of the boldest and most successful strokes ever achieved by an officer of the United States Army."[45]

It is freely acknowledged that nothing erases the memory of failure more quickly than some huge success. The border folk of Arizona and New Mexico, who had been calling for Crook's head because he had allowed Chato to raid and get away, now joined Bourke in heaping accolades upon him. One territorial paper expressed the general mood in a bold headline: "Cheers For General Crook! He catches the Indians and Makes A Fight In Mexico."[46] After a long drought, the army finally was bathed in adulation.

Still, one matter that had engaged public attention remained unresolved: where was Charley McComas? As we shall review shortly, George Crook had come back from the Sierra Madre without the boy, but with conflicting stories as to his possible fate. As long as Charley could not be accounted for, there was no hope of writing the final chapter of the McComas tragedy.

Chapter Eight

"Universal Grief and Indignation"

In March 1883, forty-two-year-old Eugene Fitch Ware of Fort Scott, Kansas, seemed to have everything going his way. He had a lovely wife, the former Miss Jeannette Huntington, who came from a prominent New England family and was a graduate of Vassar. A leader in state Republican politics, Ware was well into his second term as a Kansas senator from Bourbon County. When in the capital of Topeka, he moved freely and comfortably in the loftiest circles of power. His popular writings, particularly poetry, had caught the attention of the reading public, and his *Rhymes of Ironquill* eventually would go through thirteen editions and win him the literary title "Poet Laureate of Kansas."

The serene course of Eugene Ware's life, however, suddenly was interrupted at four o'clock on the afternoon of March 29, when he was handed a telegram from Silver City, New Mexico. Sent by the partner of his brother-in-law, Hamilton Calhoun McComas, it contained ghastly news, scarcely to be believed. The telegram read: "H. C. McComas and wife and Charles killed by Apaches yesterday. Party gone for bodies. Have telegraphed R. F. McComas. You telegraph other relatives. Ada and Mary at Mrs. Lucas's. Come at once. Will advise you further as news comes in. Answer. John M. Wright."[1]

An hour after the receipt of this wire, Senator Ware got a second one, containing a single line: "Mrs. McComas and Charley taken prisoners." That offered a ray of hope, seemingly confirmed by a Fort Scott businessman, S. A.

A portrait of Eugene Fitch Ware, made about the time of the McComas massacre.
Courtesy Kansas State Historical Society, Topeka, Kansas

Manlove, who happened to be in Tucson and who now sent a third telegram: "Messenger arrived at Lordsburg stating that Judge McComas has been killed by Apaches and his wife and child captured by Indians."[2]

These three brief telegrams, representing the first word given to the outside world about the McComas tragedy, at once were released to the newspapers, and they were printed in the press throughout the country under the heading, "Ominous Dispatches."[3] Because of the conflicting information they contained, Senator Ware expressed the forlorn hope to some of his friends that "it may not prove as bad as first reported."

Elisha M. McComas, H. C.'s elder brother who still resided at Fort Scott, did not share that optimism. In a public statement, he said, "The minute I heard the news, a terrible certainty of its truth came over me. I have no hopes of ever seeing my brother again alive." No sooner had he given voice to his feelings than Elisha received his own wire out of New Mexico. From another Fort Scott resident, now in Lordsburg, W. J. Crosby, it informed him that the McComas couple indeed had been killed the day before and their bodies recovered and sent to Silver City. "Dave [the judge's son] goes over there today to take charge of the remains. Your nephew Charley has been captured," the message concluded.[4]

As the initial press stories began to roll in from the southwestern territories, the grim reality of the disaster was firmly established. Over in St. Louis, H. C.'s former law partner, John McKeighan, also got one of Wright's thunderbolt telegrams and shortly afterward saw the first notices in the local papers. Devastated, he sent off a hurried note to Elisha McComas, asking whether the woeful news was accurate. The brief, telegraphed reply from Fort Scott read simply: "Ham and Jennie both certainly dead. Charley a prisoner.— E. W. McComas."[5]

Within two to three hours following arrival of the first Silver City telegram, the *Fort Scott Evening Herald* put an edition on the streets with the bold headline, "Horrifying Intelligence," and a subheading that announced, "H. C. McComas Killed." In a follow-up story, it declared: "The news of his horrible death and that of his wife and the undetermined fate of their little boy casts a gloom over the community. The atrocities constantly being committed by these roaming red devils are now brought home to us, and we can sympathize and excuse the feelings of those who in the past have suffered, and have come to the deliberate conclusion that all good Indians are dead."[6]

Although oppressed by his own sadness and gloom, Eugene Ware immediately had swung into action. Among his first acts, he conferred with his younger brother and law partner, Charles, who, it was agreed, should leave immediately for the family farm, where their parents were now living, and bring them the mournful news. Mindful of John Wright's admonition to "come at once," Eugene wasted no time in packing his suitcase. Then he wired H. C.'s banker-brother in Nebraska City with instructions to meet him at the Union Station in Kansas City.[7]

Ware bought a ticket on the Kansas City, Fort Scott and Gulf Railroad and reached the Union Station sometime in the afternoon on Friday. That evening he was joined by Rufus McComas, down from Nebraska, and they caught the next train leaving for the New Mexico Territory. Two days later, on April 1, they passed through Albuquerque heading south, and on the following day, Mrs. Lucas reported their arrival in Silver City.[8] It is possible that the Judge's second son, William, who had been living in Nebraska City, accompanied his two uncles. If not, he followed them on a later train, because shortly he was reported in the company of his older brother, David.

Word of the Thompson Canyon tragedy first had reached Silver City at 4 A.M. on Thursday morning, via the horseback messenger from Paschal sent by the mine superintendent, Tom Nickerson. As the report spread, men quickly pulled on their clothes and hurried into the streets. Declared the local *Enterprise*, "Nothing in the past history of Silver City has created such intense excitement as this news. When it was known for a certainty that the McComas names were added to the bloody calendar of Apache outrages, the indignation of our citizens knew no bounds."[9]

Since the town lacked its own formal militia unit, an ad hoc company of more than thirty armed volunteers was assembled under the leadership of S. H. Eckles. Among those volunteering were a physician and a surgeon, and most of those joining were prominent in the community. The group's intention was to go and help bring in the McComases' remains, but also to take the offensive against the raiders, should they have turned eastward across the Burros, as was then supposed. Upon arriving at Paschal, the party found the population behind barricades, expecting at any moment to be attacked by Chato's minions. For some reason that is as far as the volunteers went, perhaps because the men of Silver City learned that the victims' bodies were on their way in and also heard that no one had actually seen an Indian on the east slope of the mountains.[10]

With the volunteer company was Judge McComas's young partner, John Wright. Owing to his closeness to the couple, he had taken it upon himself to notify family members in the East, by telegram. The massacre affected him deeply, and in the months that followed he worked loyally and hard, first as part of the huge effort that was mounted to find Charley McComas and then in the tedious and prolonged business of settling the judge's estate.

One of the first things that Eugene F. Ware and Rufus McComas probably did, upon arrival in Silver City on April 2, was to meet with John Wright and receive an update regarding the current situation. They would have learned that, on the previous Saturday afternoon, an immense throng of friends, acquaintances, and business associates of the McComases had lined up at the Hudson Street home to file past the metallic caskets and pay their last respects.

The very next morning, on Sunday, the Reverend H. Lansdown Gamble preached a funeral oration at the Methodist Episcopal Church, speaking from the same pulpit from which he had delivered his Easter sermon the week before, when Hamilton and Juniata had been in attendance. Then a special memorial service was scheduled for Tuesday evening at 8 P.M. in the same church. So far as is known, Eugene, Rufus, son David McComas, and possibly his younger brother William (if he had arrived by this date), along with the girls Ada and Mary, filled a pew during what the papers termed "a touching and impressive service."[11]

The overflow crowd was consoled by music of the Centennial Band and by hymns from the choir (which included member John Wright). After the singing of "I Heard a Voice From Heaven," Reverend Gamble, by request, repeated his oration from the previous Sunday. Mayor Cornelius Bennett followed with a few well-chosen remarks, "in a voice full of sorrow and sympathy." To the assembled congregation, "he spoke of the horrible manner in which these two good people had lost their lives, and of their little son being carried into captivity, in a tone which brought tears to the eyes of many."[12]

Attorney Thomas F. Conway, who earlier had lost his own partner John Risque to the Apaches, brought the obsequies to a close by the reading of a set of resolutions which the mayor had commissioned him and a small committee to draft. Mr. Conway spoke feelingly of the late judge as one of the brightest legal lights of the Grant County Bar and as a man committed to public service and to his family. Specifically, he addressed the surviving daughters: "Resolved: That the children whose hearts are bowed with grief by the untimely death of both father and mother, have our sincerest sympathy and condolence in this their sad bereavement." Nor did he neglect the lost Charley, summoning Silver City residents to give "all assistance in our power to effect his recovery and return him to his family so anxiously awaiting his safe return."[13]

Similar words of condolence had been pouring into Silver City for several days. On March 29, for example, the people of Pyramid City, Shakespeare, and Lordsburg had joined in sending a message in which they "tendered to the bereaved children our profoundest sympathy in their deep affliction."[14] The same evening that Eugene and Rufus had arrived in town, Mrs. Lucas penned a sorrowful letter to Charles Ware back in Fort Scott, assuring him that "everything was being done that could be done by loving friends." And she closed with a plea: "Would you please write again and tell me of your mother, for I cannot help loving her for my dear friend's [Juniata's] sake. Ada and Mary . . . are staying overnight with a friend of their mother's, but I know they will be glad to hear from you for they talk a great deal of Grandma and Uncle Charlie."[15]

Eugene Ware also received an expression of regret from Kansas Gov. George W. Glick, who wrote from Topeka as follows: "I sympathize with you in the terrible calamity by which your sister and brother-in-law lost their lives. I fear that the little boy has also been killed; I see such statements in the papers. I hope though, it is not correct, and that you will be able to recover him."[16]

The *Enterprise* summed up prevailing sentiment among the Silver City populace. "Only a few days ago the [McComas] family were together in their own home, surrounded by all the comforts and luxuries of life, and were happy in their love for each other. All was sunshine and happiness for their little girls then, but all has changed now, and even the most sympathetic cannot realize the sorrow that has forever seared the life-spring in the hearts of these little children. It is indeed a happy thought to think that there is a bright hereafter, where a once happy family may again be united, nevermore to part."[17]

The passage is laden with the oversweet phrasing of the nineteenth century but is also eloquent in expressing the sincere distress of those who were affected in some way by the McComas story. Silver City's *Southwest Sentinel* referred to "our grief, which is universal," and that too was an accurate reflection of public feeling.[18]

As the press spread the news to the far corners of the nation, however, indignation rather than grief was the word most commonly invoked. Under the bold headline, "McComas Massacre," the *Missouri Republican* cried, "In all the previous history of Indian outrages in Arizona and New Mexico, the righteous indignation of the people has never been aroused [as it] is now."[19] A special dispatch from Globe, in the Arizona Territory, reported that "there is indignation at all points," owing to General Crook's failure to prevent the McComas slayings.[20]

From the *New York Times* through the *Chicago Tribune* to the *San Francisco Chronicle,* and in numerous papers in between, pages were filled with harsh rhetoric directed against Chato's Chiricahuas. Phrases such as these were commonplace: "blood-crazed Apaches," "the Indian hounds," "red devils," "beasts in human shape," "murderous redskins," "Apache fiends," and "filthiest brutes on the globe."

In a ringing editorial, the *St. Louis Post-Dispatch* condemned "the wanton murder by Apaches, near Silver City, of a most estimable gentleman and lady. We do not hesitate to say that the two lives which have been destroyed in cold-blooded crime were worth more than all the marauding scalpers in whose favor a sickly sentimentality is evoked throughout the East. . . . In the case of the Apaches, there is no room for any maudlin sentiment. They are born pillagers and murderers, . . . worse than wild beasts, . . . and enemies of mankind, the defenders of savagery against civilization. There is only one way to deal with these monsters, and that is to give them the same treatment they extend to others."[21]

A call for the extermination of the Apaches, once confined to the Southwest, now echoed across the land. In the desert country, inflammatory news stories fanned public hysteria and led to proliferation of wild rumors. Large bands of reservation Apaches were alleged to have joined the renegades. Other reports claimed that hordes of Indians threatened the annihilation of all whites in Grant County. Clifton, Arizona, was supposed to be under siege, with an all-out attack expected any day. None of this was true, however.[22]

Immediately following the McComas killings, Americans read in their daily papers: "The people [of the Southwest] are terribly excited, and threats of wiping out the Indians on the San Carlos Reservation are freely indulged in."[23] Such a possibility was what the peaceful Apaches at the agency had feared from the first moment when they learned that Chato had leaped the border to raid. In the explosive atmosphere, they knew that white vengeance could ricochet and catch them as secondary targets.

Eugene Ware spelled out the situation precisely in a letter he wrote to friends back in Fort Scott. "At present all is hostility," he said. "No Indian can leave the reservation without death wherever found. In fact the feeling is so intense that large bodies of men are organized in the vicinity to move upon the reservation and butcher every Indian, big and little. A feeling that seems to be universal is that the entire Apache tribe, quiet and hostile, should be exterminated."[24]

Ware's reference to vigilantism was confirmed, in fact, by news stories which declared: "Unless something positive is accomplished soon there is danger of an attempt by an organized body of citizens from Clifton, Globe and Tombstone going to San Carlos Reservation."[25] Their announced aim was "to take the administration of Indian affairs into their own hands."[26]

General Crook was sufficiently concerned over that grim prospect that he issued blanket orders to all military units for the prompt arrest of any citizen group caught marching toward the reservation with hostile intent. The measure failed to deter the outraged citizens of Tombstone, who held a mass meeting on April 3. As liquor flowed freely, they listened to community leaders call for an attack on San Carlos, saying that the miners had lost faith in the army and that reliance should be placed entirely upon their own rangers. One of the most vehement speakers was H. C. Dibble, whose brother had fallen under Chato's guns.[27]

The outcome of Tombstone's harebrained attempt to slay the Apaches of San Carlos was recorded by Lt. Britton Davis: "The Tombstone Rangers, of the same general character as the Globe Rangers and under the same or a better brand of stimulant, set out to massacre all the Indians on the Reservation." Then he informs us: "They met up with an old Indian who was gathering mescal. They fired at him but fortunately missed. He fled north and they fled south. That ended the massacre."[28] Lieutenant Bourke adds wryly that, when the whiskey taken along by the rangers was exhausted, "the organization expired of thirst."[29]

From coast to coast, reports of Chato's raid, highlighted by the McComas killings, had stirred deep feelings and sparked bitter public anger. In their dismay, people wanted to know how such a calamitous event could have occurred and who was responsible. Not surprisingly, a large share of the blame was heaped upon the government, and the press ridiculed the army mercilessly for its inability to control the marauders. But the heaviest censure, of course, descended upon Apache shoulders. An editorial printed in Fort Scott phrased the general consensus thus: "Our Indians should be treated as any other [persons] are treated when guilty of crime, and as rigorously held to account. In no other way can they be brought to a full recognition of their relations to the rest of mankind."[30]

In the widespread coverage accorded the raid, voices of moderation were few. The *El Paso Times* stood practically alone when it reminded readers that the several thousand peaceful Apaches at San Carlos ought not to be held responsible for the misdeeds of two dozen renegade invaders from Mexico. "It is far easier, and for the day to fall in with this tide of anger, or to fan the flames which deeds like the slaying of Judge and Mrs. McComas arouse in the manly breast of the outraged frontiersman," the journal editorialized. "But a movement such as is reported at Tombstone would be the height of wicked folly. . . . Let us reason together."[31] As they read accounts of the removal of the McComas bodies to Fort Scott and of the funeral that followed, however, most Americans seemed unwilling to heed that wise counsel.

In the meeting they held with John Wright upon reaching Silver City, Eugene Ware and Rufus McComas informed him that the McComas coffins would be taken back to Fort Scott for burial. Ware promptly sent his younger brother Charles the following telegram:

Silver City, N.M., April 3, 1883

C. L. Ware, Fort Scott:

Rufe will arrive at Scott Saturday afternoon with bodies. Have graves
dug in my lot in Evergreen Cemetery. Ada and Mary accompany their parents. No news from Charley. I remain to settle estate and find the boy. May
visit Old Mexico.

Eugene[32]

Early on Wednesday, April 4, following the memorial service of the previous evening, the heavy caskets of Hamilton and Juniata were gently lifted
into a horse-drawn conveyance. A huge, grieving throng composed of friends,
representatives of the legal and business community, members of fraternal
organizations, and soldiers turned out to serve as a formal escort. The procession rolled slowly through streets lined with citizens who stood solemnly, hats
in hand. The mayor had asked that all stores remain closed.

Most of the escort seems to have remained with the party on the long
ride south to the railroad at Deming. There, on the following day, Rufus saw
to the loading of the coffins on an AT&SF express car, and, after purchasing
tickets, he and his young nieces boarded for the two-day trip to Kansas City.
At that place they were joined by John McKeighan, who accompanied them
on the Gulf train down to Fort Scott, where he was to act as one of the pallbearers.[33]

The town which claimed the Apache victims to be their own was all astir.
Friends of the McComases had been pouring in from around the country, and
every hotel room in Fort Scott was occupied. The former law office of
McKeighan & McComas stood draped with crepe-covered flags. Municipal
officials worked feverishly making preparations for the enormous funeral.

The incoming train from Kansas City reached Fort Scott at 2:40 in the
afternoon on Saturday, April 7. The depot platform and adjacent streets held a
vast multitude of people, and as the New Mexico party descended from the
rail car, all eyes strained to catch a glimpse of the pair of small orphaned girls
who stood at the center of the tragedy. On hand, lending their presence to the
gravity of the moment, were the mayor, the city council, members of the Board
of Trade (that is, the Chamber of Commerce), and all representatives of the
Bourbon County Bar.[34]

Also present were three members of the Ware family: Eugene's wife
Jeannette, his brother Charles, and the father Hiram Ware. Initially, the pa-
pers reported that the McComas bodies would be taken directly to the Opera
House, where they would lie in state. However, at the family's request, that

plan was scuttled, and it was decided that Hamilton and Juniata should go instead to Senator Ware's spacious house at the corner of Birch and Eddy streets.

Willing hands transferred the coffins from the Gulf express car to a resplendent hearse waiting by the platform. Then family, the official receiving committee, and friends fell in behind, some riding in carriages and others walking. The attenuated cavalcade moved at a crawl away from the station and toward the Ware home, where Amanda Ware, Juniata's aged mother, was waiting to receive it. The girls, Ada and Mary, were told that they would be staying there. Rufus McComas soon left to lodge with his older brother Elisha, who lived on Main Street.[35]

Throughout the remainder of the afternoon, a large crowd surrounded the house, persons standing silently or, out of respect, speaking in hushed tones. Inside, family members decided to open the caskets for one last look at their loved ones. Someone passed on word that "they found the remains in a good state of preservation. Mrs. McComas' appearance was natural and lifelike. The Judge's face and features were more changed."[36] Those statements would seem to confirm the conclusion, mentioned earlier, that the bodies had not been mutilated by the Indians. Despite requests from friends, who also wanted a final viewing, the Wares elected to keep the caskets sealed during the next day's funeral.

Arrangements for that event continued apace as Saturday afternoon waned. In its pages, the *Fort Scott Monitor* had placed an obligation upon all citizens to do their part. "Let the legal fraternity turn out in a body, Board of Trade, Grand Army of the Republic, Odd Fellows, Masons, Knights of Pythias, and in fact let business be suspended and let us do honor to our honored dead," it urged.

To justify its sweeping call, the newspaper declared: "Judge McComas was as brave a soldier as ever drew a sword and served with distinction during the war. His life was devoted to helping the poor, and he was always found on the side of the toiling masses and bravely did he battle for their rights under all circumstances.

"We hope such action will be taken as will do credit to our city and ourselves as citizens."[37]

These clarion phrases must be dismissed as journalistic hyperbole, since no evidence exists that H. C. McComas ever experienced combat during the Civil War, or that he ever took the side of the poor or showed much interest in the toiling masses. The stirring words, nevertheless, served their purpose of galvanizing the entire community.

Among those who responded was the local post of the Grand Army of the Republic (GAR), of which the judge once had been an honored member. This fraternal organization of Union Army veterans had a well-defined procedure for participation in funerals. On April 7, Post Commander W. B. Shockley issued the following order: "In obedience to a resolution offered at special muster at these headquarters, the above date, all comrades of the Post, together with the members of the Drum Corps, will report for duty promptly at 12:30 P.M., Sunday, the 8th day of April. Those having uniforms will appear in such to participate at the funeral of the late Col. H. C. McComas and wife."[38]

Another group heard from was the tightly knit club of Fort Scott attorneys, which assembled at the office of one of their number on Saturday evening to draw up an appropriate set of resolutions. After the usual flowery references to the deceased's "great learning, talents, and many virtues" and the extending of customary condolences to the bereaved family, the lawyers resolved to introduce a protest. It read in part: "We . . . express our earnest censure and condemnation of the Indian policy of the government, the joint product of corrupt and heartless rings and maudlin sentimental humanitarianism which exposes our citizens upon the frontier to barbarous atrocities like this."[39] That attitude, as remarked, was surfacing all across the United States in the wake of the media coverage of the last rites for the McComases.

❧ The morning of April 8 was robed in Sunday quiet, and all households in Fort Scott awoke to a lustrous day. Budding trees and occasional notes of robins heralded the returning spring, and brilliant sunshine cast a magic light over rooftops and around the spires of churches. As one resident remembered it, that scene "suggested the bright eternal day which had dawned for the departed whom we mourned."[40]

The funeral service was scheduled to begin at 1:30 P.M., in Juniata's old Congregational church. Its pastor, the Reverend G. S. Bradley, called upon the Reverend Irving F. Davis, of the local Baptist church, to assist him. The choir of the Episcopal church also was enlisted for the occasion. By late morning, people had already begun to gather and fill the pews.

At precisely one o'clock, the caskets of Hamilton and Juniata were carried out the front door of the Ware home. Uniformed members of the fraternal Knights of Honor, standing at attention, lined the sidewalk. Among the somberly dressed pallbearers, the crowd caught a glimpse of Fort Scott's Mayor John Glunz. Close behind the caskets walked Hiram and Amanda Ware, leading their orphaned granddaughters. They were followed by Elisha W.

McComas and his wife, Charles L. Ware and his sister-in-law Jeannette, and finally by Rufus McComas and John McKeighan, who brought up the rear.

At curbside, pallbearers slid the caskets into two waiting hearses pulled by sleek horses. Then a procession formed by prearranged order. At the head marched Prothero's Silver Coronet Band (J. Prothero, leader), which routinely furnished music for all major events in Fort Scott. Then came the GAR Drum Corps and post members, the Knights of Honor (Judge McComas having been a high-standing member), the Fire Department, and representatives of the bar. The hearses were escorted, on either side, by the dashing Kansas National Guard, carrying reversed arms. Trailing them were family and friends in buggies and a throng of others on foot.

This immense concourse lurched forward and with measured tread began to move in file slowly up Birch Street, to the muffled drum of the Corps. The Congregational church by now was overflowing. Only the main aisle remained clear, and a few seats had been reserved in the front pew for family and pallbearers. Outside, the numbers of spectators and carriage teams were so great that they filled the grounds and blocked the streets. Two thousand persons were estimated to be in attendance.[41]

As the funeral procession approached, the advance units cleared a passageway and opened ranks, allowing the hearses to drive up to the front door. Reverend Bradley and Reverend Davis emerged from the vestry and proceeded up the aisle to meet the caskets at the entrance. They escorted them back to the chancel, where the caskets were placed on biers, covered with American flags, and strewn with cut flowers. As this was done, the organ piped a rueful dirge.

After the family members were seated in their pew facing the caskets, the combined Congregational and Episcopal choirs opened with the hymn "Asleep in Jesus." Reverend Bradley read some verses from scripture and then launched into the funeral sermon. In tone and sentiment, it was not unlike the one delivered earlier at Silver City. His only reference to the manner in which the McComases died was concentrated in two lines: "All the circumstances are tragic in the extreme. But it will not become me to enter into any narration of them." He added, "I am requested to make the exercises brief."[42] True to that injunction, he kept his words in check, and the choir wrapped up the service by singing "Beyond the Smiling and the Weeping."

The caskets then were borne again to the hearses, with the Knights of Honor guarding the walk from the church. The cortege left for the cemetery in the same order in which it had arrived, only now, instead of the muffled drums, Prothero's Silver Coronet Band played a solemn funeral dirge. Mrs.

McComas grave marker, Evergreen Cemetery, Fort Scott, Kansas.
Courtesy Shirley Hurd, Fort Scott, Kansas

D. E. Gardner, who as a child was present, in 1938 recalled that the McComas procession stretched two miles in length. Said the daily paper: "No similar service ever held in Fort Scott called forth such a sight."[43]

At the graveside in Evergreen Cemetery, GAR Commander Shockley and the post chaplain conducted the dramatic ritual and burial service of the organization. The crowd joined voices in the hymn "Nearer My God to Thee," and Reverend Bradley uttered a final prayer. Hamilton Calhoun McComas and Juniata Ware McComas were laid to rest in a double grave next to the burial place of their first-born son Frederick.[44]

As the day wound to a close, the McComases and Wares sadly climbed into their carriages for the ride home. Ahead of them lay the task of putting their shattered lives back into some kind of order. Being of sturdy American stock, they had stood tall, with heads high, during their ordeal and had done what was proper and expected in the matter of the funeral. That was some consolation but scarcely enough to erase the pain of their loss, which ever after would remain just below the surface as an aching memory.

The events of that day, April 8, 1883, in Fort Scott, Kansas, were the direct outcome of the Sierra Madre Apaches' need for ammunition and also of Hamilton and Juniata's innocent decision to halt under a walnut tree for a picnic beside the Lordsburg Road. How remote the New Mexico desert seemed from the peaceful, grassy sward in Evergreen Cemetery where the McComases were to spend eternity.

The final chapter in the story, however, had yet to be written. The fate of Chato's raiders, in their Mexico retreat, remained to be settled by the expeditionary force of Gen. George Crook. And Eugene Fitch Ware missed the funeral of his sister because he had stayed in the Southwest, trying to ransom her son. The attention of the nation now shifted from Kansas back to New Mexico and a new round of dramatic happenings that, in their resolution, at last would create an ending to the tale.

Chapter Nine

Little Boy Lost

A distinguished historian of the Southwest, the late Dan L. Thrapp, once wrote that the kidnapped Charley McComas became the object of the most widespread and prolonged search in the annals of Apache warfare.[1] His statement was no exaggeration. Family members, civilian posses, militia companies, and troops of U.S. soldiers all joined in scouring the country along both sides of the international boundary. Seemingly the entire nation was following the story, and the news sources eagerly pounced upon every scrap of information that hinted at the fate of the missing child.

The first published reports, based upon the erroneous telegram that Eugene Ware had received at Fort Scott, indicated that Charley had been slain with his parents. The men who went to the scene, however, made a zealous search for his body, and, not finding it, rightly concluded that he had been carried away, a captive. But almost at once rumors began to circulate that the boy had become troublesome on the trail and that, within a few miles of the massacre site, the Apaches had killed him.

The *Fort Scott Evening Herald*, for instance, ran a headline on April 2 reading: "Charley McComas's Body Found." The story, lifted from the previous day's *St. Louis Globe-Democrat*, claimed that soldiers [these would have been Forsyth's troops] had encountered the youngster's remains about two miles out and he had been brained. This was pure fiction, but it established a theme which kept resurfacing for years—that the McComas boy had been murdered within hours of his capture.

Another version appeared in the *Tombstone Republican* and was widely reprinted in southwestern newspapers.[2] It read: "The body of the little six-year-old son of Judge McComas has been found six miles from where his father and mother were killed, with his head beaten off against a rock. This is a picture for parents to look at, and then imagine he was their darling. In the face of such damnable deeds as this, that breeding-pen of San Carlos still exists."

From a Mexican who had spent his childhood with the Chiricahuas and who still maintained contact with some of the hostiles came word that, yes, Charley was dead. Almost at once "he had cried, and continued to cry, until finally [a warrior] had smashed in his head with a stone."[3] In apparent confirmation, a civilian employee at San Carlos informed a journalist that the prisoner Peaches had told him of the boy's early death, saying that he had been "knocked in the head with a rock." That same Peaches had offered to guide anyone to the place of the crime and show him the body.[4] The mule packer Anton Mazzanovich wrote in his memoirs, long after the event, that information gleaned from the Indians revealed that they had dispatched Charley rather quickly following his capture, because he had grown querulous and the pursuit became vigorous.[5]

Another account has been recorded by Jennie Parks, the niece of George Parks. It will be recalled that George, with Bramble B. Ownby, first followed Chato's trail as it led away from the walnut tree. She relates that in 1898, while a passenger on the old Concord stage that ran between Bowie and Globe, Arizona, she sat next to a Mr. Windmiller, who had been a merchant for many years at the San Carlos Agency.

> On the long, tiresome journey we talked of Indian tragedies of bygone days, and I asked him if the Indians had ever hinted at the fate of Charley McComas. Then he told me that only a month or two earlier he had heard of an old squaw who claimed to have been in the band which killed the Judge and his wife.
>
> She had told Mr. Windmiller that the little boy had cried so much and caused so much trouble that within a few hours' ride from the scene of the murder they had taken him by the feet and struck his head against a big boulder, killing him. They had then put his body in a crevice in the rocks. She gave a good description of a place that really existed in that section, but the boy's remains were never found.[6]

Perhaps the strangest recital of little Charley's fate was given by Charles R. Montgomery in 1899. At the time, he was described as a famous hunter and scout, well known throughout the territory of Arizona, and a former courier for General Crook. In an interview, he stated that he had kept his information from the public; but now, relenting, he said, "I think it is but right that history should record the facts as to what became of the McComas boy."[7]

Following Crook's expedition into the Sierra Madre and the return of the hostile Chiricahuas to San Carlos, Montgomery maintained that he had met Chato and from him obtained an account concerning Charley McComas's last hour. "He told me positively," said the scout, "that the child had been killed within three quarters of a mile from where the father and mother had fallen.

"I doubted Chato's words and accused him of lying, but he gave me all the details of the murder, which were too horrible for a white man to repeat. I afterward proved that his story was correct by going down and finding the bones, supposed to be those of a child. However, there were only a few bones of one arm, and I guess the bones of a leg."

Here in outline is what Chato allegedly related to Montgomery. When the Apaches attacked the McComas buckboard, the young boy jumped to the ground and started to run. One of the party went in pursuit, scooped him up, and tied him in front of the saddle. About then another warrior appeared and wanted the pretty jacket that the youngster was wearing, saying he wished to give it to his own son. A fierce controversy ensued, during which Charley's captor seized him by the ankles, swung him around in the air like a club, until finally the boy's head struck a rock, crushing it. After stripping the body, the Apaches threw it into the brush.

Scout Montgomery testified that, at a later date, Chato even pointed out to him the very Indian who had committed that horrible deed. Montgomery also insisted that he had provided Crook a full report of what he had learned, but that, since Chato now was a loyal government scout, the general "could not afford to have him punished." Embarrassment over that inaction, the scout infers, was part of the reason he delayed in going public.

So what are we to make of this narrative? Could any portion of it be true? It certainly would be convenient to believe so, inasmuch as this is the only instance known in which Chato is purported to have spoken about the McComas massacre. The chances seem great, nevertheless, that Charles R. Montgomery fabricated most of the yarn, perhaps to attract attention to himself, something numerous old-time frontiersmen did in their later years.

Is it plausible to believe, for example, that Montgomery was able to find some of Charley's bones almost a year after the incident, when search parties had combed the same country immediately and had been unable to locate the body? Further, why would Chato have divulged so much information to a scout he barely knew when, as all reports affirm, he never dropped so much as one word about the McComas affair to anyone else?

In fact, the other stories that have Charley succumbing to a quick death seem just as shaky, each of them being based more or less on hearsay. Yet all, curiously, have one point in common—that the boy was brained. References already have been made to several instances in which Apaches beat out the brains of captive women and children, usually with stones, although Juniata is thought to have died by the blow of a rifle butt. Attorney John Risque fell to the guns of Loco's warriors in 1882, but even after he was dead, his face was smashed with a rock.

That the Apaches often crushed the skulls of their victims is indisputable. Knowledge of the fact might have prompted whites on the New Mexico frontier, having heard rumors of Charley's murder, to suppose the he had perished in that gruesome manner. But to the present moment, not a scintilla of evidence has come to light that categorically would confirm such a conclusion.

Actually, another story exists that paints Charley's death in different terms. It derives from Deputy U.S. Marshal S. L. Sanders, who has been quoted previously. In 1890, he said that, after the massacre, Charley McComas was carried about seven miles. "As he continued to sob and cry for his parents and made considerable noise, it irritated Chief Chato to such an extent that he ordered the Indian who was carrying the boy to kill him. Acting upon the order, the Indian raised him up by the hair from the horse, plunged a knife into him, and threw his body into an arroyo."[8] The matter may have ended in that way, but there is greater reason to doubt it.

At the time, there were other conflicting accounts as well. An Arizona paper, for one, advised readers on April 4 that a fireman aboard the Southern Pacific, running between Tucson and Deming, had seen Charley McComas a few days before and even had spoken to him. "The little fellow had made his way to the railroad and was picked up by the train. He tearfully related the story of the horrible murder of his parents by the Indians, and how he escaped. He is doubtless now with his relatives in Silver City." The entire piece, of course, was contrived fiction.[9]

When Lieutenant Colonel Forsyth chased the Chiricahua marauders into the bootheel, he explicitly ordered his scouts to examine the ground carefully at the enemy's stopping places in hopes of discovering a child's shoe prints.

When none were found, he expressed the opinion that Charley long since had been slain.[10] Contrary to that, several reports held that others in pursuit were claiming to have seen the boy's tracks where the Indian trail crossed the railroad near Separ and at other points below that location.[11] The only certainty, then and now, is that the available information was inconsistent and hence unreliable.

One more comment on the question of Charley's fate was furnished by an aging Julius Caesar Brock, who stated, "I've always thought that [the Apaches] killed the McComas boy and threw his body into a well. There was a well only a hundred yards down the canyon from the walnut tree, dug by [two men] trying to get water for their sheep."[12] If there was anything to that theory, one might suppose that the original searchers would have promptly checked the well, or even Brock himself during the many subsequent years when he resided in the immediate area.

One thing seems clear: in the days right after the Thompson Canyon tragedy, when the majority of Silver City residents were saying that Charley McComas probably had died, the boy's uncle, Eugene Ware, and his two half-brothers, David and William, refused to accept that dire presumption. Joining with lawyer John Wright, they spearheaded a massive effort to mount a rescue and save Charley. Despite the flurry of reports suggesting his demise, they—like most relatives in such a situation—were unwilling to give up hope.

In writing on April 3 to his brother Charles at Fort Scott, Eugene Ware had said that, for the time being, he would remain in New Mexico, to help settle the McComas estate and to find the boy. In accomplishing the latter, he indicated that a visit to Old Mexico might be necessary.[13] What he had in mind was to explore the possibility of ransoming Charley. It was known that, on those rare occasions when the Apaches did not immediately kill their prisoners, the opportunity thereby was created for future negotiations and possible return. The *Fort Scott Daily Monitor* editorialized, "He [Charley] can never be recovered except through bribery."[14]

Perhaps owing to Ware's own firm conviction and hopefulness, the public quickly came around to the view that the McComas youngster remained alive and might yet be freed. An army man, Capt. B. F. Harover, proposed to the family one course of action. He suggested that, after money had been raised and a ransom offered, "a gentleman named Jeffery, now living at Huachuca, Arizona, be intrusted with the matter, as he is perfectly familiar with the language and has had thirty years experience among the different tribes. He was instrumental in the return of a child captured under similar circumstances, and undoubtedly could recover this boy."[15]

The captain, it would appear, was referring to the celebrated frontiersman and former Indian agent to the Chiricahuas, Thomas J. Jeffords, who had been a friend of the late Chief Cochise. Had this man been enlisted as an intermediary, there might have been some prospect of obtaining specific word regarding the condition and whereabouts of Charley McComas. But so far as we know, he never was formally approached.[16]

Charles S. Welles, a member of the Grant County Commission who had served on that board with Judge McComas, put forth another suggestion. He urged friends of the family to petition Crook's superior, Gen. William T. Sherman, to order that three, four, or five chiefs living at San Carlos be seized and held as hostages for the safe return of the child. That suggestion met with warm public approval. A Silver City journalist acknowledged, "This is a good idea and probably would work satisfactorily." And then he added, "Something should be done, as there is no doubt but what the boy is still alive and in the hands of the Indians, and if they are closely pushed they will murder him without a doubt."[17] His warning was to prove sadly prophetic.

As a first step in the family's plan of action, Ware carried a photograph of little Charley to the studio of H. C.'s friend, Harry W. Lucas, and had him print up a batch of identification cards, which besides the picture bore a description of the boy and a plea for anyone with information to contact John M. Wright in Silver City or E. F. Ware at Fort Scott, Kansas. The text on some of the cards was printed in Spanish.[18]

The cards were distributed widely on both sides of the border, with the urgent request that they be posted conspicuously in a public place. One of the cardboard flyers went into the front window of Silver City's Meredith & Ailman Bank, located downtown on Broadway, where it became the object of a great deal of curiosity. According to a contemporary report, "Many are the pitying remarks heard in front of it."[19] Over in Tucson, the photograph card was exhibited prominently in the showcase of Buehman & Company, adjoining the city's principal newspaper office.[20] And so it went, around the Southwest.

Either Ware or Wright also sent out a mailing to national publications. Two influential and widely circulated periodicals, *Harper's Weekly* and *Frank Leslie's Illustrated Newspaper,* for example, carried the story under the headline, "Stolen by Apaches." Both also ran an engraving of Charley, prepared by staff artists based on the photographic image from the flyer.[21]

Whether Eugene Ware actually made a trip south of the border at this time is unclear, although at one point he wrote, "I have caused to be distributed the photograph of the boy all around the Indian country in Mexico," which leaves open the possibility that he did.[22] With greater certainty, we can

CHARLEY W. McCOMAS,

CAPTURED BY INDIANS.

The above is a Photograph of young Charles W. McComas, whose parents, Judge McComas and wife, were killed March 28, 1883, a few miles north of Lordsburg, on the Southern Pacific R. R. The Indians carried off the boy, and his return is much desired. He is 6 1-2 years old, very large, weighs nearly 75 lbs., wears 6 3-4 hat, has light yellowish hair.

Please communicate any information to Mr. JOHN M. WRIGHT, Silver City, New Mexico, or to E. F. WARE, at Fort Scott, Kansas.

$1,000 EN DINERO DE LOS ESTADOS UNIDOS DE AMERICA

CARLOS W. McCOMAS,

DE SAN VICENTE, NUEVO MEJICO.

Llevado por los Indios, del Capitancillo Ju 1883.

Este es el retrato del joven arriba mencionado Carlos . El padre y la madre del niño fuéron matados por los Indios el dia 28 de ... de este año, cerca de Lordsburgh Nuevo Méjico, é inmediato . . . Sur Pacifico en Nuevo Méjico.

Los Indios llevaron el muchacho cons. . muchacho a Méjico. Si alguna persona pued. . . . . . muchacho de los Indios, recibe un mil pesos en moneda de los Estados Unidos de America.

La edad del muchacho es seis años y medio, es muy grande por su edad, pesa cerca de setenta libras, tiene cabello huero.

Si alguna persona puede dar informes de este niño, tenga la bondad de comunicar con Don Miguel Schutz en San Vicente Nuevo Méjico, el cual garantiza el pago de los mil pesos ofrecidos por la entriega del muchacho.

Examples, in both English and Spanish, of the cardboard flyers seeking information on Charley McComas. The Spanish version adds the offer of one thousand dollars in money of the United States of America as a reward. In McComas Family Papers, courtesy Carolyn Kimme-Smith, Los Angeles, California say that he journeyed to Santa Fe in mid-April to confer with Territorial Gov. Lionel A. Sheldon, who in the summer of 1881 had succeeded Judge McComas's old friend, Lew Wallace.

Since assuming office, Sheldon had been extremely active in building up the militia, as much to check a plague of outlaws as to bring the Apaches to heel.[23] In all likelihood, he was well acquainted with the McComas couple, probably through H. C.'s attorney-cousin Charles C. McComas, a law partner in Albuquerque with Thomas B. Catron, the political kingpin and land speculator. Charles McComas served in the territorial legislature; then, on April 21, 1883, a little over three weeks after the massacre of his kin, Governor Sheldon appointed him district attorney for Bernalillo County.[24]

In any event, Eugene Ware got right in to see the governor, whom he said treated him very kindly. As he later informed friends, "Sheldon at my request has written personal letters to the Governors of Chihuahua and Sonora, asking their good offices in the matter of the recovery of little Charley."[25] The boy's uncle was leaving no stone unturned.

By April 20, he was back in Silver City, and shortly after that date he packed up and took the train for Fort Scott, leaving John Wright and the two older McComas boys to follow up any new leads that might develop. By then Ware had become convinced that his nephew was far away in the Sierra Madre, which he described as a country "so vast and so inaccessible that it will take considerable time to find the whereabouts of the child."[26] All hopes now were pinned upon the American expeditionary force, scheduled to cross the international boundary on May 1. But since no one expected it to produce quick results, Eugene Ware decided to return to Kansas, where family and business obligations awaited him.

⚞ When General Crook's elite military force, composed of army regulars and Apache scouts, spilled over the line dividing Arizona from Sonora on May Day, the American public had the perception that its chief reason for going was the retrieval of Judge McComas's little son. That idea had taken hold as a natural consequence of all the publicity generated by the massacre, the Fort Scott funeral, and the family's search efforts. Crook's packmaster, Henry W. Daly, even said as much in 1930, the year before his death, claiming that the Sierra Madre campaign had been launched "with the expectation of rescuing Charley McComas."[27]

In reality, of course, the general was laying plans for a Mexican expedition and stockpiling supplies at Willcox on the Southern Pacific well before he got word of the Thompson Canyon killings and the abduction of the youngster.

He long since had decided that, if the southwestern territories ever were to enjoy peace and security, he would have to make the Apaches in Mexico "respect and fear the power of our government."[28] So that was uppermost in his mind.

Yet, now that the ongoing saga of Charley McComas was engaging the attention and sympathy of his fellow Americans, Crook felt constrained by both public and official pressure to shift his priorities somewhat and give that particular matter more of his attention. As he later expressed it in a letter to the adjutant general of the army at Washington, he had grown anxious about the boy's fate, and that had moved him to plan the details of his expedition with great caution, so as to avoid any act that might jeopardize a recovery.[29]

The general and his column rode southward into the Mexican wilds and almost immediately disappeared from public view. For forty-two days, no communication came from them, giving rise to rumors that the expedition had suffered catastrophe and that Crook had been slain. The War Department went so far as to issue a denial, asserting that such stories were "wholly sensational and improbable."[30] That seemed apparent, but nevertheless unease remained widespread.

Some information about Charley soon surfaced. However, it came not in a message from Crook, but in a roundabout manner and from an unexpected source. During the first week of May, two of the hostiles from Mexico showed up at Fort Thomas on the edge of San Carlos and surrendered. They were Dutchy and Gooday, both of whom had been with Chato on his raid. They told Lt. Britton Davis, who was in temporary command, that they were authorized to negotiate terms for the surrender of the remaining Chiricahuas. Evidently the pair knew nothing about Crook's being on the march.[31]

Davis remained skeptical that the renegades were ready to capitulate. But other pieces of information obtained from the two Indians seemed reliable. Dutchy put the total number of fighting men still in the Sierra Madre at 107. The largest force, with dependents, was led by Geronimo. Loco's small band had split off from Juh's and was eager to return to Arizona. Juh, yet defiant, had proclaimed that he would never surrender.[32]

When the lieutenant asked about Charley McComas, Dutchy and his companion suddenly clammed up. The only thing they would say was that they did not know his whereabouts. But from this spare admission, Davis inferred that the boy was alive and held by one of the bands in the mountains.

Back in early April, the lieutenant had received one of Eugene Ware's letters pleading for help in locating his nephew. At the time, Davis had heard the stories about the boy being brained soon after his capture. Thus, while he

Dutchy, who accompanied Chato on his raid and later returned to learn surrender terms, ca. 1886. Courtesy Smithsonian Institution

was under the impression that Charley most likely was dead, he possessed no real evidence to confirm it. Being disinclined to cause the uncle and the McComas family unnecessary grief, he delayed in responding until such time as definite news came his way.

Now that the opportunity had presented itself, in the persons of Dutchy and Gooday, he resolved to take advantage of it. Since they would not voluntarily reveal information about Charley McComas, the officer ordered them seized, placed in irons, and imprisoned. Such was not the treatment the pair of Apaches had expected, and, high-handed though it was, it quickly brought them to their senses. They talked.

Yes, as recently as eleven days earlier, they had seen the boy, alive and well, in Chato's camp, where he was under the care of Bonito. He already had become something of a pet among them; he was called by his right name, "Charley"; and, Dutchy vigorously asserted, the child was being well treated. The prisoner insisted that Chato would return the boy to his friends unhurt.

From this, Lieutenant Davis concluded that Chato and Bonito were keeping the McComas boy to use as a pawn or bargaining chip against the day when they might have to recross the border and seek terms. He mentioned that possibility in a letter dated May 6, which he wrote to John Wright in Silver City, for he knew that Ware by then had departed for Kansas. In his missive, Davis related what he had gleaned from the shackled Dutchy and also offered a recommendation.

He suggested that Wright could attempt to communicate with General Crook in the field by sending a message to the commanding officer at Fort Bowie and requesting that it be carried into Mexico by any courier who might be dispatched to the expedition. That message should advise Crook that Charley's survival was now confirmed and should ask him to so inform Mexican authorities as well as redouble his own efforts. Since there was nothing really necessary in all of this, we can surmise that the compassionate Lieutenant Davis charitably had created the small task to allow the McComas family representative a role in the continuing search for Charley.

In his letter to Wright, the officer stated that he had considered sending Dutchy or Gooday on a mission to bring the child in but finally reckoned that it would be of no avail. Maybe he realized that, after their ironing, neither Indian was apt to accommodate his wishes. Others advised him to hire several natives at San Carlos for the job, but Davis rejected that idea, telling the attorney, "I do not know of any Indian here who would risk a visit to the Chiricahua camp. Any attempt to pay them to do so would be but money wasted." And he closed by offering his sincerest sympathy to the friends of Judge and Mrs. McComas.[33]

The new word brought by Dutchy and his companion—that the McComas son was, after all, among the living—received wide media coverage and thrilled the public. Interest in the progress of the Crook campaign ascended to still a higher degree of intensity. The entire country, it seemed, anxiously awaited the outcome.

An observer at Fort Thomas told a correspondent for the *Arizona Citizen:* "I think if the troops don't surprise the [Chiricahua] camp, Charley will eventually be brought in."[34] The same concern was on the mind of experienced frontiersmen, who knew only too well that, in the event of a sudden attack, Indians almost invariably and immediately slew their prisoners.

So, through the dreamy weeks of May, a dark cloud of uncertainty hovered over the nation. Could Gen. George Crook pull off a miracle and save the angelic-faced little Charles Ware McComas? In many a church and pious household, fervent prayers were offered that it might be accomplished.

⌘ At San Bernardino, Crook left a large part of his regulars with instructions to patrol the border in his absence. For his lightning thrust into the Sierra Madre Mountains, he took 6 officers, 42 cavalrymen, 5 pack trains of 266 mules accompanied by 76 civilian packers, and, of course, the Indian scouts. The latter included men from various Apache subtribes, and also Hualapais, Mojaves, and Yumas. Among them were Chiricahuas, in high spirits and eager for the fray. Whites never understood why they so willingly went forth to fight and kill their own blood brothers.

A conspicuous frontier figure, Al Seiber, acted as chief of scouts and interpreter, but the actual command of the native unit was in the hands of Capt. Emmet Crawford. In the vanguard of the entire cavalcade rode the captive guide Peaches, whose knowledge of trails in northern Sonora Captain Bourke judged to be remarkable.[35]

One day's march brought Crook and his force to the top of a giant horseshoe bend in the Bavispe River. From that point they began to ascend the left branch, which led them upstream into the heart of the Sierra Madre. Everywhere could be viewed signs of desolation—villages in ruins, abandoned farms, and burned-out ranch houses. All had been destroyed by the Apaches. At the larger towns, the embattled Mexicans poured into the streets and onto the rooftops to greet the American column with genuine warmth.

On May 6, the expedition came to a squalid settlement called Huachinera. Peaches informed the officers that, back in early March, he had gone through this place with Chato's raiders on their way to Arizona. He said that sixteen warriors brazenly entered the plaza in broad daylight and purchased tobacco from the terrified inhabitants.[36]

Above Huachinera, the command entered true wilderness and was confronted by a bewildering succession of pine-clad ridges and yawning chasms, whose crossing wore down soldiers and mules. The Indian scouts, by contrast, bounded over the steep trails like deer, all the while laughing and jesting among themselves. Several of the laboring pack animals lost their footing and tumbled down the mountain sides.

Signs of the renegade Apaches grew common, and then a trail was struck over which they had driven stolen cattle toward their stronghold. The scouts lost their playful air and became more vigilant. On May 10, the general halted and held a council of war. By now the scouts were panting for combat and bragging that they would wipe out these Chiricahuas, starting with Juh and Geronimo, the biggest trouble-makers.[37] Since the white soldiers and pack train were slowing them down, they asked for permission to go ahead and search out the country. Crook assented.

To Captain Crawford, Al Seiber, and several other white guides who were to accompany and command the Indian scouts, he delivered very specific instructions about how the hostile camps were to be approached and entered. It seems safe to say that the general's strategy, at least in part, was designed to increase the odds of getting Charley McComas out alive. For some reason, Crook's important directions did not reach all of the 150 scouts assigned to the advance party.

After four days of hard travel, Crawford and his force spotted a main Chiricahua camp perched on a ridgetop about one mile ahead. Smoke from cooking fires drifted lazily above it, and the occupants could be seen at work, butchering and drying beef. In a note to Crook, scrawled hastily and dispatched by runner, the officer remarked that the Indians appeared to have no inkling that their enemies were in the vicinity. Evidently the Apaches had been secure so long in their mountain sanctuary that they had grown complacent and failed to post sentries.

Captain Crawford divided his command into three attack units and sent them forward to surround and surprise the Chiricahua position. It was noon of May 15. Unexpectedly, however, the trap was sprung prematurely. Bourke attributed it to the impetuosity of some of the younger scouts, who precipitated the engagement and impaired its effectiveness. A White Mountain Apache scout, known to the Americans as John Rope, claimed later that one of his companions had carried his gun cocked and it went off accidentally. But Jason Betzinez contended that the scouts had not fully understood what Crook wanted and so attacked headlong.[38]

The action, once initiated, was sharp but brief. The camp contained principally women and children, with a few men as guards, the bulk of the warriors being away on raids. As gunfire broke out, the astonished Apaches "scattered to the mountains like jackrabbits."[39] In the assault, nine Indians were killed, among them an old woman afterward identified as the aunt of Chief Chihuahua.[40]

Four children were captured, one of them the granddaughter of Cochise. Also seized was a young woman who identified herself as the daughter of Bonito. To Crawford and to Crook, who had rushed forward with the full command, she revealed valuable information. The conquered encampment belonged to Geronimo, Chato, Bonito, and Chihuahua. Their position had become so precarious recently that they had begun to consider returning to San Carlos. The two emissaries, Dutchy and Gooday, had been sent north to see what terms might be gotten. While they were away, the restive warriors had gone raiding again, the largest body accompanying Geronimo eastward toward Casas Grandes.

Her people had been utterly dismayed, the woman related, to see the Apache scouts wearing red headbands charging towards them. And there was Peaches, one of their own, in the lead. In that moment they realized that their hiding places had been made known to the white soldiers, leaving no safe havens. The informant was positive that the Chiricahua leaders would give up without further fighting.

And what about Charley McComas, she was asked? Yes, her father had brought back a six-year-old boy from Chato's raid. They called him Charley, all right, and he had the run of the camp. But when the shooting started, the child had become frightened and fled with the old women. She promised that, if allowed to go out, she would bring in the leaders and Charley McComas with them.[41]

Crook was delighted to hear that, and he gave her two days' worth of food, a horse, and the oldest captive boy as a helper and sent her on the mission. Peaches already was out in the rugged wilds trying to persuade those who had scattered from the attack to come back and submit to the soldiers. After the general moved his camp to a better location, the refugees began to dribble in and surrender. Among the early arrivals were two sisters of one of the scouts, who confirmed the story about Charley that had been given by Bonito's daughter.

Following seizure of the Apache encampment, the scouts had set ablaze about thirty wickiups, the conical shelters used by the Indians. They also collected much plunder and loaded it on pack animals. Taken from the dead were four nickel-plated, breech-loading Winchester rifles and a new-model Colt revolver, perhaps the very one that Hamilton C. McComas was carrying when he died. Of gold and silver watches recovered, several could be identified as belonging to massacre victims from Arizona. And then a McComas family album was found, furnishing proof positive that this was the camp of their killers.[42]

On Friday morning, May 18, Chief Chihuahua himself showed up and announced his readiness to end hostilities and return to San Carlos. Most of the warriors under Geronimo and Chato, he explained, were on the warpath against the Mexicans, while his own people remained dispersed in isolated camps or in hiding. General Crook granted him permission to leave and gather up the remnant of his band. Chihuahua promised a prompt return and also to bring in Charley McComas.[43]

Meanwhile, Geronimo was committing mischief on the arid plains of western Chihuahua. On a road near the village of Carmen, he swooped down upon a small party of travelers consisting of two Mexican men and six women, one of the latter nursing a baby. The men were butchered without ceremony, but the females, wives of soldiers, were taken captive, with the idea of exchanging them for some Apache children held at Casas Grandes.

The very next day, a strange incident occurred. The Chiricahuas had stopped for a meal, and Geronimo sat on the ground eating a chunk of roasted

*Some of the Sierra Madre Apaches were living in wickiups similar to this one
when Crook's scouts attacked them on May 15, 1883.*
From author's collection

beef prepared by his kinsman Jason Betzinez. Suddenly he dropped his knife, as if startled, and said aloud, "Men, our people whom we left at our base camp are now in the hands of U.S. troops! What shall we do?"

Jason in his memoirs interpreted this as an example of Geronimo's mysterious ability to tell what was happening at a distance: "I cannot explain it to this day. But I was there and saw it. No, he didn't get the word by some messenger. And no smoke signals had been made."[44]

Immediately, the war party started for the camp, 120 miles away. But progress was slow because the group was driving a small herd of stolen cattle, and because the Mexican women could not endure the usual pace kept by Apaches. Toward the end, Geronimo predicted that, on the following afternoon, an Apache would appear on a hillside and descend to verify for them that their relatives and friends were captives of the American army. It happened just as he prophesied. At that point, the Chiricahuas turned loose both their cattle and the women prisoners, then started forward to see what terms could be arranged with General Crook.

The liberated women either stumbled upon the army bivouac or were found by the scouts and brought in. Lieutenant Davis said, "The poor things were in a state of collapse, and almost insane at their unexpected deliverance."[45] After they had calmed down a bit and eaten, A. Frank Randall, a correspondent for the *New York Herald* who was accompanying the expedition, interviewed them. They told of having witnessed, on the evening before their release by the Chiricahuas, a horrifying atrocity.

The Indians had with them a young man who had been taken in southern New Mexico. Having gotten all they could from him about troop movements, they threw a rope around his neck, then mutilated and beat him with stones. As Randall related it: "In his agony he turned over on his face and the hostiles took one of their lances and ran it into his body, cutting him terribly. The poor man soon died and with the most intense suffering."[46] In his memoirs, Jason Betzinez, for obvious reasons, never mentioned this incident.

Later speculation held that the victim was a Mr. Finn, possibly a rancher or miner, who had disappeared about the time of Chato's raid. The recital of his fate by the Mexican women offered a grim reminder of what lay in store for those who found themselves in the power of the merciless Broncos of the Sierra Madre.[47] General Crook, while he might have shuddered at the story, had neither time nor inclination to pursue it further, because suddenly he faced delicate negotiations which, if successful, might end once and for all the hideous blood-letting that for so long had plagued this corner of the continent.

On May 20, Geronimo and other war leaders, including Chato, put in an appearance and opened talks that stretched over several days. With American and Mexican soldiers, aided by Apache scouts, all arrayed against them, they admitted that there was no choice but to make peace. New arrivals reached the military camp daily, most of them sent in by Chief Chihuahua. By May 2, some 220 hostiles were on hand. Rations to feed them began to run low.

Crook and his officers, of course, intently studied the growing ranks of Apache children, hopeful that Charley McComas would be found among them. But he was nowhere to be seen. Geronimo declared that he needed time to round up his stragglers, since they were not responding to his summons. Evidently they mistrusted his smoke signals, fearing that they were sent by the Apache scouts to lure them into a trap.

The general advised Geronimo, however, that he could not wait, since his agreement with the Mexicans required him to withdraw promptly once military operations had ceased. Further, he faced dwindling supplies. Geronimo responded by promising to follow after the retreating Americans, and to catch up with them as soon as possible. For good measure, he said that, in Bourke's words, "he would cause the most diligent search to be made for Charley McComas."[48] That was the best that Crook could get from the wily old raider, and he knew it.

First, Bonito's daughter, then Chief Chihuahua, and now Geronimo spoke confidently of finding the boy Charley. To this point, the American commander had seen no results, and he felt frustrated but also cautiously optimistic. To leave behind Geronimo and some of the other leaders, like Naiche, Mangus, and Chato, posed an obvious risk, but since Crook had their families in tow, he confidently believed that sooner or later they would show up. Besides, in his opinion Geronimo offered the best chance of getting the McComas youngster back.

Owing to the 384 Apache captives and the Mexican women who still were under the protection of the government, progress was slow, and it took the soldiers almost two weeks to reach the United States. With the column were Loco, Bonito, and old Nana, who had ridden with Victorio. The continued absence of Geronimo and Chato was disquieting, but it did not prevent General Crook, upon reaching the international boundary on June 9, from breaking out a good bottle of brandy and sharing toasts with his officers.

Soon after that, Crook left Captain Crawford in charge of conducting the column back to San Carlos. He started for his headquarters at Fort Whipple, going by way of Fort Grant and Fort Huachuca, where he conducted inspections. Everywhere the people were jubilant. His success produced a flood of congratulatory messages. James P. Martin, assistant adjutant general of Arizona, for instance, telegraphed these words: "Great rejoicing among your friends the world over. Your campaign universally believed to be the grandest event in Indian hostilities in America."[49]

That statement contained a good deal of hyperbole, but it correctly reflected the national mood. Ten days after reentering the United States, General Crook passed through Tucson. In that burgeoning town, with its half-Mexican and half-American look, he was given a hero's welcome by the mayor and residents, including a banquet almost royal.[50]

In the meantime, Crawford had been pushing his charges at a snail's pace northward toward the reservation. At Croton Springs south of Willcox, he encountered John M. Wright and Judge McComas's sons, David and William, who had read the first news accounts of Crook's return and had ridden from Silver City to intercept the column. Deep was their disappointment upon finding that Charley McComas had not been fetched in.[51]

They were told instead that he was expected daily, as soon as the parties led by Geronimo and Chato arrived. That sounded encouraging and served to revive their spirits. Wright soon discovered that one of the renegade warriors had in his possession McComas's two-hundred-dollar gold watch and chain, taken at the time of the massacre. He redeemed it for fifty dollars, being worth no more than that in its battered condition. But the article naturally had sentimental value for the family, and Wright afterward sent it to Eugene Ware.[52] As soon as he was able, the lawyer dispatched telegrams to McComas relatives in the Midwest, bringing them up to date on the search for Charley.

That search remained very much on the mind of General Crook, who with the passage of time began to worry over the absence of Geronimo and his followers. He said in a letter written during the last week of June to R. C. Drum, adjutant general of the army in Washington, "We have no means of communicating with them until they come in at the agency. . . . As a matter of humanity, I am anxious to get in the last one of this band, so as to leave nothing undone for the recovery of the captive boy."[53]

At the time of his brandy toasting on the border, Crook had stated in a news release: "The Chiricahuas told us they had a white boy who was in the village jumped by our scouts. He had run off with the squaws who had escaped. . . . I have such assurances that the child will be brought back alive that I am looking for him every moment."[54] But less than two weeks later, during an interview at Tucson, his confidence seemed to have slipped several degrees: "I am of the opinion that, if alive, Charley McComas will be brought in."[55]

By June 23, Captain Crawford had the renegade Chiricahuas safely corralled at San Carlos. The leaders with their remnant band, however, were still out, having failed "to catch up." If Crook possessed any misgivings, he kept them carefully concealed. In fact, he stated that Geronimo's tardiness was without significance, adding, "Indians have no idea of the value of time."[56]

According to one story, Geronimo was lingering in Mexico to conduct a few last livestock raids, so that he would have cattle for food and horses to trade to his fellow tribesmen at San Carlos. But something else, too, contributed to his dawdling. Crook had no more crossed the border than the regional press commenced to publish inflammatory editorials and letters from readers saying that the government intended to hang all the Chiricahua men and parcel out the women and children among other tribes. Territorial officials, at the very least, urged that all Apaches be removed to the Indian Territory (Oklahoma).[57]

These statements, by one means or another, reached the Indians still in the Sierra Madre and caused them to bide their time until it became clear what was to be their fate. Weeks and months went by, and, as word reached them that the Chiricahuas were settling peacefully into San Carlos, no hangings having taken place, the remaining hostiles began crossing the border in small bands to surrender.

Through October, November, and December, they trickled in. Among them were Naiche and Chihuahua. The new arrivals could not say positively when Geronimo and the other holdouts would appear, but they brought rumors, soon confirmed, that the ferocious war chief, Juh, was dead. He had gotten drunk on Mexican tequila and tumbled over a cliff, breaking his neck. Jason Betzinez commented that hard liquor had been his downfall, just as it had that of many other Apaches.[58]

By the end of the year, only a handful of Chiricahuas remained unaccounted for, but the delinquents included Geronimo and Chato, meaning that no one in either southern Arizona or New Mexico could breathe easily quite yet. And Charley McComas was still missing. All hopes now rested with Geronimo. Would he finally ride up to the door of the San Carlos Agency with the boy in his keeping? Or were the McComas family and friends destined for one last disappointment?

Chapter Ten

Hopes Fade

On April 19, 1883, less than a month after the conclusion of Chato's raid, the probate court of Grant County, New Mexico, appointed John Wright as administrator of the estate of Hamilton C. McComas. As the judge's law partner and a close personal friend, Wright was in an excellent position to handle the complicated assortment of legal matters that required settlement. In fact, the task would stretch into the next decade; Wright did not file the Administrator's Final Report and receive his formal discharge until November 18, 1892.[1] During that long interval, he performed faithful and dedicated service on behalf of the McComas family.

As was customary, Wright quickly published a notice in regional newspapers asking persons having claims against the estate to present them for settlement, and others who were indebted to the estate to make prompt payment. While far from a wealthy man, Judge McComas had left a respectable amount of assets. They included an $8,000 life insurance policy and a balance of $1,250 in his Silver City bank account. There was the Hudson Street house, plus two nearby vacant lots, and all the home and office furnishings and personal possessions. The value of his interests in mining properties and stocks amounted to almost $34,000.[2]

It was important to realize as much as possible from the liquidation of the estate, since the sum remaining after final settlement would go toward the support of the two young McComas girls, and Charley, too, should he eventually be returned. In early June, Eugene Ware made application before the probate court at Fort Scott to become the legal guardian of the three children of Hamilton and Juniata, and also the guardian of the judge's youngest son by his first marriage, William, who was still a minor.[3]

Almost at once, John Wright received several claims against the estate. One was from the Smith & Keating Implement Company of Kansas City, seeking payment for the wagon that H. C. had purchased from the firm two years earlier. That entire incident already has been described. Then the Derbyshire Brothers, Undertakers, submitted a bill for four hundred dollars due on the McComas caskets and a pair of burial robes.

Finally, John Graham, owner of the livery stable from which Judge McComas had rented his buckboard and team, put in a claim for $385. That amounted to recompense for the two horses lost and the harness, rigging, lap robe, and whip either destroyed or stolen by the Apaches. Graham also added $10 to cover his trouble in going to recover the vehicle abandoned at the walnut tree.[4]

Scarcely a month after the murders of the McComas couple, a customer entered the stable and asked for the rental of a buckboard, saying that he planned to travel the Lordsburg Road by way of Thompson Canyon. When the liveryman trotted out a conveyance and handed over the reins, he directed the gentleman's attention to the profusion of dried bloodstains on the dashboard, with the information that this was the very same buckboard in which the McComas crime had been committed. Recoiling in horror, the customer afterward wrote, "My feelings may be better imagined than defined."[5]

In his capacity as estate administrator and as a McComas family friend, John Wright played a central role in the ongoing quest for news regarding Charley's whereabouts. Expenses incurred in that effort, he dutifully charged against the estate. He also took the lead in publicizing a one-thousand-dollar reward offered for the boy's deliverance. McComas relatives put up five hundred of that; the balance, it is presumed, was provided by the Territory of New Mexico. At the time, people looked upon one thousand dollars as quite a large sum.[6]

That money brought into the picture two shadowy men of the border, D. C. Leroy and George Wilson. Back in 1880, H. C. McComas had incorporated the Leroy Silver Mining Company, but whether a connection existed between that name and D. C. Leroy is unclear. A later newspaper story refers to Leroy as a noted scout, but another account hints that both he and Wilson were shady characters who occasionally had illicit contacts with the Sierra Madre Apaches. In any case, the reward motivated them to undertake what

An engraving of Charley McComas, made from the photograph on the cardboard flyer circulated by John Wright. From Harper's Weekly, *April 28, 1883*

John Wright described as "an expedition to Casas Grandes, Mexico, for Charley's recovery."[7] The pair, evidently well armed, departed from Deming on September 18, headed south.

Wright showed interest in this mission and may even have suggested it, out of a waning faith in the army's promise to produce the missing child. Two weeks later, he received word that the men were returning, so he bought a ticket on the newly opened narrow-gauge railroad out of Silver City and rode down to Deming to meet them. Although they had no Charley McComas in hand, they did bring a tale of their suspenseful adventure.

Leroy and Wilson had steered straight for Casas Grandes, a point in western Chihuahua convenient for making contact with the few Apaches still in the mountains. There they learned from a Mexican merchant of a white boy rumored to be with Juh's little band. Riding fearlessly into the Sierra Madre, the men prowled about for several days and seem to have entered an Indian camp, where they were told of Juh's recent death. Giving notice that they wished to negotiate for the boy called Charley, they retired to Casas Grandes.

A few days later, a messenger from Geronimo slipped into town and invited the two Americans to a parley five miles away. Leroy and Wilson claimed that they met Geronimo, who was accompanied by twenty warriors. He was quite suspicious, fearing some sort of trap. Speaking through an interpreter, Leroy explained their purpose in coming. The stern old Apache seemed to know all about Charley McComas, and they began to discuss the terms of a ransom. Geronimo wanted only one thing—cartridges for his repeating rifles. In fact, right there he offered to trade the white men a horse for just ten cartridges.

At sunset they parted, with an agreement to resume talks on the following day. However, reconvening on the morrow, Geronimo showed a new nervousness and expressed fear that his old enemies, the Mexicans, might be planning treachery. Abruptly he broke off negotiations, signaled his men, and they all rode away in a cloud of dust. In spite of this inauspicious ending, Leroy and Wilson upon their arrival in Deming on October 3, tried to convince John Wright that another trip south might succeed in winning Charley's release.[8]

But the lawyer by this time had lost confidence in their ability to pull anything out of the hat, and hence he began casting about in other directions We know that within a couple of weeks, for instance, he dealt with a man in El Paso named Sidney Alan Eady, who proposed to make his own visit to Casas Grandes in pursuit of the boy. This proved yet another straw in the wind, and nothing came of it.[9]

Meanwhile, in Arizona, Apache bands small and large continued to dribble into San Carlos. One of Wright's contacts below the reservation, the Fort Bowie telegraph operator, Alfred F. Simz, wrote him a letter on October 31. In it, he advised that Charley McComas was not with the latest party of Indians that had passed by on the way to surrender. But he added that others were yet due, and he promised to "make rigid inquiries of those that come in, and if the boy is with them I will telegraph to you immediately."[10]

On November 16, the largest group of all, numbering ninety Chiricahuas, entered San Carlos. And accompanying them was a white boy! The army officers and government officials took one look at the thin, ragged lad and shook their heads. Was he Charley or not? He did not look much like the picture on the McComas flyer, nor did he seem to understand English. But no one was ready to say for sure. So a telegram hastily was dispatched to John Wright in Silver City.

Upon receipt of the astonishing news, Wright bought a train ticket that same day for Willcox, Arizona. From the railroad, he went either by stage or buckboard to Fort Thomas and San Carlos. As he walked into military headquarters, four officers were just completing their examination and questioning of the boy. Three agreed that he was not McComas, but the fourth dissented. Now, suddenly, here was someone who could settle the whole matter.[11]

In all likelihood, John Wright took a single glance at the youngster and felt his heart plummet. The small figure had hollow cheeks and light hair that was matted and tangled, and he stood garbed entirely in Indian costume. He appeared frightened and bewildered at finding himself the center of so much attention. Wright had to "hire him to stand still," so as to make a close study. In the end, he announced disappointedly to the people in the room: "Positively he is not Charley McComas."[12]

Kaahteney (sometimes written Cayotene), one of the leaders of the newly arrived band, was consulted next. He stated that the white boy, who now considered himself an Indian, had been seized near a salt lake in the Navajo country several years before. Kaahteney expressed his willingness to give up the child if his friends came and recognized him. But no clue could be found as to his identity. The best guess seemed to be that he was a Mormon boy whose parents had been killed and about whom no relatives ever had inquired.

Wright stayed on at San Carlos so as to be present on November 22, when the Apaches came from various parts of the reservation to receive their regular rations at the agency headquarters, and also to be tallied and accounted for. He wanted to quiz anyone who might prove helpful. As it happened, the attorney got an earful when someone introduced him to Bonito.

Uncharacteristically, Chato's second-in-command on the raid furnished ready information. Indeed, he had been with the war party that encountered the McComas family. But he was not present at the killings, having come up afterwards. (That may have been a self-protective lie, since Bonito, and all Apaches, now understood the anger that these particular murders had caused among the whites.) Anyway, he maintained that he found two warriors quarreling over possession of Charley and therefore claimed the boy for himself, in consequence saving his life. (Again, this statement could have been calculated to put Bonito in a favorable light.) He carried the little captive off to Mexico and kept him in his wickiup. That part of his testimony, at least, was confirmed by others.

Bonito insisted that Charley McComas had been well cared for until the day in mid-May when General Crook's scouts had attacked their camp and scattered the residents. Then, with everyone else, the boy had become frightened and run away into the hills on his own hook. Afterward, all the Chiricahua leaders kept their promise to Crook that they would look for the boy, each devoting several days to the search. Nevertheless, no trace of him could be found.

⍟ By November 28, John Wright was back home, and he provided the *Silver City Enterprise* with a detailed recital of his experience at San Carlos. It is clear that he had been deeply moved by the plight of the white youngster who had turned out not to be Charley. As for Bonito's description of Charley's flight at the time of the attack, Wright told the press, "This account of his disappearance is corroborated by the rest of the Indians."[13] That suggests that he was coming around to the view that the son of his late partner probably was lost for good.

Notwithstanding, John Wright continued to go through the now all-too-familiar motions of following up every possible lead. On the last day of December, he exchanged telegrams with General Crook, and a few days later he received another wire from Captain Crawford at San Carlos. We gather that both men were reassuring him of the eventual arrival of Geronimo.[14]

Actually, Chato came in and surrendered first, on February 7, 1884. He rode at the head of a pitifully small band of nineteen followers. Geronimo, leading twenty-six warriors and seventy women and children, trailed into San Carlos on March 16. Aside from one last, tiny party that arrived the next May, all of the Arizona Chiricahuas for the first time were on the reservation, as Crawford pointedly noted in an official report. That result had been a long and anxious time in coming.[15]

No one truly was more relieved than Gen. George Crook. The delays in Geronimo's capitulation had prompted the regional press once more to shower his policies with criticism and make him a target of ridicule. But now, with the belated surrender, the Crook campaign in Mexico and the strategies he had formulated to draw the hostiles, one and all, into San Carlos seemed brilliantly conceived. New Mexico and Arizona were gladdened.

John Wright and the McComas family, however, found no cause for rejoicing. Captain Crawford wrote to them as follows: "Chato had no white boy with him. Geronimo has [only] a Mexican boy in his band. . . . I am afraid you will never hear anything more of Charley. He was undoubtedly lost in the fight with the Indians in the Sierra Madre. This is what they all say and I am now satisfied that it is so."

In a follow-up letter, the general, from his headquarters at Prescott, addressed Wright in these terms:

> I am just in receipt of a telegram from Capt. Crawford stating that Geronimo's Indians make the same report regarding Charley McComas that all the remainder of the Chiricahuas have, to-wit: That he was never found after the fight. The night after the fight there was a cold rain, which made us men huddle around our fires, although we were warmly clad. I can't express to you the sad disappointment this gives me, for I could not have felt deeper interest in his recovery had he been my own child. While it makes our hearts bleed to think of his sad fate, it is some consolation to believe he was not tortured.
>
> Very Sincerely your friend,
> George Crook[16]

Capt. John G. Bourke and Lt. Britton Davis, both of whom were on the scene and interviewed the Apache prisoners, made brief statements about the matter. Wrote Bourke: "Charley McComas was never found. The Chiricahuas contend, and I think truthfully that in the [fight] . . . he escaped terror-stricken to the depths of the mountains."[17] And Davis said, "Little Charley McComas was in the camp when it was attacked, but he either ran away in fright and subsequently perished in the mountains, or was killed at some distance from the camp by the fleeing women."[18]

Two more brief reports soon surfaced as to what had become of Charley. One originated with a U.S. consular officer in northern Mexico, who indicated that several women from Juh's disintegrating band had been apprehended by the Mexicans. Under interrogation, they divulged that the boy had been killed by his captors.[19]

An entirely different story was circulated by Mickey Free, the chief interpreter at San Carlos, however. In mid-May 1884, he and some scouts escorted the very last parcel of Chiricahua renegades—six warriors and their families—from the border to the agency on the reservation. In his words: "They report that Charley McComas died this winter in the Sierra Madre from sickness caused by extreme cold." That is, by this version, the child survived the May 15 attack, escaped with some of the Indians, and lived among them for another six months.[20]

"So Charley McComas is dead!" concluded a Silver City newspaper. "He died, probably, from exposure, but the redskins are answerable for the lad's cruel end. Poor Indians! Resolutions denouncing Charley McComas are in order at [Indian rights] meetings in Boston."[21] The last two sentences, uttered in bitter sarcasm, reflected the anger of southwesterners over misplaced sympathy for the Apaches in the East, Boston being a hotbed of such sentiment.

Under the circumstances, John Wright considered the weight of evidence overwhelming. On March 27, 1884, he closed the running account he had been keeping of expenses related to the search for Charley. That simple act, in its finality, must have pained him. By way of explanation, he said, "The return of Chief Geronimo to San Carlos bringing the last band of his renegade Chiricahuas and Warm Springs ends all hope of the child being alive."[22] That became both the official and the family view.

Wright had not been able to get out of his thoughts the tragic image of the little white boy he had examined at San Carlos the previous November. For the time being, the child remained with the Indians, as the authorities waited to see whether relatives might not come forward. None did. As a result, the attorney took a hand and enlisted the assistance of Judge McComas's old business associate, Gen. John Boyle, with whom he was now linked in various mining ventures.[23] Through their Missouri connections, the two men arranged to have the youngster sent to the Methodist Episcopal Orphan Home and School at St. Louis. One account, in the saccharine phrasing of the time, declared that "his physical, mental and spiritual training will be looked after by the managers of that institution of love and learning."[24]

Now that the question of Charley McComas had been put to rest, both John Wright and Eugene F. Ware urged that action be taken against those guilty of the original crime that had led to his loss. Nor were they the only ones calling for punishment of Chato, Bonito, Naiche, Mangus, Dutchy, and all others who could be identified as parties to the 1883 raid. A journalist expressed the widespread popular feeling that Crook, "instead of giving them cold lead, as justice and right called for, receives these murderers of Judge McComas and forty odd other American and Mexican citizens with open arms, and in all probability gave them a grand banquet in honor of their return!"[25]

The residents of Silver City, who had known the McComases as friends and neighbors, were particularly incensed that the killers were not immediately arrested and placed on trial. If the civil courts did not have the authority, they firmly believed that the U.S. government should take the matter in hand, mete out justice, and make an example of these "fiends in human form," as they were accustomed to call the Apaches.[26]

General Crook chose to ignore the calls for summary justice. While in the Sierra Madre, he had made pledges to Geronimo and other leaders to settle them peacefully once more on their reservation. Finally they all had come in and been placed in camps near Turkey Creek, southwest of Fort Apache. Seeds and plows were given them, with the idea that warriors could learn to be farmers. Any attempt to arrest individual chiefs and charge them with their past misdeeds, Crook knew, might provoke a massive breakout.

He sent Lieutenant Davis and the Apache scouts to camp at Turkey Creek to keep order. Ironically, Chato, Bonito, and Dutchy now were enrolled as scouts, a wise move on the part of the army but one that infuriated the critics of General Crook. Chato rose to the rank of first sergeant of Company B, and, through his loyalty and attention to duty, won Davis's firm admiration.

In this connection, a curious incident occurred in September 1885. John Wright had gone to Lordsburg on business and was returning over the same route the McComases had been traveling when massacred two years earlier. By chance, he ran into Lieutenant Davis and some of his scouts out patrolling. There on the Lordsburg Road, Wright came face to face with Chato, the very man responsible for the death of his friend and law partner. Not too far, either, from the place where the macabre deed had been done. History fails to record the attorney's reaction, but it must not have been hostile, because he purchased a string of beads from Chato![27]

Davis was in New Mexico because Geronimo, along with Chihuahua, Naiche, Mangus, and Nana, had left the reservation again. On May 15, exactly two years to the day after the attack on their camp in the Sierra Madre, they had struck out for Mexico with a total of forty-three warriors and one hundred and one women and children. Before decamping, Geronimo had instructed three of the Apache scouts, who were relatives of the escapees, to assassinate Lieutenant Davis and Chato. Fortunately, the plan failed.

Soon after the renegades were on the trail, the chiefs had a falling out. Chihuahua and Mangus, each with his people, split and went their separate ways. Chihuahua's band swung into New Mexico, committed depredations, and then disappeared south of the border. For the people in that corner of the

Chato transformed, as an Army scout with the rank of sergeant.
Photo taken at San Carlos, 1884, the year after he killed the McComases.
Courtesy Arizona Historical Society, Tucson, Arizona

territory, the event was all too reminiscent of Chato's raid in 1883. Only now Chato was on their side.

White men who knew Geronimo said that he could not tolerate restraint and that reservation rules, such as prohibitions on drinking of *tizwin* (Apache beer) and wife-beating, deeply angered him. His young cousin, Jason Betzinez, declared that it was crowding which the free-spirited old warrior found un-bearable.[28] The real cause of this last breakout, however, probably could be traced to Geronimo's deep love of raiding, which had become the traditional Apache way of making a living. The majority of the Chiricahuas were ready to give it up, recognizing that a new day had overtaken them. But not Geronimo and the slim number of others who succumbed to his blandishments and fol-lowed him on the warpath one final time. Their foolish escapade soon would bring unimaginable tragedy upon the heads of all Chiricahuas.

Under the hot-pursuit agreement with Mexico, recently renewed, both Captain Crawford and Lieutenant Davis led units across the boundary on the trail of the renegades. Later, warriors under Chihuahua broke off and returned to New Mexico. They crossed the railroad tracks between Deming and El Paso, headed north, and near the mining town of Lake Valley killed rancher Brady Pollock. Then the marauders turned west, skirting the lower end of the Black Range and butchering a woodcutter in the Mimbres Valley. They also came upon the young sons of John McKinn, out herding. The older boy was murdered and mutilated, while the younger, twelve-year-old Jimmy (also called Santiago), was carried into captivity.[29]

By the time Davis and his company of Apache scouts reached the South-ern Pacific tracks east of Deming, their horses were exhausted, and they were out of supplies. So he broke off the chase and rode to El Paso to reprovision. There Chato and his companions attracted much curious attention and readily posed for a formal photograph after persuading Davis to buy them some clean clothes. Upon picking up the trail of the hostiles once more, the lieutenant found it cold. It was while riding west toward San Carlos that he chanced to meet John Wright on the Lordsburg Road and, in a brief conversation, brought him up to date on this particular band of raiders.

Not until September 4, 1886, did Geronimo and his pathetically small remnant make their final surrender. But by then, General Crook had resigned (the previous April 1) under pressure, and Brig. Gen. Nelson A. Miles was the new commander of the Department of Arizona. During this last Apache out-break, thirty-nine whites were slain in New Mexico, mainly within a one-hundred-mile radius of Silver City, while another thirty-four died in Arizona. That was more than twice the number that had perished in Chato's raid, but since none of the new victims was as prominent as the McComases had been, the casualty figures did not have quite the same impact on the nation at large.

On orders from Washington and in response to public pressure, all of the Chiricahuas were loaded on railway cars and shipped eastward to Florida as prisoners of war. That included even the loyal Apache scouts who had been instrumental in bringing Geronimo to bay. General Crook, when he heard of it, was outraged; and his aide, Captain Bourke, described the act as a "disgraceful page in the history of our relations with the American Indians."[30]

In midsummer of 1886, Chato had gone to Washington with a delegation of Chiricahua leaders to meet with national officials. On that occasion, he was presented with a peace medal which he would treasure and wear to the end of his life. But while returning to Arizona, the Apaches were stopped at Fort Leavenworth and diverted to Florida, to join the first contingents of their exiled tribesmen.

The Florida imprisonment, with its damp climate, took a toll on the ranks of the Chiricahuas. By 1887 they were moved to an even more unhealthy site in Alabama, where Dutchy was killed during a drunken brawl with soldiers in 1893. The following year, the much-diminished tribe was sent to Fort Sill, Oklahoma, where Geronimo died in 1909. Then in 1913, some 187 Chiricahuas got permission to transfer to New Mexico's Mescalero Apache Reservation. The remainder stayed at Fort Sill. Chato went with those who relocated at Mescalero, and that was as close as they ever would get to their own lost homeland in Arizona.

⚐ Through the passage of years, the Chiricahua remained silent on the subject of the McComas massacre and the fate of little Charley, not wishing to open old wounds. But then, around the middle of the twentieth century, with most of the older generation gone, several aged survivors of the 1880s, who had direct knowledge of Chato's raid, made statements for the historical record.

One was Jason Betzinez, who at age ninety-nine published his recollections under the title *I Fought with Geronimo*. It will be remembered that Jason had accompanied Geronimo on a raid into western Sonora at the time Chato's war party had set out for Arizona. In his book, Jason states that, when that party returned, it brought back a white child captured near Lordsburg. In his words, "this boy, named Charles McComas, quickly learned to speak Apache, and was well liked and kindly treated by the Indians. The family who took him in charge behaved toward him as if he were their own boy."

When Crook's scouts attacked the Chiricahua base camp on May 15, Jason continues, they killed an old woman, mother of an Apache named Speedy. This warrior became so enraged that he picked up a rock and brained the small white captive. "The Apaches later told the soldiers that the little boy had run off into the brush and was never found. . . . They were protecting one of their own band from possible punishment, so they lied about what happened to the poor little boy even though they disapproved of the murder."[31]

Jason admits that he was away from the camp at the time of the attack but says that he got the true story of Charley's death from an eyewitness, Ramona Chihuahua, daughter of the chief. The trouble with that is that Ramona later denied the story to historian Eve Ball, asserting that she knew nothing about the killing of the McComas youngster.[32] Was that actually the case, or was she reverting to the standard Apache practice of disavowing to an outsider any knowledge of a sensitive matter?

Whatever the truth, Jason Betzinez's version of Charley's end, since its publication in 1959, has been widely quoted and now seems to be accepted by the majority of writers and scholars who deal with the Apache wars. Wide acceptance, of course, is no guarantee of truth.

Ramona Chihuahua's husband, Asa Daklugie (son of Juh), before his death in 1955, told Eve Ball this: "There have been many different accounts of the fate of Charley McComas. I saw that child once, but I do not know what family had taken him and was rearing him to be a warrior. I was not present when the [scouts] attacked that camp, but in the escape Charley was killed."[33]

While there is nothing new in this statement, we are, nevertheless, offered reaffirmation by an Apache that Charley died violently during the assault by Crook's scouts. Daklugie seemed to believe, or at least he wanted others to believe, that the boy had been hit by a stray bullet. He makes no reference to his braining by someone named Speedy.

Perhaps the most intriguing information concerning Charley McComas comes from Sam Haozous, the warrior apprentice and youngest member of Chato's raiding party. In 1941 he informed a white neighbor of his, Martin Christensen of Apache, Oklahoma, that he was the last living Indian who had seen the captive child alive. Then he gave an account of the McComas massacre.

Two years later, Christensen wrote a letter that was published in the western magazine *Frontier Times,* in which he attempted to summarize the story given him by Haozous. Evidently he failed to keep notes, and, as he relied on memory, his description of the whole episode came out quite garbled.[34]

On January 27, 1955, not long before his death, Sam Haozous told his tale again, this time to Indian writer Angie Debo, who subsequently made use of the material in her biography of Geronimo. Haozous related that, on May 15, the attacking scouts wantonly killed an old woman, whose son then, in grief and anger, picked up a stone and beat the McComas child on the head, but without killing him.

The next day, Haozous's mother and aunt were making their way down the mountainside through rocks and brush toward Crook's camp to surrender, when they encountered the gravely wounded boy. The aunt was upset, having become greatly attached to him. According to Debo, the voice of Sam Haozous grew tender and compassionate as he quoted his aunt's precise words in that tragic moment: "'Poor little fellow. We can't let him die here. Let's take him along.' But my mother said, 'If we bring him in, the soldiers will blame us,' so they left him. Nobody else went that way, so no doubt he died there."[35]

Ruey Darrow, daughter of Sam Haozous, in 1960 added a few details that she had gleaned from her father. He thought it likely that Charley had succumbed from exposure rather than his wound. In fact, he said that the women had tried to lift and carry the bleeding boy, but without success. Therefore, they laid him unconscious on the ground, and he seemed to have stopped breathing, but his mother could not be sure. So long as she lived, she reproached herself for abandoning him in that condition.[36]

In the main, the accounts of the death of Charley McComas revealed by Betzinez and Haozous reinforce one another and undoubtedly offer the best explanation of his last hours that we are ever likely to have. Still, questions remain, and some doubt must always exist as to the actual circumstances that led to his demise.

⌇ No history of the McComas tragedy would be complete without some recounting of a bizarre aspect of the case that surfaced early and continues to puzzle writers and scholars to this day. It has to do with the so-called Lost Apaches, a remnant band of Chiricahuas who evaded capture, remained free in the wildest precincts of the Sierra Madre, and continued, well into the twentieth century, to live and raid in the old way. Through the 1920s and the early part of the 1930s, they even occasionally crossed the border into the United States to commit depredations.

The Lost Apaches usually were identified as stray members of Geronimo's old band, who, having slipped away singly or in twos and threes, fled to the Mexican mountains where eventually they found one another. Close scrutiny of the evidence, however, strongly suggests that the core of the group was probably made up of Juh's people, the Nednhi or Bronco Apaches whose original homeland, as we have seen, was the Sierra Madre. To them were joined the few Chiricahuas who somehow managed to escape as the tribe was being shipped off to Florida.

The total number of Lost Apaches must have been exceedingly small, perhaps no more than two or three dozen. Over time, the population was augmented by captured Mexican children and by the infrequent addition of an old-line warrior from some other branch of the Apache tribe who, hungry for freedom, drifted south from San Carlos.

On August 9, 1892, eight warriors crossed the international boundary into New Mexico's bootheel and raided the Frank Davenport ranch southwest of Deming. They sacked the headquarters, killed two cowboys, and, mounted on fresh horses, headed northwest toward Stein's Pass on the Arizona line. Pursuers were unable to overtake them before they dropped back into Mexico. Outraged, the *Silver City Enterprise* reminded readers that "a season has scarcely passed when some citizens of Grant County have not lost their lives to this band of cutthroats."[37]

The sporadic killing, in incidents such as this, would continue for another thirty years in southern Arizona and New Mexico, and for a much longer time in neighboring Mexico. A news bulletin from Tucson, dated April 23, 1930, for example, gave the following account:

> Riding out of their wilderness hideout, high in the Sierra Madre Mountains, a band of wild Apache Indians scalped three persons, April 10, in a settlement near Nácori Chico, Sonora, it was reported today by V. M. White, a mining engineer.
>
> The three victims were Mexicans who opened fire on the marauders while the latter were looting the village. Armed parties immediately set out to trail the painted savages and attempt to engage them in battle before they reached their impregnable and historic cliffs.[38]

Four years later, another encounter occurred in a mountain pass above Cumpas, Sonora. Apaches making off with a pack train of stolen goods were intercepted by cowboys, and in a fight five Indians—one man and four women—were slain. They were carrying bloody scalps, lifted earlier in Cumpas.

In that same year, 1934, a young Arizona anthropologist, Grenville Goodwin, stated in a letter to a colleague, "[These Apaches] are fighting a losing battle in Mexico, and it seems only a question of time till they will be exterminated."[39] About this time, several of the Lost Apaches are reported to have found their way to New Mexico's Mescalero Reservation and, from concealment in the forest, made their presence known to some of the Chiricahuas resident there. Daklugie and others went out and spoke with them, but the subject of their conversation is unknown.

Could the renegades have been exploring the possibility of coming into the reservation for good? More likely, they were simply curious or just longing to speak to some of their own people, especially the son of Juh. In any case, they promptly headed back to the place from whence they had come and soon were swallowed up by the forbidding canyons of the Sierra Madre. When Jason Betzinez published his book in 1959, he wrote, "I understand that these outlaws or their descendants are still hiding out in Old Mexico."[40] As late as the 1980s, a published statement indicated that the Sierra Madre Apaches, still free, were being supplied AK47s and light machine guns by drug smugglers and leftist guerrillas.[41]

Now comes the McComas connection. Back in the early 1890s, when the public first became aware of the Lost Apaches' existence, stories began to circulate that Charley McComas was alive and living among them. Since the reports of his death during or immediately after the 1883 Sierra Madre attack were strictly hearsay, many people seemed to believe that he had survived and had been taken by some of the fleeing Indians to a new mountain refuge, where he was adopted and raised as an Apache.

Over the next several decades, reported sightings of an adult Charley McComas appeared periodically in the press. Most were fanciful in the extreme, but not all. At the very least, they demonstrated that the McComas calamity, now fading into the past, had left a deep impression upon southwesterners, whose interest in the fate of little Charley had not abated.[42]

In 1923, prospector John Hughes, operating out of Douglas, Arizona, caught a glimpse of a Lost Apache war party in the mountains below the Chiricahua range. He got close enough to observe that the band leader was a white man with a long beard who wore a buckskin breechcloth and high-topped Apache moccasins. Citizens of Douglas at once jumped to the conclusion that this white Indian must be Charley McComas, who by then would have been with the Apaches for forty years.[43]

The following year the marauders were back, sweeping across the lower half of the bootheel. As they crossed into the United States, they chanced upon hapless cowboy Frank Fisher, shooting him dead and leaving his body at trailside. A Mexican vaquero soon found the corpse and sounded the alarm. Instantly the country was up in arms, and posses swarmed over the desert basins and into the rock-ribbed mountains.

High in the Animas, where Chato's raiders had rested after killing the McComases, the Apaches pillaged a ranch house, whose owners luckily were away. Among their stolen plunder was a rifle and cartridges. Then, after a quick passage through the Playas Valley, they slipped into the craggy Big Hatchet Mountains and went into camp.

A twenty-four-man posse from Lordsburg spotted the Apaches and attempted to surround and capture them. But upon charging the camp, they found that the wily Indians had gotten wind of their approach and run, leaving meat roasting on the fire. It proved a disappointing near-miss, although some twenty rustled horses and mules were recaptured.

The party of hostiles, after regrouping, swung southwestward and, right after slipping over the Sonora line, they were seen by a pair of Arizona ranchers, the Hunt brothers. The white men counted six warriors, five of whom appeared to be small, swarthy Apaches. But the sixth, obviously the leader, was fair, with blonde hair and a waist-length beard. He was much taller than the others. The *El Paso Post* speculated that this remarkable individual was "none other than the kidnapped boy [Charley McComas], raised by the Indians from infancy until he has become a renegade and leader among them."[44] That romantic theory strongly appealed to the people of the border country.

In 1938, a Norwegian anthropologist, Dr. Helge Ingstad, appeared on the scene and announced his intention to make contact with the Lost Apaches. He seemed especially enamored of the stories that McComas had become a chief of the band. His inquiries led him to interview a young woman named Lupe, born and raised with these Apaches but captured by the Mexicans when she was fourteen. By her testimony, "A white man, an American, lived with us. For a long time he had lived with my kin, but in the end he disappeared." And Lupe added that the American had red hair and startling blue eyes.[45]

With a couple of Mescalero Apaches he enlisted as interpreters and a Yaqui Indian named Mora for a guide, Dr. Ingstad ventured into the mountainous country along the Sonora-Chihuahua line. Once he met a Mexican on the trail who told of finding red hairs in a crude comb he had picked up in one of the Apache camps. At some point, Ingstad claimed that he had gotten a quick look at five of the Lost Apaches. By his description, "They were healthy, husky, erect, defiant—the very opposite of the Indians upon whom the crushing weight of civilization has been laid." And he noted that so many of the males had been killed that their women were dressing as men and fighting as warriors.[46]

Apparently, by the time Helge Ingstad visited the Sierra Madre, the white Apache already was dead. The circumstances of his demise were related later at Mescalero by Rogers To-clanny, an aging Chiricahua army scout. How he acquired the information is not known.

> I knew that boy [Charley McComas]. He became like one of us. When he grew up, we called him Red Beard.... He could fight and raid just like an Apache. When he was a man, his beard came in red.
>
> He began to like one of our Indian girls. But one of our warriors . . . liked the same girl. The two men were jealous of each other. They had a fight, and the warrior stabbed Red Beard, who died.[47]

To-clanny's story is partially confirmed by a statement taken from a Lost Apache woman captured by the Mexicans in late 1937. She related that the white man who had been living with her people had been brought in as a child by Chato's war party. He was raised to follow the customs and habits of the Apaches and became a real fighter and hunter. His skin was pale and his beard so thick that it could not be plucked out with tweezers, as was the custom of the Indians.

Not long before she was made a captive, the woman declared, their band leader had a fight with the white man over a woman and killed him. That little detail aroused considerable interest among her listeners, and subsequently she guided an American mining engineer from Douglas and a group of Mexicans to the spot where the bearded warrior had been buried. A skeleton was recovered and taken to Arizona. A doctor allegedly identified it as that of a white man.[48]

All of the assorted pieces of the puzzle presented here, being fragmentary and of dubious validity, in no way provide convincing proof that Hamilton and Juniata McComas's little boy survived to become a fighting man among Mexico's Lost Apaches. They only suggest a slim and highly unlikely possibility that he did so.

Jason Betzinez spoke of the numbers of white boys who, in the early 1880s, were incorporated into Juh's and Geronimo's bands.[49] Any one of them could have matured to become the Indianized raider leading the Lost Apaches. Historian Dan Thrapp suspected that, rather than Charley McComas, he probably was a young captive American rumored to have been the son-in-law of Juh. Thrapp was reported to be following that historical thread when he died in 1994.

It is certainly curious that reports of the earlier sightings refer to the white Apache as a blonde, while later on, by the 1930s, he has been transformed into a red-head. Actually, in traditional Chiricahua tales there can be found several men known as Red Beard. As often occurs in oral history, similar figures merge and become fused with the passage of time, so that later it is difficult or even impossible to sort them out.[50]

In the same manner, the Apaches, having been quizzed so often about Charley McComas, eventually would have come around to identifying him as the white man with the Sierra Madre raiders, whether or not they had any evidential basis for saying so. Indeed, all the known Indian accounts that relate to Charley and his captivity contain confusing and conflicting details, leading us to believe that they must be regarded with skepticism and used with utmost caution.

In summary, therefore, what conclusions can be drawn? Was little Charley Ware McComas brained within hours of his capture on March 28, 1883, as some of the first reports indicated? Did he die from exposure after fleeing the Apache camp the following May 15, during the attack by Crook's scouts? Or, on that same occasion, did he receive a mortal wound at the hands of a warrior called Speedy? And can any credence be given to the legend that Charley lived to become a prominent leader of the last free Sierra Madre Apaches?

An Arizona journalist, in 1909, after recounting the complete McComas episode for his newspaper, summed up the matter handily: "One narrator describes the manner of the child's death, while another pictures him as growing to manhood, having adopted the customs and life of the Indians. It is finally determined that no reliance can be placed on any of the stories."[51] Today, that remains the only certain statement that can be made concerning the fate of Charley McComas.

Chapter Eleven

Massacre's Legacy

In the history of warfare between red man and white along the United States–Mexican border, the tale of the McComas family came to occupy an especially memorable place. The reasons were several: the prominence of the victims; the lateness of the episode, occurring as it did when the country was just settling into the comfortable belief that the Indian wars were over; and, of course, the persistent mystery about what really happened to Charley McComas. As long as people were living who had any direct connection with events surrounding the massacre, the dramatic story was told and retold.

At Malone, a mining camp that grew up in the Burro Mountains a few miles south of the death site, residents assembled on January 21, 1885, and organized a movement to raise funds to build a suitable monument at Thompson Canyon in memory of Judge McComas, his wife, and the child Charley. They voted to make an appeal for contributions to all miners in the territory and to Americans nationwide, who, it was felt, would be stirred by this noble and fitting project. To that end, committees were set up in Silver City, Lordsburg, Paschal, Malone, and other mining communities.[1]

Folks at Pinos Altos, above Silver City, thought that was a splendid idea, but one that did not go far enough. They wanted to see a monument erected in honor of some five hundred men, women, and children slain by Apaches in recent years. In their enthusiasm, they issued "an appeal to everybody throughout the world," asking that each person and business firm send twenty cents to the project's collection center, located at the Pioneer Meat Market, Pinos Altos, New Mexico.[2]

While expectations were high for both monuments, the results proved disappointing. The money failed to flow, at least in the quantity needed, and the effort collapsed. A 7,681-foot mountain just outside Silver City already had been named McComas Peak, back in 1883, so that would have to serve, in place of a formal monument, as a kind of natural memorial to the family.[3]

With the advent of the automobile age in the following century, a new paved State Highway 90 was built between Silver City and Lordsburg. It stayed several miles east of the old stagecoach road used by the McComases and then cut westward over the Burros at a point some five miles south of Thompson Canyon. In 1935, the New Mexico State Highway Department and the Tourist Bureau began placing historical markers along the roadways.

One such marker, entitled "McComas Massacre" and carrying a brief text, was installed beside Highway 90, although the actual site where Hamilton and Juniata died was more than ten miles to the west. By 1984, when all the state markers were revised and repainted, attitudes toward the past had changed. Indiscriminate killings by Indians, being quite remote, now were viewed in a more sympathetic light, partly on the assumption that the intruding whites got what they deserved. That represented a curious reversal of the sentiment that had prevailed on the frontier.

As a result, the "McComas Massacre" marker was retitled "McComas Incident," and the term *massacre* was eliminated from the text. In 1883, territorial newspapers commonly had characterized the McComas deaths as a massacre, but a bare century later, that harsh word had fallen out of public favor, insofar as it was linked to Indian behavior.[4]

❦ In assessing both the immediate and long-term consequences of the McComas massacre, or McComas incident, if one prefers, it seems fair to say that they were substantial. Certainly the widespread publicity and anger that were generated at the time helped to prepare public opinion, as did other massacre reports, to accept and even approve the government's drastic decision in 1886 to send the entire Chiricahua Apache tribe to a Florida imprisonment. That severe punishment, owing to its lengthy term, led within a generation or two to much loss of the native language and the disintegration of the core of traditional culture—an extraordinarily high price exacted for Chato's and Geronimo's misdeeds.[5]

The former, who in later years was known as Alfred Chato, had plenty of time to ponder what his hostility and then his friendliness toward the whites

Historical marker beside the new Lordsburg Road, 1993.
Photo by author

had cost him. When Gen. George Crook visited Chato in his Florida captivity, the old scout showed him the presidential medal and asked: "Why was I given that to wear in the guard house? I thought that something good would come to me when they gave it to me, but I have been in confinement ever since I have had it."[6] To that, the general had no ready answer.

Even when the Apaches were transferred to Oklahoma and gained some freedom of movement, Chato's own fortunes remained bleak, mainly because he was shunned by most of his fellow tribesmen. The standard explanation is that other Chiricahuas regarded him as a traitor for having cooperated so completely with their enemies as a government scout. But numerous Apaches filled the army ranks and later were forgiven, so that hardly can be the sole cause of the animosity shown to Chato.

Some of it may be traced to his old rivalry with Geronimo, the tribal memory of which would have worked to his discredit during the depressing reservation years. Or, as seems more likely, perhaps his personality and attitudes just clashed with those of other Apache leaders. Daklugie, for instance, despised him for his faults, even while admitting that Chato had been a brave and formidable warrior.

Among the Chiricahuas who moved from Fort Sill to New Mexico's Mescalero Reservation in 1913 were Chato and Naiche, the last surviving major players in the raid of 1883. Naiche, youngest son of Cochise, died of influenza at the Mescalero hospital in 1921. Chato, having taken to the bottle, lived on for another thirteen years.

In his new home, the aging warrior continued to be ostracized, not only by his own people but also by their Mescalero hosts, who had been fully informed of Chato's loss of status. In the face of rejection, he and his wife withdrew to an isolated home at Apache Summit, in the center of the mountainous reservation. Drinking water had to be hauled from a distance of ten miles. Situated thus, apart from the world and with liquor glass in hand, did an outcast Chato while away his final years reflecting upon that one brief, shining moment in his career when he rode out of Mexico at the head of two dozen warriors, spread terror across the land, and slew a man and woman by a walnut tree on the Lordsburg Road? We have no way of knowing, of course.[7]

On August 16, 1934, Chato drove his Model-T Ford to the outlying Indian village of White Tail. Returning late at night by a high road with treacherous curves, he went off a cliff and suffered fatal injuries. For a man raised as an equestrian nomad, it was a strange way to die. Perhaps he had taken one drink too many. Or maybe he just fell asleep at the wheel. Chato at the time of his death was eighty years old.

Just as the Chiricahuas for years suffered from the effects of Chato's bloody work on the Lordsburg Road, so too did those whites who had some connection to the tragic affair long experience its reverberations. Assuredly, until their own deaths, often many years later, the story of the massacre never was far out of mind.

J. M. Dennis and his wife, who had accommodated the McComases at their hostelry, never reoccupied the Mountain Home after their initial flight to Paschal and Silver City. The place was haunted by memories of that terrifying night when they learned of the massacre, and so the property was sold. In the early morning hours of May 13, 1885, the Mountain Home caught fire and burned to the ground, along with all its outbuildings and the wagons and buggies parked nearby. It was the first of several landmarks associated with the McComas saga to be lost.[8]

On the evening of March 27, 1884, exactly one year after the McComas family had stopped at the Mountain Home, friends of the Harry Lucases in Silver City gave them "a very pleasant party in honor of their second wedding anniversary."[9] On what otherwise would be a joyous occasion, Mrs. Lucas must have been saddened by the unhappy recollection that, on the same day a year ago, she had said good-bye for the last time to her cherished friend Juniata

Skeleton of the walnut tree at the McComas massacre site, 1993.
Photo by author

McComas. "She was like a dear sister to me," the woman had said in a letter to Juniata's brother, Charles.[10]

Of her husband Harry Lucas, who had photographed the McComases and later prepared the handbills for the lost Charley, an odd footnote remains. In 1884, he opened a second photography studio in Deming, thereafter dividing his time between that town and Silver City. A sociable man, he belonged to six local fraternal organizations, including the Masons. Then, in December 1893, his career ended and his reputation crashed when Mr. Lucas absconded with the Silver City Masonic Lodge treasury and fled to Mexico. The presumption is that he abandoned his devoted wife to her fate.[11]

Julius Caesar Brock, whose life at age nineteen had intersected with the McComas tragedy, recorded his own recollections of the event on tape shortly before his death on March 19, 1952, at age eighty-eight. Elder residents of Lordsburg to this day recall the eccentric, loquacious, and grizzled old-timer who had seen the McComas bodies lying bloodied on the roadside.[12]

In 1890, Brock established a ranch headquarters at the mouth of Thompson Canyon, in time expanding his boundaries to take in thirty sections of land. He also was an organizer of the New Mexico Cattle Growers Association and a member of its executive board.[13] During the late 1920s and early 1930s, burl hunters came through the country, uprooting the walnut trees to harvest the burls, or hard knots, which could be sold to the manufacturers of smoking pipes and wooden salad bowls. Brock, it is reported, stood guard on more than one occasion over the ancient giant where the McComases had died and which grew a half-mile below his ranch house. He always called it the "Massacre Tree," and, after the burl hunters were finished, it was the only walnut left in the vicinity.[14]

※ In assembling the scattered data of history that relate to Chato's raid and examining the aftereffects upon survivors, it becomes clear that the shattered McComas family never recovered from the appalling occurrences of 1883. Life went on for the kin of H. C., Juniata, and little Charley, but the weight of their losses cast a perpetual cloud of gloom over those who were left behind, down to the next generation.

H. C.'s older brother, Elisha W. McComas, passed the remainder of his days at Fort Scott, engaging in railroad promotion, serving as the first president of the Chamber of Commerce (then called the Board of Trade), and writing religious tracts. At his son Gordon's farm six miles north of town, he succumbed to heart failure on March 3, 1890.[15]

Younger brother Rufus McComas of Nebraska City continued his activity with mining properties and investments in southwestern New Mexico. By 1890, he had become owner and manager of the Last Chance Mining Company, which was milling fifty tons of ore a day. At its operation in the Mogollon Mountains outside Silver City, he suffered a fatal mishap on January 20, 1891. According to a news bulletin: "Mr. McComas slipped upon the ice near the mine, and being a man of more than common proportions, the force of the fall was sufficient to burst a blood vessel. He died before medical aid could be summoned." It was a sad blow to his family, lamented the press notice, and a loss to the community, since he was a thorough businessman and a perfect gentleman.[16]

Eugene Fitch Ware devoted the remainder of his career to politics, public service, and writing. After leaving the Kansas State Senate in 1884, he twice served as a delegate to the National Republican Convention. President Theodore Roosevelt appointed him U.S. Commissioner of Pensions in 1902; and, during his three-year term in Washington, Ware streamlined that office and worked diligently for adoption of an age disability rule. Among his other contributions, he sat as president of the Kansas State Historical Society and founded the first public library in Fort Scott.[17]

In 1891, Ware filed a petition before the U.S. Court of Claims on behalf of Ada and Mary McComas, for losses their parents' estate had suffered as a result of the Apache attack on March 28, 1883. Although Ware's guardianship had lapsed, both girls now being of legal age, he continued to represent their legal interests. Not until 1927 did Ada learn that the claim had been dismissed by the court.[18]

One of Ware's last accomplishments was the publication in 1911 of his highly regarded book, *The Indian War of 1864,* an account of his youthful military experiences. The McComas affair in no way figures in the narrative, but the author's strong anti-Indian attitude, apparent therein, surely was shaped by that event. Ware believed that Indians deserved extermination, a view he found common on the southwestern frontier and one that must have been strongly reinforced in his own mind by the massacre of his relatives. In his seventieth year, while vacationing in Cascade, Colorado, with his wife and daughter, Eugene Fitch Ware died suddenly. His body was returned to Fort Scott, Kansas, for burial.[19]

Of those tied in some way to the Thompson Canyon tragedy, none was affected more profoundly than the McComas children—David, William, Ada, and Mary. With the massacre, the central pillars of their young lives were suddenly removed. Gone, too, was the small brother, Charley, upon whom the entire family had lavished attention and affection. Anguish caused by Chato's violent act lessened with the passage of years, but the deep scars would always remain.

Although our information on the eldest son, David, is the thinnest, we have some reason to believe that the traumatic loss took its heaviest toll upon him. Perhaps he felt some responsibility for what had happened, since it was his telegram summoning his father to Lordsburg that had led to the fatal trip.

After spending several months with John Wright tracking leads on Charley, David McComas returned to his job with the Pyramid Mining and Milling Company. He was now a resident of Shakespeare, but on one or more occasions he paid a visit to Silver City, either to see friends or on business concerning settlement of his father's estate. If the journey was made by horseback or stagecoach, rather than by the new roundabout railroad route, he could not have avoided passing directly by that grim specter of the walnut tree.[20]

A public notice appearing on November 15, 1884, revealed that David McComas had been selected a constable for the Shakespeare precinct.[21] Evidently this new position as a county peace officer, to his way of thinking, offered more reward or opportunity. However, scarcely enough time was left to him to realize either.

The *Silver City Enterprise* of May 21, 1886, ran a bulletin as shocking as it was brief: "Monday morning attorney J. M. Wright received a telegram from Lordsburg announcing the death of David McComas, son of the late Judge McComas. The deceased, who was only 25 years old, was engaged in mining until recently."

No other details about the young man's sudden passing have ever come to light. Since he died without leaving a will, the court appointed Wright, recognized as the McComas family attorney, to be the administrator of his estate.[22] One recent historian has speculated that "his father's death was too much for David, who never recovered from the shock and died [three] years later."[23] Omission of reference at the time to a cause of death leads us to wonder whether David McComas might have taken his own life, thus becoming a belated casualty of Chato's raid.

William McComas, David's younger brother, was another story. For three years, he continued on his own to search for Charley, refusing to believe that he was dead.[24] About midsummer of 1884, Silver City friends learned that he had taken up residence at the mining center of Bisbee, down in the southeastern corner of the Arizona Territory.[25] He had gone there, at the tender age of twenty, to assume duties as a schoolteacher upon opening of the next term.

His employment soon led to a scandal. Handsome, athletic, graceful, and tall like his father, Will McComas had a keen eye for the ladies. Within three

William McComas, last living male heir of Judge McComas, toward the end of his life. In McComas Family Papers, courtesy Carolyn Kimme-Smith, Los Angeles, California

months, his attentions to the older girls in his classes led the Bisbee school trustees to dismiss the young Don Juan and replace him with a serious, matronly woman.

That proved to be merely the first of many romantic escapades in the adult life of Judge McComas's son. Those who knew him would claim later that, in his youth, Will had learned to take advantage of women and girls who felt sympathy for his family's tragedy, becoming in the process a philanderer without conscience. His looks and debonair manner won and broke many hearts, and he had numerous relationships.[26]

From Bisbee, Will drifted back to Grant County, New Mexico, took odd jobs in the mines, became proficient with a six-gun, and dealt faro on the side. That was leading him nowhere, so, probably at the urging of his Uncle Rufus, he went off to college (exactly where is unknown) and graduated a few years later with honors as a mining engineer. Once again in New Mexico, he was put to work, as near as we can determine, with the Last Chance Mining Company, headed by Rufus McComas, who well may have paid his nephew's college bills.[27]

In 1892 Will suffered an injury in a bizarre incident that all but blinded him in one eye. At a mine site one day, he was blasting out a prospect hole twenty feet underground. He lit the fuses for six rounds of dynamite and scampered up the ladder to the surface. As his head emerged level with the ground, he found himself exchanging stares with a huge coiled rattlesnake. Horrified, he quickly pondered the unpalatable choices: go ahead and risk being struck in the face by those deadly fangs, or hold back and take his chances with the dynamite.

In the next instant, the dynamite decided for him. The explosion rocked the ground and sent Will McComas flying into the air. When he regained consciousness, lying prone on the desert floor, he found that a rock had whacked him in the left eye, taking his sight. That he had survived at all was practically a miracle.[28]

Shortly afterward, Will departed for Chicago, where a cousin, Mrs. W. H. Lyford, wife of a prominent railroad attorney, had offered help in getting treatment for his injury. The couple was shocked to observe that "his eye was clear out of the socket and looked like fresh liver."[29] McComas spent four months recuperating at their home, the first two in total darkness. He healed but lost 98 percent of his vision in the damaged eye. He also suffered from severe hearing impairment.

While in Illinois, Will made contact with his mother, Louisa McComas, who then was living in Danville. Judge McComas, we believe, had severed all connection with her after the divorce for adultery in Monticello. Whether the boys, David and William, even had been allowed to receive letters from her seems doubtful. By the time of the judge's death, they may not have known her whereabouts.

In the settlement of H. C.'s and David's estates, however, her name came up in the disposition of their property, quite likely causing administrator Wright to communicate with her. That would have produced an address, giving Will the opportunity, upon returning east, to renew familial ties. With his father, two brothers, and Uncle Rufus now dead, doing that might have assumed new importance for him. Louisa McComas, we know, made at least one trip to New Mexico.[30]

In the *Enterprise,* a social note appeared on March 10, 1893. It informed readers: "Will McComas, one of Silver City's most popular young gentlemen in days gone by, returned from Chicago on yesterday's train. His many old acquaintances will be delighted to meet him." His arrival back in New Mexico fell within a few days of the tenth anniversary of the Thompson Canyon massacre.

For the next few years, Will worked his way from one mining operation to another. After a period in Arizona, he wandered into Mexico, where he spent some time at Mazatlán on the west coast. It probably was soon after the turn of the century that he showed up in California, establishing headquarters in Los Angeles for his "mining interests." There, on February 28, 1908, William P. McComas shot and killed Charlotte L. Noyes, a wealthy divorcee to whom he had been attentive for several months. His subsequent trial became one of the biggest news stories of the decade.

Mrs. Noyes was addicted to gambling and regularly took the Pacific Electric streetcars to the Santa Anita Race Track to play the horses. Will McComas often escorted her. On Friday evening, they were alone in her fashionable apartment at 671 Little Street when a quarrel developed. Apparently Mrs. Noyes had lost a considerable sum of money and wanted McComas to extend her a loan. Court testimony characterized her as "a highly emotional woman" who "possessed a violent temper." Once she was said to have attacked her ex-husband with a hat pin, injuring him severely.[31]

Now, she became infuriated with her companion and rushed to a cabinet to take out a cup of sulfuric acid. This she flung in Will McComas's face. With the blind instinct of a wounded Arizona gunfighter (the defense he would later use), Will jerked out the pistol he habitually wore and fired. A bullet pierced the heart of Mrs. Noyes. After dousing the terrible acid wound with olive oil from the kitchen, he went to the telephone and made two calls: the first to the police and the second to an acquaintance, Earl Rogers, who happened to be one of the day's most celebrated trial lawyers.[32]

The case created a sensation, especially when Will was indicted for murder by a coroner's jury. At his trial the following May, mobs stormed the courthouse and broke down the front door, trying to get a seat for the proceedings. Some women fainted upon viewing the romantic figure of the accused. Since the killing, he had remained free on bond, which had been posted by powerful friends, including former Los Angeles Mayor A. C. Harper.[33] The *New York Times,* in its coverage, identified Will McComas as "one of the most prominent mining engineers on the Pacific Coast."[34]

The lengthy trial became a classic duel between prosecuting and defense attorneys. As Rogers pulled out all stops on behalf of his client, in building a case for self-defense, McComas remained suave, composed, even defiant.[35] The result, however, was a hung jury and the declaration of a mistrial. But when the matter was retried shortly afterward, the defendant won acquittal. Earl Rogers's daughter, many years later, declared that the McComas trial was her father's masterpiece.[36]

The furor surrounding this episode brought to the fore once more the story of the McComas massacre, now almost twenty-five years old. News dispatches providing background information about the accused almost invariably mentioned it, but with the facts routinely garbled. In one instance, the young Will even was represented as having been present during Chato's attack upon his father's buckboard, with himself wounded and left for dead by the Apaches. Such tale-telling helped sell newspapers, but it also earned Will McComas public sympathy, which he did nothing to discourage.[37]

Will's later years are obscured in a dim twilight. Most of that time was spent in California, with periodic business stays in Mexico. William McComas died in a Los Angeles hospital in late 1927 or early 1928.[38]

The McComas daughters, Ada and Mary, like their half-brothers, lived out the remainder of their lives under the shadow of the terrible calamity that had taken Hamilton and Juniata. Their elderly grandparents, the Wares, were unable to care for them, so, soon after the funeral, they were sent to live with McComas aunts in West Virginia. Before long, however, they were returned to relatives in Fort Scott, who placed Ada at a boarding school in Topeka but kept Mary at home, owing to her affliction with scoliosis.[39]

The people of Silver City remained interested in the status of the girls, and one of them, on a trip east, stopped by in the summer of 1886. Said the

Enterprise: "J. M. Smith, who returned last week from a visit to Fort Scott, met the McComas children while there. The oldest one of the girls is a young lady now. They are in good health and spirits."[40]

The following decade, Ada married Ulysses Grant Hazelton. Her first child was a son whom she named Charles, in honor of her long-lost little brother. When he died at age three, she was devastated. A daughter, Mildred, was born to Ada at Fort Scott on November 15, 1900.[41]

Sometime before 1910, the Hazeltons moved to California. Mary McComas, who never married, went with them. Indeed, because of her infirmity, she spent the rest of her life under the domineering care of her sister. It must be assumed that the relocation to California had something to do with William McComas. Back in 1892, Eugene Fitch Ware, in filing the Indian Depredation Claim on behalf of his nieces, mentioned in that document that William "has long since been unheard from, but may be living."[42] That is a curious statement, since Ware hardly could have been ignorant of the fact that his nephew was associated with the late Rufus McComas's mine outside Silver City. Maybe William's reckless ways had prompted the Wares, strict Congregationalists all, to disown him and cut off communication? Of course, we don't know.

In California, Ada and Mary reestablished a close relationship with their brother. One or both of them testified in his behalf at the 1908 murder trial.[43] Whether they were already living in Los Angeles, or, as seems more likely, they came out to help William and decided to remain, is not recorded. Small daughter Mildred called him Uncle Bill, and within the family circle, that nickname became shortened to the initials "U. B." Both Ada and Mary, as the saying went, were crazy about him. He was not only a charmer, but also the last male McComas relative with whom they had regular contact.[44]

Grant Hazelton, Ada's husband, began working with U. B., perhaps more as a factotum than as a partner. At some point, the men went off to Mexico for an extended sojourn related to their mining business. Mary accompanied them to perform housekeeping chores. At the time, the Mexican Revolution was raging, the country was in turmoil, and living conditions were more dangerous and unhealthy than usual.

According to family tradition, McComas and Hazelton were kidnapped by revolutionaries, a misfortune not all that uncommon among Americans working in remote mining districts of Mexico. Hazelton won release fairly quickly, but Will McComas lingered in captivity for more than six months, during which time he received severe beatings. Further, when the pair returned to California, they were suffering from malaria. Hazelton's heart was weakened by the experience, and this debility proved a factor in his premature death in 1934, at age fifty-four. Will's passing also may have been premature, for the same reason.[45]

Ada, we have reason to think, grieved her entire life for the loss of her brother Charley. At the time of the massacre, well-meaning relatives and friends attempted to shield both girls from pain by keeping specific details of Chato's attack from them. Consequently, they grew up blaming their parents for an imagined failure to protect Charley from the Apache raiders. Only decades later did Ada and Mary gain peace of mind, when they read published accounts which made clear that Hamilton and Juniata had done what they could to save their son.

To her granddaughter (Mildred's child, Carolyn), Ada often related stories of her happy childhood in Fort Scott before the tragic deaths of the senior McComases. But she never spoke of the event itself. Then, in 1944, an article about the McComas affair appeared in a popular adventure magazine. Taking considerable liberties, it represented Charley as having survived to grow up and become a white savage in the mountains of the Southwest. Ada was stunned, upset, angered. The sensationalized piece, in suggesting that Charley had gone native, cast a stigma upon his name. Indignantly, she wrote a strong letter of protest to the magazine's editors.[46]

That incident released painful memories, long repressed. It also may have given Ada the courage to seek closure by undertaking a return trip to scenes of her childhood. With her second husband, W. F. Taylor, Ada traveled back to Fort Scott in September 1945 for a visit with the few Ware relatives still there. Sixty-three years had passed since she and her family climbed aboard a train at the Fort Scott station for the long ride out to Silver City. Now she was seventy-five years old.

In returning to California by car, the Taylors paused for a weekend in Silver City. Ada talked with several pioneer residents who could recall the tragedy of her girlhood, although none actually had known the McComases. She mentioned that the family had lived briefly in the ornate Exchange Hotel, but that building, along with its livery stable, long since had been torn down. In fact, Ada declared that she was unable to find any landmarks she remembered as a child.

One significant building still stood—the red brick house on Hudson Street that H. C. had bought for his brood in December 1882. Although the structure was much altered by time, Ada hardly could have overlooked it. Quite likely, she deliberately passed the home by, upon learning that it now sheltered a bordello. In 1970, seven years after Ada's death, the McComas house was razed and a new Silver City post office constructed on the site.

Before leaving town, Ada was advised to drive by way of Caesar Brock's ranch at Thompson Canyon, since the old fellow had known her father and found her parents' bodies. She promised to do that. If the two actually met, we can imagine that the rancher guided Ada and her husband to the nearby walnut tree, and she would have viewed for the first time the bloody ground where the course of her life was forever changed.[47]

A short time after Ada arrived home in California, her sister Mary died. Stooped and hunchbacked from the long affliction with scoliosis, she finally had been felled by cancer. Ada McComas Taylor, following a series of strokes, passed away in 1963. She was the last living soul who had been personally involved in the dramatic events of 1883 that unfolded on the Lordsburg Road.

☙ Chapter Twelve ❧

A Personal Epilogue

On the afternoon of August 26, 1994, I attended the memorial service for Allan Houser (son of Sam Haozous), Chiricahua Apache sculptor and artist who had died the previous Monday in Santa Fe. The open-air event, attended by hundreds of people, including representatives of numerous tribes, took place at Houser's studio and "sculpture garden" located a dozen miles south of the Santa Fe city limits, on the edge of the Galisteo Basin.

Houser had been a neighbor, his studio lying just over the hill from my canyon-locked adobe home. But my only contact with him was the brief interview conducted several months earlier, when he shared with me recollections of what his father years ago had told him about the McComas affair. As mentioned earlier in this book, a ten-year-old Sam Haozous had ridden north from Mexico with Chato in 1883, thereby becoming an eyewitness to a tragic chapter in history.

"As long as my father was alive, we did not speak about Charley McComas outside the family, for he always feared reprisal," Allan Houser had told me during my interview. Such reticence was common among old-time tribesmen who had taken part in the last Indian wars. Author Evan Connell quotes a Sioux warrior who fought Custer at the Little Big Horn as saying: "We had done more than we thought we ever could do, and we knew that the whites were very strong and would punish us."[1] As late as the 1920s and 1930s, some of Sitting Bull's aging warriors worried that they might yet be rounded up and hanged. Like them, Sam Haozous, rightly or not, dreaded a belated retribution.

The day of Allan Houser's burial, his cousin Lupe Gooday from Apache, Oklahoma, reminded those present that neither bitterness nor the dark burden of history had prevented Houser from fulfilling his lifelong mission of creating uplifting art. In a like manner, the father, Sam Haozous, had refused to permit his years in captivity to deter him from building a productive, responsible, and rewarding life. Now, in the sad, waning days of the twentieth century, men of strong character and individual achievement such as these seem like quaint relics of an age that is gone and beyond recovery.

I entered the sculpture garden through an adobe entranceway with an opening in the form of a T, plainly modeled after the door style seen today in prehistoric ruins across the Southwest. The winding walk led through scattered piñons and junipers, past a pavilion where food was being prepared to feed the enormous crowd. On every hand, tucked with loving care into the natural setting, rested one example after another of Allan Houser's art in stone and bronze. No other place on earth possibly could resemble this garden.

Five miles to the south, dark storm clouds billowed over the purple crest of the Ortiz Mountains, and the faint rumble of thunder warned of possible rain. Little bursts of wind, cool and sweet-smelling, set the piñon limbs trembling and caused multicolored strips of paper suspended from each branch to flutter wildly. These "tree notes" had been placed earlier in the day by Houser grandchildren, and persons attending the service were asked to take one, in recollection of the man. The tree notes bore this inscription:

> *In Honor and Memory*
> *of*
> *Allan*
> *Houser*
> *(Haozous)*
> ARTIST
> *1914–1994*
> *A Man Of*
> *Simplicity*
> *Vision*
> *Courage*
> *Creativity*
> *Nobility*
> *Love*
> *August 26, 1994*

The walkway led to an outdoor amphitheater which was flanked by the white cones of twin teepees. Folding chairs had been set up inside the circle facing a speaker's stand and a walnut casket draped with a bright Pendleton blanket, of the kind much favored by Indians. Speaking with gravity and force, Wendell Chino, the venerable chairman of the Mescalero Apache Tribe, opened the tributes. He was followed by family members, friends, former art students, and tribal representatives—Picuris, Hopi, Navajo, Kiowa, Comanche, and the Warm Springs of Oregon, who had brought their medicine woman. Throughout, the service was enriched by the singing of traditional songs and flute playing, Houser having been strongly attached to music and the native flute.

Mostly, simple, unvarnished recollections of Allan Houser were offered by people who knew him best. What began to emerge was the picture of a man as described on the tree notes, but one possessing the added characteristic of generosity. Houser was not just a creator, but a generous creator who gave abundantly to young apprentice artists and to the community as a whole. How different was the configuration of the life of this Chiricahua Apache from the lives of those men who had come raiding out of the Sierra Madre with Chato some 110 years ago.

Sitting directly behind the Houser family during the long service, I kept seeing historical connections that tied this solemn event to the past. I was in the presence of people—Fort Sill and Mescalero Apaches—who actually had known Chato, Sam Haozous, and perhaps other participants in the 1883 tragedy. I had spent that same morning at my typewriter, by sheer coincidence, writing up the Kansas funeral of the McComases, in part using records supplied me by Hamilton and Juniata's great-granddaughter. Now, attending, as it were, my second funeral of the day, I keenly felt that I myself had become another link in a long chain that stretched backward through time to a distant, fateful day on the Lordsburg Road.

A central thesis of this book is that the McComas massacre played a major role in bringing the Chiricahua way of life to an end. The eldest of the tribal elders, here to honor the memory of Allan Houser, seemed to be the last remnant living spiritually in the past. I sensed that one corner of their grief was reserved for the realization that things can never again be the same and that something precious has slipped away. Of exactly what the Apaches lost, their descendants in the future will have only the faintest idea.

As Pueblo artist Dan Namingha was addressing the crowd, lightning cracked, peals of thunder shook the earth, and a few drops of rain fell. He remarked somberly: "A dark sky opening to rain means a man has been accepted into the spirit world."[2]

In driving away from Allan Houser's sculpture garden, I remembered, as I so often have in the past, that history is at its best when revealing the drama of human events and highlighting the dignity and courage of individuals. From first to last, my tracing of the McComas story had opened for me new vistas of understanding and led to experiences I would not exchange for any others. A fond hope I nursed was that readers, having followed my narrative of events, might gain a new awareness of the costs involved in settling the Southwest, and what exactly had been won.

In the final analysis, however, my chief task has been to pull from the dark shadows the personal history of Hamilton, Juniata, and Charley McComas and for the first time to place it in full sunlight. Their sorrowful tale deserved better than to be buried and forgotten. At least now they can ride once more across the New Mexican landscape in the imaginations of those who knew them not. And thus, in the fullness of time, the McComases' circle is definitively closed.

Notes

Chapter 1. A Proper Beginning

1. According to James G. Leyburn, *The Scotch-Irish: A Social History* (Chapel Hill: Univ. of North Carolina Press, 1962), 200: "Two counties in the Valley of Virginia, Augusta and Rockbridge, claim to be the most Scotch-Irish counties in the present United States." He adds, "Telephone books list names beginning with 'Mac' in a separate category from those under 'M'."

2. Mildred Hazelton Rice (granddaughter of H. C. McComas), "McComas Family History," typescript, in McComas Family Papers, in possession of Carolyn Kimme-Smith (daughter of Mildred Hazelton Rice), Los Angeles, California. The collection is cited hereinafter as McComas Family Papers.

3. Leyburn, *Scotch-Irish*, 333; Mildred Rice, "McComas Family History."

4. Mildred Rice, "McComas Family History."

5. Biographical sketch of Elisha Wesley McComas, in William Connelley, *A Standard History of Kansas and Kansans* (Chicago: Lewis Publishing Co., 1918), 3:1346.

6. Mildred Rice, "McComas Family History"; Francis B. Heitman, *Historical Register and Dictionary of the United States Army* (Washington, D.C.: U.S. Government Printing Office, 1903), 1:658.

7. Jun Comstock, ed., *The West Virginia Heritage Encyclopedia* (Richwood, W.Va.: Privately published, 1974), 6:90.

8. Connelley, *Standard History of Kansas*, 3:1346.

9. Biographical sketch of Hamilton Calhoun McComas, in C. E. Cory, "The Osage Ceded Lands," *Transactions of the Kansas State Historical Society* 8 (1904): 191.

10. Edwin E. Sparks, *The Lincoln-Douglas Debates of 1858* (Springfield: Illinois State Historical Library, 1908), 67–68. The Lincoln visit to Monticello is also described in the *Missouri Republican* [St. Louis], Aug. 1, 1858.

11. Mildred Rice, "McComas Family History."

12. *New York Weekly Tribune,* May 28, 1850.

13. Emma C. Piatt, *History of Piatt County, Together with a Brief History of Illinois* (Evansville, Ind.: Privately printed, [ca. 1883]), 243.

14. Allan Nevins, *Ordeal of the Union* (New York: Charles Scribner's Sons, 1947), 2:397.

15. Connelley, *Standard History of Kansas,* 3:1346.

16. Ibid., 3:1347.

17. Franklin William Scott, *Newspapers and Periodicals of Illinois, 1814–1879* (Springfield: Illinois State Historical Library, 1910), 65, 73.

18. Mildred Rice, "McComas Family History"; Connelley, *Standard History of Kansas,* 3:1346.

19. A search of Monticello municipal records failed to produce a McComas marriage certificate. Lisa Winters, Piatt County Historical and Genealogical Society, to Marc Simmons, Cerrillos, N.M., Apr. 15, 1993. But see U.S. Census of Population, 1860, Piatt County, Ill., on file at Piatt County Historical and Genealogical Society, Monticello, Ill.

20. Mildred Rice, "McComas Family History."

21. Otis K. Rice, *West Virginia: A History* (Lexington: Univ. Press of Kentucky, 1985), 114–15.

22. Mildred Rice, "McComas Family History."

23. Muster Papers, in Hamilton C. McComas, Compiled Service Record, Military Branch, National Archives, Washington, D.C.; Piatt, *History of Piatt County,* 196. On the history of the 107th, see State of Illinois, Adjutant General, "Report on Participation of Illinois Men in the War of the Rebellion," vol. 6, on file at Newberry Library, Chicago.

24. Correspondence in H. C. McComas, Compiled Service Record.

25. Allen Johnson, ed., *Dictionary of American Biography* (New York: Charles Scribner's Sons, 1929), 2:532.

26. Letter of Resignation, H. C. McComas, Compiled Service Record.

27. Discharge Papers, H. C. McComas, Compiled Service Record.

28. Letter of Resignation, H. C. McComas, Compiled Service Record.

29. Carolyn Kimme-Smith to Marc Simmons, Cerrillos, N.M., Oct. 25, 1992. The recollections of this descendant are the only information available on the breakup of the McComas marriage. On Louisa McComas's retaining her married name, see *Silver City Enterprise,* Aug. 18, 1892.

30. Kimme-Smith to Simmons, Oct. 25, 1992.

31. Biographical details are drawn from John Boyle, Compiled Service Record, Military Branch, National Archives, Washington, D.C., esp. John Boyle, Declaration for Pension, Jan. 23, 1907. John Boyle, *Boyle Genealogy* (St. Louis: N.p., 1909), *passim* (reference courtesy of Janaloo Hill Hough, Shakespeare, N.M.).

32. Boyle, Declaration for Pension, May 27, 1912, and Boyle, Cover Summary, Bureau of Pensions, Dec. 3, 1904, both in Boyle, Compiled Service Record.

33. Johnson, *Dictionary of American Biography,* 2:532.

34. Boyle, *Boyle Genealogy, passim;* Questionnaire submitted by John Boyle to Bureau of Pensions, Nov. 30, 1904, in Boyle, Compiled Service Record. This questionnaire, coincidentally, is signed by H. C. McComas's brother-in-law, E. F. Ware, then U.S. pension commissioner.

35. Charles McIntosh, *Past and Present of Piatt County, Illinois* (Chicago: S. J. Clarke

Co., 1903), 19–20; Francis Shonkwiler, *Historical Encyclopedia of Illinois and History of Piatt County* (Chicago: Munsell Publishing Co., [ca. 1917]), 642.

36. Mabel E. Richmond et. al., *Centennial History of Decatur and Macon County, 1829–1929* (Decatur, Ill.: Decatur Review, 1930), 109, 151. According to one report, H. C. McComas lived briefly in Decatur in 1860. *Chicago Tribune*, Mar. 28, 1883. For reference to Charles C. McComas in New Mexico, see Victor Westphall, *Thomas Benton Catron and His Era* (Tucson: Univ. of Arizona Press, 1973), 190, 388n.

37. *Southwest Sentinel*, Mar. 31, 1883.

38. Cory, "Osage Ceded Lands," 190.

39. Anna Heloise Abel, "Indian Reservations in Kansas and the Extinguishment of Their Title," *Transactions of the Kansas State Historical Society* 8 (1904): 107–108.

40. Cory, "Osage Ceded Lands," 191.

41. A. T. Andreas, *History of the State of Kansas* (Chicago: Published by the author, 1883), 1072–75.

42. Connelley, *Standard History of Kansas*, 3:1345–46.

43. S. D. Myres, ed., *Pioneer Surveyor, Frontier Lawyer: The Personal Narrative of O. W. Williams, 1877–1902* (El Paso: Texas Western Press, 1968), 145. Reference to the McComas marriage date is found in the *Fort Scott Evening Herald*, Apr. 9, 1883.

44. *Fort Scott Evening Herald*, Mar. 30, 1883.

45. *Fort Scott Monitor*, Oct. 25, 1902.

46. Gracy Lowry, "Life of Eugene Ware" (M.S. thesis, Kansas State Teachers College, Pittsburg, Kans., 1936), 3, 7.

47. Ibid., 4. In the records of the day, Juniata is sometimes spelled with two Ts. Where the family got her unusual name is unclear, but a Juniata River and Juniata County exist in Pennsylvania. The birth date of Mar. 7 is given in the register book in the Evergreen Cemetery, Fort Scott, Kans. The tombstone, however, gives the day of birth as Mar. 4, 1846. At her funeral service, the minister said it was Mar. 8, 1846; see *Fort Scott Daily Monitor*, Apr. 10, 1883. Genealogical information from the Ancestral File (TM-Version 4.11), Latter-Day Saints Church, Salt Lake City, Utah, gives the date as Mar. 4 (reference courtesy of Mel and Mary Cottom). These discrepancies remain unexplained.

48. From a biographical sketch, "Eugene Fitch Ware," in Dan L. Thrapp, *Encyclopedia of Frontier Biography* (Glendale, Calif.: Arthur H. Clark Co., 1988), 3:1512. Eugene Fitch Ware, *The Indian War of 1864* (Topeka, Kans., 1911; reprint, Lincoln: Univ. of Nebraska Press, 1963).

49. Lowry, "Life of Eugene Ware," 31–32.

50. Ibid., 6, 25–27.

51. William E. Connelley, "Acceptance on Behalf of the Historical Society," in *Collections of the Kansas State Historical Society, 1913–1914* 13 (1915): 46.

52. Inventory and Appraisement of the McComas Estate, 1883, Grant County Probate Records, Silver City, N.M.

53. Judson S. West, "Eugene Ware," in *Collections of the Kansas State Historical Society, 1913–1914* 13 (1915): 70.
54. *Fort Scott Daily Monitor,* Apr. 10, 1883.
55. Personal letter, Carolyn Kimme-Smith to Marc Simmons, Cerrillos, N.M., May 29, 1993. For aid in interpreting Juniata McComas's clothing, I am indebted to Janaloo Hill Hough of Shakespeare, N.M.
56. See reference to Jennie McComas in the *Silver City Enterprise,* Aug. 6, 1886. The U.S. Census, 1870, for Bourbon County, Kansas, Microfilm Edition, M593-429, gives "Juney" as the first name of Mrs. McComas. The sound of that is very close to Jennie, the latter perhaps being what friends understood her nickname to be.
57. Connelley, "Acceptance on Behalf of the Historical Society," 46–47.
58. Lowry, "Life of Eugene Ware," 4A.
59. Personal letter, Carolyn Kimme-Smith to Marc Simmons, Cerrillos, N.M., Feb. 27, 1993. The residency of the McComas boys and Roxey Scott is established by the U.S. Census, 1875, Bourbon County, Kansas, Microfilm Edition, K-002, p. 50 (reference courtesy of Mel and Mary Cottom).
60. Information courtesy of Shirley Hurd, Fort Scott, Kans. Frederick's name appears on the grave monument of his parents.
61. Myres, *Pioneer Surveyor,* 206. Birthdays of the children are given in the *Fort Scott Monitor,* Apr. 8, 1883.
62. Biographical sketch of Judge H. C. McComas, *Silver City Enterprise,* Mar. 30, 1883; and *Fort Scott Herald and Record,* Apr. 5, 1883.

Chapter 2. Apaches

1. For an expression of this idea, see Edward H. Spicer, *Cycles of Conquest* (Tucson: Univ. of Arizona Press, 1962), 594.
2. Richard J. Perry, *Western Apache Heritage* (Austin: Univ. of Texas Press, 1991), 164–73, contains a discussion of the raiding complex.
3. Quoted in Morris Opler, *An Apache Life-Way* (Chicago: Univ. of Chicago Press, 1970), 119–20.
4. Jason Betzinez, *I Fought with Geronimo* (Harrisburg, Pa.: Stackpole, 1959), 102. Readers should note that some of Betzinez's statements cannot be corroborated independently.
5. Eve Ball, *In the Days of Victorio* (Tucson: Univ. of Arizona Press, 1970), 119–20.
6. Eve Ball, *Indeh: An Apache Odyssey* (Provo, Utah: Brigham Young Univ. Press, 1980), 58.
7. Ball, *In the Days of Victorio,* 119.
8. Michael E. Melody, *The Apache* (New York: Chelsea House Publishers, 1989), 64. For the period 1820–35, it is reported that 5,000 Mexicans were killed by the Apaches. Perry, *Western Apache Heritage,* 170.

9. Dan L. Thrapp, *General Crook and the Sierra Madre Adventure* (Norman: Univ. of Oklahoma Press, 1972), 117.

10. Ralph A. Smith, "Apache Plunder Trails Southward, 1831–1840," *New Mexico Historical Review* 37 (Jan. 1962): 32. See also Ralph A. Smith, "The Scalp Hunter in the Borderlands, 1835–1850," *Arizona and the West* 5 (Spring 1964): 5–22.

11. Betzinez, *I Fought With Geronimo*, 3.

12. Keith H. Basso, ed., *Western Apache Raiding and Warfare* (Tucson: Univ. of Arizona Press, 1971), 143–44.

13. *Fort Scott Monitor*, Apr. 1, 1883.

14. *Fort Scott Evening Herald*, Mar. 31, 1883.

15. The episode is described in Kenneth L. Holmes, *Ewing Young: Master Trapper* (Portland, Ore.: Binfords & Mort, Publishers, 1967), 26–27.

16. Frederick Russell Burnham, *Scouting on Two Continents* (Garden City, N.Y.: Garden City Publishing Co., 1926), 3.

17. Ball, *In the Days of Victorio*, xiv; Morris E. Opler, "Chiricahua Apache," in *Handbook of North American Indians: Southwest*, ed. Alfonso Ortiz (Washington, D.C.: Smithsonian Institution, 1983), 10:401.

18. Ball, *In the Days of Victorio*, xiv.

19. S. M. Barrett, ed., *Geronimo: His Own Story* (New York: Ballantine Books, 1971), 65–66.

20. Betzinez, *I Fought with Geronimo*, 15.

21. Dan L. Thrapp, *Juh: An Incredible Indian* (El Paso: Texas Western Press, 1973), 6.

22. Betzinez, *I Fought with Geronimo*, 14–17.

23. Melody, *The Apache*, 21.

24. Jason Hook, *Geronimo: Last Renegade of the Apaches* (Dorset, England: Firebird Books, 1989), 6.

25. Nelson A. Miles, *Personal Recollections and Observations of General Nelson A. Miles* (Chicago: Werner Co., 1897), 445.

26. Quoted in Thrapp, *General Crook*, 117.

27. Britton Davis, *The Truth about Geronimo* (New Haven, Conn.: Yale University Press, 1929), 80.

28. Betzinez, *I Fought with Geronimo*, 60.

29. Davis, *Truth about Geronimo*, 80.

30. Richard I. Dodge, *Our Wild Indians* (reprint, New York: Archer House, 1959), 46.

31. Miles, *Personal Recollections*, 447; John G. Bourke, *An Apache Campaign in the Sierra Madre* (New York: Charles Scribner's Sons, 1958), 46.

32. Opler, "Chiricahua Apaches," 411.

33. Basso, *Western Apache*, 253.

34. Kimberly Moore Buchanan, *Apache Women Warriors* (El Paso: Texas Western Press, 1986), 18–24.

35. Basso, *Western Apache*, 253.

36. Interview with Allan Houser, Santa Fe, Mar. 30, 1993. Haozous was about ten years old at the time of Chato's raid. In 1986, his son Allan told *Arizona Highways* (Sept. 1986, p. 10), "My father was forty-six when I was born. And I'm seventy-two now."

37. Davis, *Truth about Geronimo*, 59; Betzinez, *I Fought with Geronimo*, 85, 88.

38. Betzinez, *I Fought with Geronimo*, 77–80, 107.

39. J. P. Dunn, Jr., *Massacres of the Mountains* (reprint, New York: Archer House, n.d.), 310.

40. Miles, *Personal Recollections*, 445.

41. George Novack, *Genocide Against the Indians* (New York: Pathfinder Press, 1988), 20.

42. Dodge, *Our Wild Indians*, 524.

43. Ball, *Indeh*, xviii, 78.

44. Miles, *Personal Recollections*, 445.

45. Burnham, *Scouting on Two Continents*, 53.

46. In other instances, Apaches capturing a pioneer wagon cut off the feet of puppies and left them alive to be discovered by a rescue party; and cut out the tongues of draft oxen. See Dodge, *Our Wild Indians*, 534; Jennie Parks Ringgold, *Frontier Days in the Southwest* (San Antonio: Naylor, 1952), 17.

47. For an example, see *Silver City Enterprise*, June 5, 1885.

48. Ball, *Indeh*, 104.

49. Burnham, *Scouting on Two Continents*, 53.

50. Davis, *Truth about Geronimo*, 116.

51. Opler, *Apache Life-Way*, 343.

52. Jerry D. Thompson, ed., "With the Third Infantry in New Mexico, 1851–1853: The Lost Diary of Private Sylvester W. Matson," *Journal of Arizona History* 31 (Winter 1990): 376.

53. Betzinez, *I Fought with Geronimo*, 67. On women's noses, see Dodge, *Our Wild Indians*, 211. Several photographs were made of Apache females with mutilated noses. For an example, consult H. Henrietta Stockel, *Women of the Apache Nation* (Reno: Univ. of Nevada Press, 1991), 20.

54. A. C. Greene, *The Last Captive* (Austin: Encino Press, 1972), 99.

55. Dan L. Thrapp, ed., *Dateline Fort Bowie: Charles Fletcher Lummis Reports on an Apache War* (Norman: Univ. of Oklahoma Press, 1979), 111.

56. Lieutenant Bascom long has been represented as the villain of this episode. For a discussion that places his actions in a somewhat more favorable light, see Donald E. Worcester, *The Apaches: Eagles of the Southwest* (Norman: Univ. of Oklahoma Press, 1979), 77.

57. Ball, *In the Days of Victorio*, 28.

58. Thomas Cruse, *Apache Days and After* (Lincoln: Univ. of Nebraska Press, 1987), 86.

59. The best study of Old Vic is Dan L. Thrapp, *Victorio and the Mimbres Apaches* (Norman: Univ. of Oklahoma Press, 1974). On Nana, see Stephen H. Lekson,

Nana's Raid (El Paso: Texas Western Press, 1987). The figure of one thousand casualties (disputed by other sources) is given by Cruse, *Apache Days and After,* 86.

60. Dan L. Thrapp, *The Conquest of Apachería* (Norman: Univ. of Oklahoma Press, 1967), 231; Col. H. B. Wharfield, *Cibicue Creek Fight in Arizona,* 1881 (El Cajon, Calif.: Privately printed, 1971), 18–20.

61. Ralph Hedrick Ogle, *Federal Control of the Western Apaches* (Albuquerque: Univ. of New Mexico Press, 1970), 209–10.

62. Thrapp, *Juh,* 26.

63. Betzinez, *I Fought with Geronimo,* 56–57.

64. Thrapp, *Conquest of Apachería,* 239.

65. Betzinez, *I Fought with Geronimo,* 60.

66. James T. King, "George Crook, Indian Fighter and Humanitarian," *Arizona and the West* 9 (Winter 1967): 335; Frank C. Lockwood, *Pioneer Days in Arizona* (New York: Macmillan, 1932), 190.

67. The "hot pursuit accord" is published in *U.S. Statutes at Large,* 22:934., according to a note in Martin F. Schmitt, ed., *General Crook: His Autobiography* (Norman: Univ. of Oklahoma Press, 1946), 246. An official copy, with text in English and Spanish, is included in John G. Bourke, Diary, Library of the U.S. Military Academy, West Point, N.Y., vol. 69. A bound facsimile of the entire diary is in the Library, Univ. of New Mexico, Albuquerque. In his official message to Congress on Dec. 4, 1883, President Chester A. Arthur spoke favorably of the accord, noting that it had resulted in the capture or dispersal of several of the most dangerous bands of Apaches. James D. Richardson, *A Compilation of the Messages and Papers of the Presidents* (Washington, D.C.: U.S. Government Printing Office, 1898), 8:173.

Chapter 3. Silver City

1. J. A. Dacus and James W. Buel, *A Tour of St. Louis; or, The Inside Life of a Great City* (St. Louis, Mo.: Western Publishing Co., 1878), 22, 26–27.

2. *Missouri Republican,* Mar. 30, 1883.

3. *Fort Scott Daily Monitor,* Mar. 30, 1883.

4. Boyle's move to St. Louis is referred to in Boyle, Declaration for Pension, in Boyle, Compiled Service Record, Aug. 19, 1900, Military Branch, National Archives, Washington, D.C.

5. *The Los Angeles Evening Express,* Apr. 23, 1880; Rita Hill and Janaloo Hill, "Alias Shakespeare: The Town Nobody Knew," *New Mexico Historical Review* 42 (July 1967): 220.

6. *Arizona Citizen,* Apr. 11, 1879 (reference courtesy of Janaloo Hill Hough).

7. See, e.g., *Silver City Herald,* Apr. 5, 1879, wherein it is stated that "the Colonel is not disposed to be communicative in regards to his purposes and movements."

8. Rita Hill, *Then and Now: Here and Around Shakespeare* (Lordsburg, N.M.: Privately printed, 1963), 13.

9. Ibid., 14.

10. Charles van Ravenswaay, *St. Louis: An Informal History of the City and Its People, 1764 to 1865* (St. Louis: Missouri Historical Society Press, 1991), 529–30; *Missouri Republican*, Mar. 30, 1883. A story in the *Grant County (N.M.) Herald*, Jan. 3, 1880, on the mining prospects at Shakespeare, states: "Ex-governor B. Gratz Brown of Missouri has purchased a half interest in the Wide West, Silver Bell, Salero, and Golden Gate [mines], agreeing to place them all in dividend paying condition."

11. Janaloo Hill, *The Ranch on Whitewater Creek* (Silver City, N.M.: Privately printed, 1984), 12, states specifically that McComas came to New Mexico to perform legal work for the Shakespeare Mining Co.

12. *Grant County Herald*, Mar. 20, 1880, noted the arrival in Silver City of H. C. McComas on his way to Shakespeare with a St. Louis party "who own large mining interests" there. The same paper, Apr. 3, 1880, mentioned that the Boyle party left St. Louis for Shakespeare on Mar. 28.

13. Joseph A. Stout, Jr., *Apache Lightning: The Last Great Battles of the Ojos Calientes* (New York: Oxford Univ. Press, 1974), 195.

14. James E. Sherman and Barbara H. Sherman, *Ghost Towns and Mining Camps of New Mexico* (Norman: Univ. of Oklahoma Press, 1974), 195.

15. *San Francisco Post*, Apr. 22, 1878.

16. The *Grant County Herald* of Silver City, N.M., May 1, 1880, printed the first rumor of Col. William G. Boyle's death.

17. H. C. McComas to Mary McComas, Shakespeare, N.M., Apr. 16, 1880, in McComas Family Papers.

18. *Chicago Tribune*, Mar. 31, 1883. Oscar W. Williams, who met McComas soon after his arrival, mentioned that the judge had been ailing. Myres, *Pioneer Surveyor*, 206.

19. A good discussion of health seekers, as the phenomenon relates to St. Louis business and professional men, is provided by Barton H. Barbour, *Reluctant Frontiersman: James Ross Larkin on the Santa Fe Trail, 1856–1857* (Albuquerque: Univ. of New Mexico Press, 1990), 45–51.

20. *Missouri Republican*, Mar. 20, 1883.

21. Mildred Rice, "McComas Family History." The mine purchase is referred to in the *Missouri Republican*, Mar. 30, 1883.

22. On Elkins, see Adrienne Christopher, "The Life of Stephen Benton Elkins," *Westport Historical Quarterly* 4 (Dec. 1968): 28–32. For Catron, the standard source is Westphall, *Thomas Benton Catron*. Elkins's biography fails to place him in Nebraska City, Nebraska, but notes that his mother died there in 1866. Oscar Doane Lambert, *Stephen Benton Elkins: American Foursquare* (Pittsburgh, Pa.: Univ. of Pittsburgh Press, 1955), note on p. 3.

23. Rita Hill and Janaloo Hill, "Alias Shakespeare," 218.

24. The letter is preserved in the McComas Family Papers. It is addressed to 2312 Chestnut Street, St. Louis. As noted earlier, the U.S. Census, 1880, gave the

McComas residence as being on Cass Street. One possibility is that the family was staying with friends while the judge was absent in New Mexico.

25. Myres, *Pioneer Surveyor,* 179–80.

26. Ibid., 124–25, 145.

27. Ibid.

28. Quoted in Conrad K. Naegle, "The Rebellion in Grant County, New Mexico, in 1876," *Arizona and the West* 10 (Autumn 1968): 226.

29. Dorothy Watson, *The Pinos Altos Story* (Silver City, N.M.: *The Enterprise,* 1960), 5–6.

30. R. S. Allen, "Pinos Altos, New Mexico," *New Mexico Historical Review* 23 (Oct. 1948): 305–306.

31. Watson, *Pinos Altos Story,* 13.

32. Helen Lundwall et al., *This Is Silver City* (Silver City, N.M.: Privately printed, 1970), 1.

33. Elliott Gillerman, *Mineral Deposits of Western Grant County New Mexico,* Bulletin 83 (Socorro, N.M.: New Mexico Institute of Mining and Technology, 1964), 1; Susan Berry and Sharman Apt Russell, *Built to Last: An Architectural History of Silver City, New Mexico* (Silver City, N.M.: Silver City Museum, 1986), 10.

34. This positive characterization is explicitly set forth in the *Las Cruces Borderer,* Mar. 30, 1871.

35. Paul Wellman, *Death in the Desert* (New York: Macmillan, 1935), 95.

36. Letter from Eugene F. Ware, published in the *Fort Scott Daily Monitor,* Apr. 8, 1883.

37. Berry and Russell, *Built to Last,* 10–11; *New Southwest and Grant County Herald,* May 6, 1882.

38. Berry and Russell, *Built to Last,* 13–14.

39. Patti Unger, ed., *True Tales* (Silver City, N.M.: Sun Dog Publishing, 1991), 50.

40. *Grant County Herald,* July 19, 1880.

41. *Silver City Enterprise,* May 28, 1886, reported: "Gen. Lew Wallace and his son are now at their mine near Stein's Pass. They will take out five carloads of ore and will ship to Kansas City."

42. Lew Wallace, *An Autobiography* (New York: Harper and Brothers, 1906), 2:919.

43. *Grant County Herald,* as early as July 10, announced the coming of the governor.

44. *Grant County Herald,* July 25, 1880.

45. Letter in McComas Family Papers.

46. Myres, *Pioneer Surveyor,* 206.

47. Examples of the stock certificates are located in McComas File, Grant County Probate Records, Silver City, N.M.

48. Other references to McComas and his Arizona mine are in *Grant County Herald,* Feb. 4 and Nov. 5, 1881.

49. Eugene Carter Anderson, *The Metal Resources of New Mexico and Their Economic Features Through 1954,* Bulletin 39 (Socorro, N.M.: State Bureau of Mines and Mineral Resources, 1957), 98.

50. Refer to stock certificates in McComas File, Grant County Probate Records, Silver City, N. M.

51. Myres, *Pioneer Surveyor*, 199.

52. Letter in McComas Family Papers.

53. *Grant County Herald*, May 8, 1880.

Chapter 4. Prelude to Disaster

1. *New Southwest and Grant County Herald*, Sept. 3, 1881.

2. James H. Cook, *Fifty Years on the Old Frontier* (New Haven, Conn.: Yale Univ. Press, 1923), 163.

3. Ibid., 163–64.

4. Dale F. Giese, *Echoes of the Bugle* (Silver City, N.M.: Phelps Dodge Corp., 1976), 16–18; Robert W. Frazer, *Forts of the West* (Norman: Univ. of Oklahoma Press, 1965), 95–98.

5. *Prescott [Ariz.] Courier*, Apr. 1, 1882.

6. *New Southwest and Grant County Herald*, May 13, 1882.

7. Cruse, *Apache Days and After*, 185.

8. Quoted in Lockwood, *Pioneer Days in Arizona*, 190.

9. Ibid., 190.

10. Bourke, *Apache Campaign*, 51.

11. Hook, *Geronimo*, 33.

12. The stock term "Crook's Pets" or even "Uncle Sam's Pets" was used frequently by the territorial press. *Silver City Enterprise*, Mar. 30, 1883. See also Thomas B. Dunlay, *Wolves for the Blue Soldiers: Indian Scouts and Auxiliaries with the United States Army, 1860–1890* (Lincoln: Univ. of Nebraska Press, 1982), 65–66.

13. Cruse, *Apache Days and After*, 64.

14. Burnham, *Scouting on Two Continents*, 54.

15. Davis, *Truth about Geronimo*, 27.

16. Rules of militia service appear in the *New Southwest and Grant County Herald*, May 6, 1882.

17. Emma M. Muir, "The First Militia," *New Mexico Magazine* 30 (Oct. 1952): 19. See also Myres, *Pioneer Surveyor*, n. 100, p. 172.

18. C. B. Phillips, Shakespeare, N.M., to Gov. Lionel Sheldon, Santa Fe, Apr. 2, 1883, Territorial Archives of New Mexico, roll 99, frame 599, New Mexico State Records Center and Archive, Santa Fe.

19. Ralph E. Twitchell, *The Leading Facts of New Mexican History* (Cedar Rapids, Iowa: Torch Press, 1917), 3:254.

20. Susan Nelson and David Nelson, eds., *The Silver City Book* (Silver City, N.M.: Silver Star Publishers, 1978), 14–15.

21. Helen J. Lundwall, ed., *Pioneering in Territorial Silver City* (Albuquerque: Univ. of New Mexico Press, 1983), 177.

22. Berry and Russell, *Built to Last*, 85.

23. *New Southwest and Grant County Herald,* June 12, 1880. The same paper reported on June 5, 1880, that "J. P. Risque is improving his property on Bullard Street." The reference seems to be to his law office.

24. Myres, *Pioneer Surveyor,* 198–99.

25. Jay J. Wagoner, *Arizona Territory, 1863–1912* (Tucson: Univ. of Arizona Press, 1970), 149.

26. Betzinez, *I Fought with Geronimo,* 60.

27. Thrapp, *Conquest of Apachería,* 237.

28. A detailed account of the attack upon the Risque party appears in the *New Southwest and Grant County Herald,* Apr. 29, 1882. A summary of the incident, with added details, is given in Thrapp, *Conquest of Apachería,* 238.

29. Myres, *Pioneer Surveyor,* 198.

30. *Santa Fe Daily New Mexican,* May 4, 1882.

31. *New Southwest and Grant County Herald,* May 6, 1882. Upon Risque's death, his partner, Thomas F. Conway, closed out their Santa Fe business and moved to Silver City to occupy the vacant office there. Lundwall, *Pioneering in Territorial Silver City,* 177.

32. Inventory of the Property of Hamilton C. McComas, Grant County Probate Records, Silver City, N.M. At the time of McComas's death, the syndicate still owed him half of the fee.

33. *New Southwest and Grant County Herald,* May 6, 1882.

34. *Silver City Enterprise,* Jan. 11, 1883.

35. Background on Wright is gleaned from these issues of the *Silver City Enterprise:* Jan. 11, 1883; Oct. 15 and Dec. 24, 1886.

36. Documents related to the Smith & Keating claim are available in McComas File, Grant County Probate Records, Silver City, N.M.

37. The McComas family's stay in the Exchange Hotel (or Timmer House) was referred to by daughter Ada McComas when she returned to the town for a visit in 1945. *Silver City Enterprise,* Sept. 27, 1945.

38. Conrad Keeler Naegle, "The History of Silver City, New Mexico, 1870–1886" (M.A. thesis, Univ. of New Mexico, 1943), 4.

39. *Silver City Enterprise,* Feb. 22, 1883.

40. Naegle, "History of Silver City," 152, 167, 170–72.

41. The purchase date is recorded in property deeds, of which copies are located in the Silver City Museum, Silver City, N.M. Grant County Tax Assessment records show that, at the time of his death, McComas in addition owned two vacant city lots with a combined value of $12.

42. Inventory of the Property of Hamilton C. McComas, Grant County Probate Records, Silver City, N. M.

43. *Silver City Enterprise,* Mar. 30, 1883.

44. Myres, *Pioneer Surveyor,* 199.

45. *Southwest Sentinel,* Sept. 8, 1883. On Lucas's arrival in Silver City, see *Southwest and Grant County Herald,* Apr. 1, 1882. Also consult Richard Rudisill, comp.,

Photographers of New Mexico Territory, 1854–1912 (Santa Fe: Museum of New Mexico, 1973), 40.

46. *Silver City Enterprise,* Mar. 28, 1884, and May 14, 1886.

47. The letter is printed in full in *Fort Scott Monitor,* Apr. 8, 1883.

48. *Silver City Enterprise,* Feb. 15 and July 4, 1884.

49. Juniata's letters home and the photographs are referred to briefly in *Fort Scott Monitor,* Mar. 30, 1883.

50. A copy of this photo in the Arizona Historical Society Archives, Tucson, identifies the woman at the far right as Juniata McComas. An examination of the evidence, however, leads me to believe that Juniata is the woman closest to the judge.

51. *Silver City Enterprise,* Feb. 22, 1883.

52. Ibid.

53. James E. Sherman and Barbara H. Sherman, *Ghost Towns,* 170; *Southwest Sentinel,* Mar. 31, 1883.

54. *Silver City Enterprise,* Feb. 22, 1883.

55. Unger, *True Tales,* 80.

56. *Silver City Enterprise,* Feb. 22, 1883.

57. *Southwest Sentinel,* Mar. 31, 1883.

Chapter 5. The Raid

1. Betzinez, *I Fought with Geronimo,* 77, 102.

2. Bourke, *Apache Campaign,* 32.

3. Betzinez, *I Fought with Geronimo,* 84.

4. Thrapp, *Conquest of Apachería,* 263.

5. Betzinez, *I Fought with Geronimo,* 78.

6. Ibid., 80.

7. Ball, *Indeh,* 50–51.

8. See, e.g., statements by contemporary observers: Anton Mazzanovich, *Trailing Geronimo,* 3rd ed. (Hollywood, Calif.: Privately printed, 1931), 235; and the captured Apache, Tzoe (Peaches), in Thrapp, *Conquest of Apachería,* 272. Both assign leadership to Chato.

9. A Wilcox letter, with such a reference, was published in *Tombstone (Ariz.) Republican,* Mar. 29, 1883. See also *Arizona Daily Star,* Mar. 25, 1883. *Southwest Sentinel,* Apr. 7, 1883, spoke of Juh, even that late, as head of the raiders.

10. Wellman, *Death in the Desert,* 207.

11. Eve Ball, "The Apache Scouts: A Chiricahua Appraisal," *Arizona and the West* 7 (Winter 1965): 320n.

12. Ball, *Indeh,* 50.

13. H. W. Daly, "The Geronimo Campaign," *Arizona Historical Review* 3 (July 1930): 36. Betzinez goes into detail regarding rivalries among chiefs. See Betzinez, *I Fought with Geronimo,* 67.

14. Betzinez, *I Fought with Geronimo,* 102.

15. Frank C. Lockwood, *The Apache Indians,* (reprint, Lincoln: Univ. of Nebraska Press, 1987), 243.

16. Davis, *Truth about Geronimo,* 71–72; Thrapp, *Conquest of Apachería,* 273. Mangus's participation in the raid is reported in Wellman, *Death in the Desert,* 237.

17. Daly, "Geronimo Campaign," 28. Dutchy's presence on the Chato raid is confirmed in *Southwest Sentinel,* May 9, 1883.

18. Worcester, *The Apaches,* 284.

19. Davis, *Truth about Geronimo,* 58.

20. Bourke, *Apache Campaign,* 52–53.

21. Peaches asserted that he had been forced against his will to go with his wife to Mexico. Worcester, *The Apaches,* 269. According to him, the name *Beneactiney* in Apache meant "the Crazy Man." Bourke, Diary, 68:22.

22. Betzinez, *I Fought with Geronimo,* 107.

23. Woodrow B. Skinner, *As The Apache Rock Crumbles* (Pensacola, Fla.: Skinner Publications, 1987), 34.

24. *Arizona Daily Star,* Mar. 27 and 30, 1883.

25. Mazzanovich, *Trailing Geronimo,* 239; *Silver City Enterprise,* July 6, 1883.

26. Testimony of Peaches, as recorded in Bourke, Diary, 68:21.

27. *Tucson Daily Star,* Mar. 27, 1883.

28. Cruse, *Apache Days and After,* 185.

29. Davis, *Truth about Geronimo,* 56.

30. Undated news clipping from Bourke, Diary, 67:77.

31. *Tombstone Republican,* Mar. 28, 1883.

32. Thrapp, *Dateline Fort Bowie,* 102.

33. Davis, *Truth about Geronimo,* 56.

34. *Tombstone Republican,* Mar. 27 and 29, 1883; *Las Vegas (N.M.) Daily Gazette,* Mar. 25, 1883.

35. *Arizona Daily Star,* Mar. 24, 1883; Bourke, Diary, 68:22.

36. Thrapp, *Conquest of Apachería,* 267–68.

37. *Arizona Daily Star,* Mar. 24, 1883; Bourke, Diary, 68:22.

38. Cornelius C. Smith, Jr., *Fort Huachuca: The Story of a Frontier Post* (Washington, D.C.: U.S. Government Printing Office, 1981), 38.

39. *Arizona Daily Star,* Mar. 25 and 30, 1883.

40. The slayings in and near the Whetstones are described in *Arizona Daily Star,* Mar. 25 and 28, 1883; and in *Las Vegas (N.M.) Gazette,* Mar. 25, 1883.

41. *Arizona Daily Star,* Mar. 30, 1883.

42. Bourke, Diary, 68:22; *Arizona Daily Star,* Mar. 30, 1883; Lockwood, *Apache Indians,* 264.

43. Full text of the extensive letter is preserved in Bourke, Diary, 68:5–7.

44. *Tucson Daily Star,* Apr. 5, 1883.

45. *New York Herald,* Mar. 29, 1883.

46. *Prescott (Ariz.) Courier,* Apr. 2, 1883.

47. Bourke, Diary, 67:89.

48. *New York Times,* Apr. 1, 1883.

49. *Arizona Daily Star,* Mar. 28, 1883.

50. *Tombstone Epitaph,* 2 Mar. 25, 1883.

51. *Tombstone Republican,* Apr. 5, 1883.

52. For an account of some of the American deaths, see *Tombstone Republican,* Mar. 27, 1883.

53. The dispatch from Sonora was printed in *Santa Fe Daily New Mexican,* Apr. 1, 1883, as well as other southwestern newspapers.

54. *Arizona Daily Star,* Mar. 28, 1883; *Silver City Enterprise,* Mar. 30, 1883.

55. *Tombstone Republican,* Mar. 27, 1883; *Arizona Daily Star,* Mar. 24, 1883.

56. *Southwest Sentinel,* Apr. 14, 1883; *Arizona Daily Star,* Apr. 4, 1883.

57. Betzinez, *I Fought with Geronimo,* 103–107.

58. *San Francisco Chronicle,* Apr. 12, 1883.

59. Bourke, Diary, 68:22.

60. *Arizona Daily Star,* Mar. 30, 1883; *Southwest Sentinel,* Mar. 31, 1883.

61. Bourke, Diary, 68:22; Edwin R. Sweeney, *Merejildo Grijalva: Apache Captive, Army Scout* (El Paso: Texas Western Press, 1992), 60.

62. On the scattering of the war party, see Thrapp, *Dateline Fort Bowie,* 101; Lockwood, *Apache Indians,* 264.

63. Betzinez, *I Fought with Geronimo,* 116–17.

64. Peaches' testimony is found in Bourke, Diary, 68:25.

65. *Southwest Sentinel,* Apr. 4, 1883.

66. *Southwest Sentinel,* Mar. 30, 1883.

67. *Santa Fe New Mexican,* Apr. 1, 1883. The same paper, Mar. 30, 1883, referred to York's death as occurring in Oct. 1881, when he led a party across the New Mexico line in pursuit of hostiles, and he and a man named Moore were killed.

68. *Silver City Enterprise,* Mar. 30, 1883; *Southwest Sentinel,* Mar. 31, 1883.

69. *Arizona Daily Star,* Mar. 31, 1883; *Southwest Sentinel,* Mar. 31, 1883.

Chapter 6. The Massacre

1. Of this telegram, *Albuquerque Review,* Apr. 5, 1883, noted that "Judge McComas had been sent for by a mining Company to go to Pyramid City in a professional capacity." Eugene F. Ware, in a letter published in *Fort Scott Daily Monitor,* Apr. 8, 1883, said only that "Judge McComas received a telegram on Monday from Lordsburg."

2. The Rufus McComas quotation was carried in *St. Louis Daily Globe–Democrat,* Apr. 8, 1883. Juniata's brother, Eugene F. Ware, said that she desired to accompany her husband to enjoy the trip. *Fort Scott Daily Monitor,* Apr. 8, 1883. See also Mazzanovich, *Trailing Geronimo,* 234.

3. Mrs. Harry Lucas to Charles Ware, letter printed in *Fort Scott Daily Monitor,* Apr. 8, 1883. According to a family tradition, Ada and Mary were left at home to

practice the piano for a coming recital. Jean Ware Nelson to Marc Simmons, Cerrillos, N.M., Jan. 29, 1996.

4. The judge's telegram is referred to in both *St. Louis Post-Dispatch*, Mar. 30, 1883, and *Arizona Daily Star*, Mar. 30, 1883. The document concerning his buckboard rental is contained in McComas File, Grant County Probate Records, Silver City, N.M. On the Stock Exchange Corral's practice of delivering rental vehicles, see *Las Vegas Daily Gazette*, May 4, 1883.

5. The willow basket, clothes, and rainwear are listed in Indian Depredation Claim, no. 7473, U.S. Court of Claims, Apr. 29, 1892, copy in McComas Family Papers.

6. Physical data on Charley from his reward circular, in McComas Family Papers.

7. Cruse, *Apache Days and After*, 185.

8. Myres, *Pioneer Surveyor*, 204.

9. Ibid., 131.

10. *St. Louis Daily Globe–Democrat*, Apr. 1, 1883.

11. For an editorial comment justifying the warning, see *Southwest Sentinel*, Apr. 4, 1883.

12. *Missouri Republican*, Mar. 30, 1883. The judge's rashness was the principal cause of the tragedy, according to his brother-in-law, Eugene F. Ware. Jean Ware Nelson (granddaughter) to Marc Simmons, Cerrillos, N.M., Jan. 29, 1996.

13. Heitman, *Historical Register*, 2:958.

14. Capt. William Alexis Thompson, Report to Post Adjutant, Fort Bayard, N.M., Aug. 13, 1883; in Letters Received by Headquarters, District of New Mexico, Sept. 1865–Aug. 1890, National Archives Microfilm Publication, Reel 52. On Julius Caesar Brock, see short biographical sketch in *Historical Encyclopedia of New Mexico* (Albuquerque: New Mexico Historical Association, 1942), 2:1437; and Elliott West, *Growing Up with the Country* (Albuquerque: Univ. of New Mexico Press, 1989), 23–24. Brock's stepfather was Jack Yeamans (or Yamens), formerly the post sutler at Fort Selden, N.M. Many years later, Brock claimed that Captain Thompson sent him to warn the settlers, but the officer's report, a contemporary document, makes no reference to that.

15. The raiders' change of course is outlined in *St. Louis Daily Globe–Democrat*, Apr. 1, 1883. Reports in *Southwest Sentinel*, Mar. 31, 1883, establish that the Apaches were headed toward Burro Springs.

16. *Southwest Sentinel*, Apr. 4, 1883, claimed that Captain Thompson missed discovering the Indian trail running between the Gila and Burro Springs because of darkness.

17. "Statement of H. E. Muse," 1928, typescript on file in Old-Timers' Recollections, Silver City Museum, Silver City, N.M. On Paschal, see James E. Sherman and Barbara H. Sherman, *Ghost Towns*, 169.

18. Hill, *Ranch on Whitewater Creek*, 9. Personal information on Dennis and his family appears in U.S. Census, 1880, Grant County, N.M., Microfilm Edition, Roll no. 802.

19. Deputy Sheriff Muse mentioned Moore, leading to this conclusion; "Statement of H. E. Muse."

20. Ringgold, *Frontier Days in the Southwest*, 69.

21. The McComas encounter with the stage is referred to in *Albuquerque Review*, Apr. 5, 1883. The clipping was pasted in Bourke, Diary, 67:92.

22. Mazzanovich, *Trailing Geronimo*, 235.

23. *St. Louis Daily Globe–Democrat*, Apr. 1, 1883.

24. *Albuquerque Review*, Apr. 5, 1883. Some of the first newspaper reports of the murders listed only four wounds for the judge. See, e.g., wire dispatch in *Fort Scott Daily Monitor*, Mar. 31, 1883.

25. *Albuquerque Review*, Apr. 5, 1883. Deputy U.S. Marshal S. L. Sanders is the source for the off-wheeler being the one killed. *Arizona Daily Citizen*, Feb. 22, 1890.

26. Basso, *Western Apache*, 312.

27. Bonito afterward made a statement about his seizure of Charley McComas that was published in *Silver City Enterprise*, Nov. 30, 1883. Speculation at the time that Juniata had taken Charley in her arms and attempted to run with him seems unwarranted, as he weighed 75 lbs. That suggestion appears in *St. Louis Daily Globe–Democrat*, Apr. 8, 1883; and in Mazzanovich, *Trailing Geronimo*, 236. Ball, "Apache Scouts," 322, mentions Bonito tying Charley to his belt.

28. Bourke, Diary, 68:24.

29. Reference to the articles stolen and the condition of the bodies can be found in Indian Depredation Claim, copy in McComas Family Papers; and in *Albuquerque Review*, Apr. 5, 1883.

30. See *St. Louis Post-Dispatch*, Mar. 30, 1883, for an early reference that the McComases "were murdered and scalped." Jennie Parks Ringgold, in her recollections of the tragedy, states that both McComases were "horribly mutilated"; Ringgold, *Frontier Days in the Southwest*, 70. Emma M. Muir, who was a child at Shakespeare in 1883, wrote in 1952 that, "The bodies of the Judge and his wife were mutilated"; Muir, "First Militia," 44. See Horatio O. Ladd, *The Story of New Mexico* (Boston: D. Lothrop Co., 1891), 371.

31. *Albuquerque Review*, Apr. 5, 1883. Mazzanovich, *Trailing Geronimo*, 236, suggests that time was not taken for mutilation "because the assault was made upon a well-traveled highway, where discovery was imminent at any moment."

32. *Santa Fe Daily New Mexican*, Mar. 30, 1883.

33. *Fort Scott Daily Monitor*, Apr. 8, 1883; *St. Louis Daily Globe–Democrat*, Apr. 8, 1883. For Daklugie's words, see Ball, *Indeh*, 51.

34. *Arizona Daily Star*, Mar. 30, 1883.

35. Dodge, *Our Wild Indians*, 529–30. In fact, instances did exist of white captives' not being raped. For example, Mary Fletcher, captured by Cheyennes in 1865, claimed good treatment and, upon rescue, made no mention of sexual abuse. George E. Hyde, *Life of George Bent* (Norman: Univ. of Oklahoma Press, 1967), 251.

36. *Courier*, Apr. 1, 1883; *Enterprise*, July 3, 1885.

37. *Arizona Enterprise*, Feb. 22, 1890.

38. A written statement by John Moore was published in *Southwest Sentinel*, Mar. 31, 1883.

39. The figure of 45 minutes is given in *Las Vegas Daily Gazette*, Mar. 30, 1883.

40. Julius Caesar Brock, Tapes and Transcripts (1952), ed. Lou Bachley, in Pioneer Foundation Collection, Library, Univ. of New Mexico, Albuquerque. While this is the principal source for Brock's experience, some additional details can be found in Doug Dinwiddie, "The McComas Massacre Retold," *Silver City Enterprise*, Mar. 31, 1983, an issue published to commemorate the 100th anniversary of the event and containing the comments of Harry McCauley, Brock's son-in-law. Also see an undated (ca. 1953) news clipping in McComas File, Public Library, Silver City, N.M. Janaloo Hill, interviewed by Marc Simmons, Shakespeare, N.M., Feb. 6, 1993, clarified several points about Brock's story; she knew him. Brief mention of Brock's encounter with the two Apache scouts appeared in *Las Vegas Daily Gazette*, Mar. 30, 1883, and *Southwest Sentinel*, Mar. 31, 1883.

41. On this, see *Tombstone Republican*, Mar. 29, 1883.

42. *Silver City Enterprise*, Apr. 13, 1883.

43. *Albuquerque Review*, Apr. 5, 1883.

44. The comments of Rufus McComas were published in *Fort Scott Daily Monitor*, Apr. 8, 1883, and *St. Louis Daily Globe–Democrat*, Apr. 8, 1883.

45. Ringgold, *Frontier Days in the Southwest*, 45.

46. The letter from Mrs. Lucas, published in *Fort Scott Daily Monitor*, Apr. 8, 1883, gives the time of Moore's late arrival at the Mountain Home.

47. The text of the Nickerson message is published in *Southwest Sentinel*, Mar. 31, 1883.

48. "Statement of H. E. Muse."

49. *Silver City Enterprise*, Mar. 30, 1883; *Albuquerque Review*, Apr. 5, 1883. Eugene Ware, in a letter published in *Fort Scott Daily Monitor*, Apr. 8, 1883, described the judge as having been riddled with bullets.

50. Mazzanovich, *Trailing Geronimo*, 235.

51. On the mile-wide search for Charley, see *Silver City Enterprise*, Mar. 30, 1883.

52. The smoke signal is mentioned in *Silver City Enterprise*, Mar. 30, 1883.

53. Janaloo Hill, *Ranch on Whitewater Creek*, 15; Dinwiddie, "McComas Massacre Retold."

Chapter 7. The Pursuit

1. Ringgold, *Frontier Days in the Southwest*, 70.

2. *St. Louis Daily Globe–Democrat*, Apr. 1, 1883.

3. *Arizona Weekly Citizen*, Apr. 8, 1883; *St. Louis Daily Globe–Democrat*, Mar. 31 and Apr. 1, 1883.

4. *El Paso Times*, Mar. 31, 1883; *Santa Fe Daily New Mexican*, Mar. 31, 1883.

5. Quotation from *St. Louis Daily Globe–Democrat*, Apr. 1, 1883, which contains a full account of the attack upon Devine and Anderson. The same paper on

Apr. 6 refers to the theft of 11 bottles of whiskey. See also *Denver Tribune*, Apr. 3, 1883; *Santa Fe Daily New Mexican*, Apr. 3, 1883.

6. George A. Forsyth, *Thrilling Days in Army Life* (New York: Harper, 1900): 79–86; for a biography, see David Dixon, *Hero of Beecher Island: The Life and Military Career of George A. Forsyth* (Lincoln: Univ. of Nebraska Press, 1994).

7. *Silver City Enterprise*, Mar. 30, 1883.

8. *Silver City Enterprise*, Apr. 6, 1883.

9. Ringgold, *Frontier Days in the Southwest*, 70.

10. William Alexis Thompson, Report to Post Adjutant; *St. Louis Daily Globe–Democrat*, Mar. 31, 1883.

11. *St. Louis Daily Globe–Democrat*, Apr. 6, 1883.

12. *Silver City Enterprise*, Mar. 30, 1883.

13. Mazzanovich, *Trailing Geronimo*, 237.

14. *St. Louis Daily Globe–Democrat*, Mar. 31, 1883.

15. Janaloo Hill, *Ranch on Whitewater Creek*, 16, identifies James Black as a saloon keeper. For references to his bravery and lack of Indian-fighting experience, see *Arizona Weekly Citizen*, Apr. 8, 1883. Mazzanovich, *Trailing Geronimo*, 237–38, provides the names of 19 regular Guards in the expedition (from Lordsburg, Shakespeare, and Pyramid City) and indicates that the remaining members were volunteers. He also says that two more Lordsburg men joined the party later, near the Animas Mountains. Black's figure of 26 men appears in James Black, Report to the [Territorial] Adjutant General, Apr. 10, 1883, Territorial Archives of New Mexico, Santa Fe, Roll 72, Frame 87.

16. Black, Report to Adjutant General.

17. William Alexis Thompson, Report to Post Adjutant.

18. Ibid.; *St. Louis Daily Globe–Democrat*, Apr. 6, 1883; *Santa Fe Daily New Mexican*, Apr. 3, 1883.

19. Black, Report to Adjutant General.

20. Ibid.

21. *Silver City Enterprise*, Apr. 20, 1883.

22. *Santa Fe Daily New Mexican*, Mar. 31, 1883.

23. *Southwest Sentinel*, Apr. 4, 1883.

24. For examples of this report, see *Denver Tribune* and *Arizona Daily Star*, both Apr. 3, 1883.

25. Lockwood, *Apache Indians*, 264.

26. Bourke, Diary, 68:24.

27. Betzinez, *I Fought with Geronimo*, 107.

28. *Arizona Daily Star*, Mar. 28, 1883; *Tombstone Republican*, Mar. 28, 1883. For background on Mackenzie as New Mexico's district commander, see Michael D. Pierce, *The Most Promising Young Officer: A Life of Ranald Slidell Mackenzie* (Norman: Univ. of Oklahoma Press, 1993), 214–19.

29. *Albuquerque Review*, Apr. 4, 1883.

30. The complete telegram is published in Thrapp, *Dateline Fort Bowie*, 103.

31. *St. Louis Daily Globe–Democrat,* Apr. 8, 1883.
32. Davis, *Truth about Geronimo,* 57.
33. Bourke, Diary, 67:67. Crook's arrival time in Willcox is mentioned in *St. Louis Daily Globe–Democrat,* Apr. 8, 1883.
34. Thrapp, *General Crook,* 123.
35. Ball, *Indeh,* 51.
36. *Southwest Sentinel,* Apr. 21, 1883.
37. Thrapp, *General Crook,* 123.
38. *St. Louis Daily Globe–Democrat,* Mar. 31 and Apr. 5, 1883.
39. Bourke, Diary, 68:65.
40. Bourke, *Apache Campaign,* 34.
41. Joseph C. Porter, *Paper Medicine Man: John Gregory Bourke and His American West* (Norman: Univ. of Oklahoma Press, 1986), 152; *Las Vegas Daily Gazette,* Apr. 17, 1883.
42. *El Paso Times,* Apr. 17, 1883.
43. Bourke, *Apache Campaign,* 33.
44. *Arizona Daily Citizen,* undated clipping (ca. Apr. 7, 1883) in Bourke, Diary, 68:18–19.
45. John G. Bourke, *On the Border With Crook* (New York: Charles Scribner's Sons, 1891), 453. The most thorough accounts of the Crook expedition are found in Bourke, *Apache Campaign,* and Thrapp, *General Crook.*
46. *Las Vegas Daily Gazette,* May 26, 1883.

Chapter 8. "Universal Grief and Indignation"

1. *Fort Scott Evening Herald,* Mar. 29, 1883.
2. *Fort Scott Daily Monitor,* Mar. 30, 1883.
3. See, e.g., *St. Louis Daily Globe–Democrat,* Mar. 30, 1883.
4. *Fort Scott Daily Monitor,* Mar. 30, 1883.
5. *St. Louis Daily Globe–Democrat,* Mar. 31, 1883.
6. *Fort Scott Evening Herald,* Apr. 5, 1883.
7. *Fort Scott Daily Monitor,* Mar. 31, 1883.
8. *Fort Scott Banner,* Apr. 5, 1883; *Santa Fe Daily New Mexican,* Apr. 3, 1883; *Fort Scott Daily Monitor,* Apr. 8, 1883.
9. *Silver City Enterprise,* Mar. 30, 1883.
10. *Southwest Sentinel,* Mar. 31, 1883.
11. *Silver City Enterprise,* Apr. 16, 1885.
12. *Southwest Sentinel,* Apr. 4, 1883; *Silver City Enterprise,* Apr. 16, 1885. The full text of the funeral sermon was published in *Southwest Sentinel,* Apr. 7, 1883.
13. The full text of the municipal resolutions of condolence appears in *Silver City Enterprise,* Apr. 16, 1883.
14. *Southwest Sentinel,* Mar. 31, 1883.
15. *Fort Scott Daily Monitor,* Apr. 8, 1883.

16. Gov. George W. Glick, Topeka, to Eugene F. Ware, May 5, 1883, in Eugene Fitch Ware Papers, Abby Ware Nies Collection, Kansas State Historical Society, Topeka.

17. *Silver City Enterprise,* Apr. 4, 1883.

18. *Southwest Sentinel,* Mar. 31, 1883.

19. *Missouri Republican,* Mar. 31, 1883.

20. Quoted in *Missouri Republican,* Mar. 30, 1883.

21. *St. Louis Post-Dispatch,* Mar. 30, 1883.

22. *Denver Republican,* Mar. 29, 1883; *St. Louis Post-Dispatch,* Mar. 30, 1883; and *New York Times,* Mar. 30, 1883.

23. *St. Louis Daily Globe–Democrat,* Mar. 31, 1883.

24. Eugene Ware to unnamed friends, n.d., printed in *Southwest Sentinel,* Apr. 25, 1883.

25. *St. Louis Globe-Democrat,* Mar. 31, 1883.

26. *Fort Scott Evening Herald,* Mar. 31, 1883.

27. Thrapp, *Conquest of Apachería,* 273.

28. Davis, *Truth about Geronimo,* 55–56.

29. Bourke, *Apache Campaign,* 30. See also *New York Times,* Apr. 1, 1883.

30. *Fort Scott Evening Herald,* Mar. 31, 1883.

31. *El Paso Times,* Apr. 19, 1883.

32. Eugene Ware to Charles L. Ware, Fort Scott, Kans., Apr. 3, 1883 [telegram], published in *Fort Scott Banner,* Apr. 5, 1883.

33. *Silver City Enterprise,* Apr. 6, 1883; *St. Louis Daily Globe–Democrat,* Apr. 8, 1883.

34. *Fort Scott Banner,* Apr. 12, 1883.

35. *Fort Scott Daily Monitor,* Apr. 8, 1883.

36. *St. Louis Daily Globe-Democrat,* Apr. 1, 1883. A press statement reported that "owing to the elapse of time since death, it has been thought best not to uncover the caskets." *Fort Scott Evening Herald,* Apr. 7, 1883.

37. *Fort Scott Daily Monitor,* Apr. 4, 1883.

38. *Fort Scott Daily Monitor,* Apr. 8, 1883. A letter from the family to the GAR post, published in *Fort Scott Evening Herald,* Apr. 7, 1883, specifically asked that body "to turn out and escort the remains to Evergreen Cemetery and to take such further action as you may deem proper."

39. *Fort Scott Daily Monitor,* Apr. 8, 1883.

40. The sunshine, budding trees, and robins are referred to in *Fort Scott Daily Monitor,* Apr. 10, 1883.

41. *Fort Scott Evening Herald,* Apr. 9, 1883.

42. *Fort Scott Daily Monitor,* Apr. 10, 1883.

43. *Old Fort Log* (Old Fort Genealogical Society, Fort Scott, Kans.) (Summer 1981), 23; *Fort Scott Banner,* Apr. 12, 1883.

44. *Fort Scott Daily Monitor,* Apr. 10, 1883.

Chapter 9. Little Boy Lost

1. Dan L. Thrapp, *Al Sieber, Chief of Scouts* (Norman: Univ. of Oklahoma Press, 1964), 269.

2. *Arizona Weekly Citizen,* Apr. 4, 1883.

3. *Silver City Enterprise,* Nov. 2, 1883.

4. *Southwest Sentinel,* May 9, 1883.

5. Mazzanovich, *Trailing Geronimo,* 239.

6. Ringgold, *Frontier Days in the Southwest,* 71.

7. *Tucson Daily Star,* Apr. 16, 1899. All quotations that follow are from this source.

8. Loose typed note, in C. M. Wood Photo Collection, album 3, Arizona Historical Society, Tucson (reference courtesy of John P. Wilson). A portion of Sanders's account appears in *Arizona Enterprise,* Feb. 22, 1890. Captain Bourke, a man not unsympathetic to the Apaches, once wrote: "Where their captive was of tender years . . . , it was promptly put out of its misery by having its brains dashed against a convenient rock or tree." Bourke, *On the Border With Crook,* 128.

9. Bourke, Diary, 67:89. *Silver City Enterprise,* Apr. 13, 1883, carried the same news item but noted that the *Arizona Weekly Citizen,* which originally published it, was misinformed.

10. *Southwest Sentinel,* Apr. 21, 1883.

11. *Fort Scott Evening Herald,* Apr. 25, 1883; *Silver City Enterprise,* Apr. 13, 1883.

12. Brock, Tapes and Transcripts, 1952.

13. *Fort Scott Banner,* Apr. 5, 1883.

14. *Fort Scott Daily Monitor,* Apr. 8, 1883.

15. *Silver City Enterprise,* Apr. 6, 1883.

16. "Jeffords, Thomas Jonathan," in Thrapp, *Encyclopedia of Frontier Biography,* 3:723–24.

17. *Silver City Enterprise,* Apr. 6, 1883.

18. Lucas's bill for $9.00 is listed in "Expenses Incurred by McComas Estate," Mar. 17, 1884, McComas File, Grant County Probate Records, Silver City, N.M.

19. *Southwest Sentinel,* Apr. 7, 1883.

20. *Arizona Weekly Citizen,* Apr. 15, 1883.

21. "Stolen By Apaches," in *Harper's,* Apr. 28, 1883, p. 260; "Stolen By Apaches," in *Leslie's,* Apr. 28, 1883, p. 158. *Silver City Enterprise,* May 11, 1883, reported that, besides these two journals, "several sporting papers of recent date contain a very correct picture of Charley."

22. *Fort Scott Daily Monitor,* Apr. 21, 1883.

23. For accounts of militia activity against Indians and outlaws, 1882–84, see Territorial Archives of New Mexico, Microfilm Edition, Roll 99, in New Mexico State Records Center and Archives, Santa Fe.

24. "Charles C. McComas," entry in biographical file, New Mexico State Records Center and Archives, Santa Fe; *Southwest Sentinel,* Apr. 25, 1883.

25. *Fort Scott Daily Monitor,* Apr. 21, 1883; *Southwest Sentinel,* Apr. 25, 1883.

26. *Fort Scott Daily Monitor,* Apr. 21, 1883.

27. Daly, "Geronimo Campaign," 36; Cory, "Osage Ceded Lands," 191.

28. *Albuquerque Daily Democrat,* June 6, 1883.

29. The letter was published in *Fort Scott Evening Herald,* June 28, 1883.

30. Thrapp, *Conquest of Apachería,* 277.

31. Fort Thomas to Asst. Adj. Gen. J. A. Martin, Fort Whipple [telegram], May 2, 1883; printed in *Las Vegas Daily Gazette,* June 8, 1883.

32. *Southwest Sentinel,* May 9, 1883; *Las Vegas Daily Gazette,* June 8, 1883.

33. Britton Davis to John Wright, printed in *Silver City Enterprise,* May 11, 1883. Wright at once passed the news on to Eugene Ware in Fort Scott, emphasizing that Charley was being treated well by his captors. *Fort Scott Evening Herald,* May 11, 1883.

34. Quotation from *Arizona Daily Citizen,* in *Southwest Sentinel,* May 9, 1883.

35. Bourke, *Apache Campaign,* 52.

36. Thrapp, *Conquest of Apachería,* 284.

37. Porter, *Paper Medicine Man,* 155.

38. Bourke, *Apache Campaign,* 93; Basso, *Western Apache,* 159; Betzinez, *I Fought with Geronimo,* 118.

39. *Albuquerque Daily Democrat,* June 14, 1883.

40. Thrapp, *General Crook,* n. 23, p. 144.

41. Bourke, *Apache Campaign,* 94–95.

42. *Albuquerque Daily Democrat,* June 14, 1883; Bourke, *Apache Campaign,* 93–94.

43. Thrapp, *Conquest of Apachería,* 287; Bourke, *Apache Campaign,* 101.

44. Betzinez, *I Fought with Geronimo,* 113.

45. Davis, *Truth about Geronimo,* 68.

46. Randall's dispatch containing this account was dated June 15 and appeared in *El Paso Times,* after which it was reprinted in *Albuquerque Daily Democrat,* June 21, 1883.

47. *Silver City Enterprise,* Nov. 2, 1883.

48. Bourke, *Apache Campaign,* 113.

49. Quoted in Thrapp, *General Crook,* 174.

50. *Arizona Daily Star,* June 20, 1883.

51. *Arizona Daily Star,* June 19, 1883.

52. Recovery of the watch is referred to in Indian Depredation Claim, copy in McComas Family Papers; in *Silver City Enterprise,* Oct. 26, 1883; and in *Arizona Daily Star,* June 19, 1883.

53. Gen. George Crook to R. C. Drum, adjutant general, U.S. Army, Washington, D.C., June 1883, in *Fort Scott Evening Herald,* June 28, 1883.

54. Quoted in *Las Vegas Daily Gazette,* June 13, 1883.

55. *Albuquerque Daily Democrat,* June 27, 1883.

56. Quoted in Angie Debo, *Geronimo, The Man, His Time, His Place* (Norman: Univ. of Oklahoma Press, 1976): 192.

57. Bourke, *Apache Campaign,* 127; *Arizona Daily Star,* June 13, 1883.
58. Betzinez, *I Fought with Geronimo,* 122; Thrapp, *Juh,* 39.

Chapter 10. Hopes Fade

1. The document of Wright's appointment as administrator and an official notice published in *Deming (N.M.) Headlight,* Apr. 21, 1883, as well as Final Report of the Estate, submitted to the probate clerk, are preserved in McComas File, Grant County Probate Records, Silver City, N.M. See also *Silver City Enterprise,* May 4, 1883.
2. The insurance policy is mentioned in *Las Vegas Daily Gazette,* Apr. 11, 1883. The two lots (Block 25, Lots 10 and 12) in Silver City are recorded in Grant County Tax Assessment Rolls, 1884, County Clerk's Office, Silver City, N.M. The remainder of the assets appear in McComas Estate Inventory and Appraisal, Grant County Probate Records, Silver City, N.M. Wright soon rented the McComas house, to bring income to the estate.
3. Application for Guardianship, Bourbon County, Kans., June 2, 1883, copy in McComas File, Grant County Probate Records, Silver City, N.M.
4. Documents for all these claims are in the McComas File, Grant County Probate Records, Silver City, N.M. The Graham claim also is entered in Indian Depredation Claim, copy in McComas Family Papers.
5. The incident is described in *Las Vegas Daily Gazette,* May 4, 1883.
6. On the family's posting half the reward, see *Arizona Daily Citizen,* Apr. 21, 1883, and *Fort Scott Daily Monitor,* Apr. 15, 1883. The full reward of $1,000 was referred to frequently in the press, e.g., *Silver City Enterprise,* Apr. 13, 1883.
7. This reference appears in the affidavit, [John M. Wright], "Expenses Incurred and Paid by Administrator in the Matter of the Search for Charley McComas," in McComas File, Grant County Probate Records, Silver City, N.M. The same file holds a certificate for the Leroy Silver Mining Co. Mention of Leroy as a "noted scout" can be found in *Arizona Daily Star,* Aug. 14, 1909.
8. The main account of this episode, containing several inconsistencies, is in Skinner, *Apache Rock,* 35–36. The author fails to cite his source. An even more garbled account was printed long afterward in *Arizona Daily Star,* Aug. 14, 1909. Some added details are revealed in [John M. Wright], "Expenses Incurred and Paid by Administrator." How much of the Leroy-Wilson story is true cannot now be determined.
9. The contact with Eady is mentioned briefly in [John M. Wright], "Expenses Incurred and Paid by Administrator."
10. The complete Simz letter is quoted in *Silver City Enterprise,* Nov. 9, 1883.
11. On the arrival of the Apache band on Nov. 16, 1883, see Thrapp, *General Crook,* 176. Wright's itinerary, Silver City to Fort Thomas, is given in [John M. Wright], "Expenses Incurred and Paid by Administrator."

12. *Silver City Enterprise,* Nov. 30, 1883.

13. Two days after Wright's return, the story appeared in the issue of Nov. 30, 1883. Lt. Britton Davis made reference to another captive boy, a Mexican, brought in by the Apaches, who some thought might be Charley. But later he was identified as a child from northern New Mexico and was restored to an uncle who came for him. Davis, *Truth About Geronimo,* 68.

14. The telegrams, without reference to their contents, are referred to in [John M. Wright], "Expenses Incurred and Paid by Administrator."

15. Debo, *Geronimo,* 202.

16. The texts of both the Crawford and Crook letters were published in *Silver City Enterprise,* Mar. 24, 1884. Earlier Crook had cited, as the chief reason for his failure to rescue Charley, the premature gunshot by one of the scouts at the May 15 attack, which allowed many of the Apaches to escape. *Arizona Weekly Star,* June 19, 1883.

17. Bourke, *Apache Campaign,* 128.

18. Davis, *Truth about Geronimo,* 68.

19. *Silver City Enterprise,* Apr. 18, 1884.

20. *Silver City Enterprise,* May 2, 1884.

21. *Silver City Enterprise,* Apr. 4, 1884.

22. See [John M. Wright], "Expenses Incurred and Paid by Administrator."

23. *Silver City Enterprise,* Mar. 7, 1884. Two years later, Wright was a director of the Peerless Mining Co., which Boyle served as vice president. *Silver City Enterprise,* Oct. 15, 1886.

24. *Silver City Enterprise,* Feb. 1, 1884.

25. *Arizona Weekly Citizen,* Oct. 27, 1883.

26. *Silver City Enterprise,* May 9, 1884.

27. *Silver City Enterprise,* Sept. 18, 1885.

28. Betzinez, *I Fought with Geronimo,* 77.

29. Davis, *Truth about Geronimo,* 152–53; *Silver City Enterprise,* Sept. 18, 1885. Jimmy McKinn, unlike Charley McComas, subsequently was rescued and returned to his family. The incident is described in Marc Simmons, *Ranchers, Ramblers, and Renegades* (Santa Fe: Ancient City Press, 1984), 65–68.

30. Bourke, *On the Border with Crook,* 485.

31. Betzinez, *I Fought with Geronimo,* 109, 118, 120.

32. Eve Ball to Angie Debo, Feb. 27, 1973, cited in Debo, *Geronimo,* 190n.

33. Ball, *Indeh,* 51.

34. Martin Christensen, "Fate of the McComas Family," *Frontier Times* 20 (Feb. 1943): 86.

35. Debo, *Geronimo,* 190.

36. Versions by Ruey Darrow, containing some conflicting details, appear in Ball, *Indeh,* 51, and in Skinner, *Apache Rock,* 35.

37. *Silver City Enterprise,* Aug. 12, 1892.

38. Quoted in Wellman, *Death in the Desert*, 175.

39. This quotation, as well as reference to the Cumpas episode, appear in Lynda A. Sánchez, "The Lost Apaches of the Sierra Madre," *Arizona Highways* 62 (Sept. 1986): 25–26. Also see Jack Rowe and Lynda A. Sánchez, "A Short Stay in Paradise," *Journal of Arizona History* 28 (Spring 1987): 1–16. Sánchez is preparing a full study of the Lost Apaches, forthcoming.

40. Betzinez, *I Fought with Geronimo*, 145.

41. Sánchez, "Lost Apaches," 26.

42. For miner Jack Stockbridge's 1913 meeting with a redheaded Indian out of Mexico, who he thought might be Charley McComas's son, see Elizabeth Fleming McFarland, *Wilderness of the Gila* (Albuquerque: Univ. of New Mexico Publication Office, 1974), 18.

43. *Fort Scott Tribune-Monitor*, May 30, 1942.

44. The *El Paso Post* story was reprinted in *Silver City Enterprise*, Feb. 5, 1928. For the details of this particular raid, I have relied upon Douglas V. Meed, *They Never Surrendered: Bronco Apaches of the Sierra Madres, 1890–1935* (Tucson, Ariz.: Westernlore Press, 1993), 55–58.

45. Lupe's statement, as recorded by Ingstad, generously was shared in Lynda A. Sánchez to Marc Simmons, Mar. 3, 1993, in possession of Marc Simmons, Cerrillos, N.M.

46. "The Lost Apache Tribe," undated story from *El Paso Times*, reprinted in *Frontier Times* 20 (Oct. 1942): 28.

47. Ruth McDonald Boyer and Narcissus Duffy Gayton, *Apache Mothers and Daughters* (Norman: Univ. of Oklahoma Press, 1992), 64.

48. *Fort Scott Tribune-Monitor*, May 30, 1942.

49. Betzinez, *I Fought with Geronimo*, 77.

50. Boyer and Gayton, *Apache Mothers and Daughters*, 363.

51. *Arizona Daily Star*, Aug. 14, 1909.

Chapter 11. Massacre's Legacy

1. *Silver City Enterprise*, Feb. 6, 1885; *Southwest Sentinel*, Feb. 7, 1885.

2. *Silver City Enterprise*, Feb. 13, 1883.

3. *Southwest Sentinel*, Apr. 11, 1883. The news story stated specifically that the mountain was named in honor of H. C. McComas. In the early 1950s, a new effort was launched to establish a McComas monument, but it too failed. See undated news clippings (ca. 1953), McComas File, Public Library, Silver City, N.M.

4. Compare the marker texts in the two editions of the following book: N. Delgado and D. Delgado, comps., *Guide to Historical Markers in New Mexico* (Santa Fe: Delgado Studios, 1984), 35; and Stanley M. Hordes and Carol Joiner, comps., *Historical Markers in New Mexico* (Santa Fe: Delgado Studios, 1984), 30.

5. Allan Houser, in an interview by Marc Simmons, Santa Fe, N.M., Mar. 30,

1993, stated that, as a boy at Apache, Okla., he could understand the elderly people when they spoke in Chiricahua, but that he could not speak the language himself.

6. C. L. Sonnichsen, *The Mescalero Apaches* (Norman: Univ. of Oklahoma Press, 1958), 202.

7. On Daklugie's opinion of Chato and Chato's treatment at Mescalero, see Ball, *Indeh*, 50–51, 282.

8. Janaloo Hill, *Ranch on Whitewater Creek*, 20–21.

9. *Silver City Enterprise*, Mar. 28, 1884.

10. *Fort Scott Monitor*, Apr. 8, 1883.

11. *Silver City Enterprise*, Dec. 12, 1884; and Rudisill, *Photographers of the New Mexico Territory*, 40.

12. Brock, Tapes and Transcripts, 1952.

13. *Historical Encyclopedia of New Mexico*, 2:1437.

14. "Ada McComas Taylor Revisits City," undated news clipping (ca. 1953), McComas File, Public Library, Silver City, N.M.

15. Connelley, *Standard History of Kansas*, 3:1346–47. Regarding Elisha McComas's railroad promotion, see *Fort Scott Evening Herald*, July 11, 1883. His death date is recorded in Burial Register, Evergreen Cemetery, Fort Scott, Kans. (reference courtesy of Shirley Hurd).

16. *Silver City Enterprise*, Jan. 23, 1891; Fleeta Cook, *More Footprints: Mogollon through Cook's Peak* (Silver City, N.M.: Privately printed, n.d.), 131.

17. Lowry, "Life of Eugene Ware," 4; *Fort Scott Tribune*, Nov. 2, 1962.

18. Indian Depredation Claim, copy in McComas Family Papers; J. Bradley Tanner, chief clerk, U.S. Court of Claims, Washington, D.C., to Ada McComas Hazelton, Oct. 21, 1927, in McComas Family Papers.

19. Ware's death occurred on May 31, 1911. For details, see *Colorado Springs Gazette*, June 1 and 2, 1911.

20. *Silver City Enterprise*, July 25, 1884.

21. *Southwest Sentinel*, Nov. 15, 1884.

22. Letter of Administration, Estate of David McComas, Aug. 2, 1886, in McComas File, Grant County Probate Records, Silver City, N.M.

23. James E. Sherman and Barbara H. Sherman, *Ghost Towns*, 171.

24. This detail is mentioned in *Arizona Sentinel*, Mar. 4, 1908.

25. *Silver City Enterprise*, July 25, 1884.

26. Alfred Cohn and Joe Chisholm, *"Take the Witness!"* (Garden City, N.Y.: Garden City Publishing Co., 1934), 168–69.

27. More than a year after his uncle's death, Will McComas was still at the Last Chance Mine in the Mogollons; *Silver City Enterprise*, Mar. 11, 1892. Temporarily at least, he may have taken over management of the property.

28. Cohn and Chisholm, *"Take the Witness!"* 175–76.

29. *Los Angeles Times*, May 22, 1908. Mrs. Lyford was the daughter of Rufus McComas.

30. See, e.g., the reference to Louisa McComas in mining deeds left by H. C. McComas to sons David and William, Sierra County Records, McComas File, Silver City Museum, Silver City, N.M. *Silver City Enterprise,* Aug. 18, 1892.

31. *Los Angeles Times,* Mar. 2 and May 22, 1908.

32. The daughter of Earl Rogers, Adela Rogers St. Johns, was present when Will McComas's call came, and she describes it in detail in her book, *Final Verdict* (Garden City, N.Y.: Doubleday, 1962), 345. She also wrote: "Everyone knew Mac [McComas] as one of the fastest guns in the West," an obvious exaggeration (326).

33. *Los Angeles Times,* Mar. 20 and 30, 1908.

34. *New York Times,* Mar. 1, 1908.

35. Rogers's strategy in the McComas case is spelled out in his biography by Cohn and Chisholm, *"Take the Witness!"* 168–79.

36. St. Johns, *Final Verdict,* 344. On the conclusion of the first trial, see *Los Angeles Times,* May 30, 1908. The retrial is referred to in Cohn and Chisholm, *"Take the Witness!"* 178.

37. For examples of press references to the McComas massacre, see *New York Times,* Mar. 1, 1908; *Los Angeles Times,* May 30, 1908; *Arizona Star,* Mar. 5, 1908. On Will as a supposed witness to the massacre, see St. Johns, *Final Verdict,* 328.

38. Kimme-Smith to Simmons, May 29, 1993.

39. Kimme-Smith to Simmons, Oct. 25, 1992.

40. *Silver City Enterprise,* June 11, 1886.

41. Kimme-Smith to Simmons, Oct. 25, 1992; and Kimme-Smith to Simmons, Mar. 21, 1993, Cerrillos, N.M. The second letter refers to some confusion over the exact year of Mildred's birth.

42. Indian Depredation Claim, copy in McComas Family Papers.

43. Cohn and Chisholm, *"Take the Witness!"* 175.

44. Kimme-Smith to Simmons, Feb. 27, 1993.

45. Kimme-Smith to Simmons, Feb. 27 and Mar. 21, 1993.

46. Kimme-Smith to Simmons, Oct. 25, 1992. The magazine was *True.* A search was made by the author and Santa Fe librarian Elizabeth West, but no back file of the periodical, dating to the early 1940s, could be located.

47. Ada's trip is described in *Silver City Enterprise,* Sept. 27, 1945.

Chapter 12. A Personal Epilogue

1. Evan Connell, *Son of the Morning Star* (San Francisco: North Point Press, 1984), 312.

2. *Santa Fe New Mexican,* Aug. 27, 1994.

❧ Bibliography ❦

Documents

Adjutant General Records. Territorial Archives. New Mexico State Records Center and Archives, Santa Fe.

Ancestral File (TM-Version 4.11). Latter-Day Saints Church, Salt Lake City, Utah.

Bourke, John G. Diary. 128 volumes. Library, United States Military Academy, West Point, New York. Facsimile set at University of New Mexico Library, Albuquerque.

Boyle, John. Compiled Service Record, Military Branch. National Archives, Washington, D.C.

Brock, Julius Caesar. Tapes and Typescripts, 1952, edited by Lou Bachley. Pioneer Foundation Collection. Library, University of New Mexico, Albuquerque.

Grant County Tax Assessment Records, Silver City, New Mexico.

McComas Family Papers. In possession of Carolyn Kimme-Smith, Los Angeles, California.

McComas File. Grant County Probate Records, Silver City, New Mexico.

McComas, Hamilton C., Compiled Service Record. Military Branch. National Archives, Washington, D.C.

Old-Timers' Recollections. Typescripts on file. Silver City Museum, Silver City, New Mexico.

Sanders, S. L. Typescript. C. M. Wood Photo Collection, Album 3. Arizona Historical Society, Tucson.

Territorial Archives of New Mexico. New Mexico State Records Center and Archives, Santa Fe.

Thompson, Capt. William Alexis. Report to Post Adjutant, Fort Bayard, New Mexico, August 13, 1883. Letters Received by Headquarters, District of New Mexico, September 1865–August 1890. National Archives Microfilm Publication, Reel 52.

U.S. Census. Bourbon County, Kansas, 1870. Microfilm Edition, M593-429.

U.S. Census. Bourbon County, Kansas, 1875. Microfilm Edition, K-002.

U.S. Census. Grant County, New Mexico, 1880. Microfilm, Edition, Reel 802.

Ware, Eugene Fitch. Papers. Abby Ware Nies Collection. Kansas State Historical Society, Topeka.

Newspapers

Albuquerque (N.M.) *Review*
Arizona Daily Citizen (Tucson)
Arizona Daily Star (Tucson)
Arizona Enterprise (Tucson)
Arizona Sentinel (Yuma)
Chicago Times and Herald
Chicago Tribune
Colorado Springs Gazette
Deming (N.M.) *Headlight*
Denver Republican
Denver Tribune
El Paso (Tex.) *Times*
Fort Scott (Kans.) *Banner*
Fort Scott (Kans.) *Evening Herald*
Fort Scott (Kans.) *Monitor*
Grant County (N.M.) *Herald*
Las Cruces (N.M.) *Borderer*
Las Vegas (N.M.) *Daily Gazette*
Los Angeles Evening Express
Los Angeles Times
Missouri Republican (St. Louis)
New York Times
New York Weekly Tribune
Prescott (Ariz.) *Courier*
San Francisco Post
Santa Fe Daily New Mexican
Silver City (N.M.) *Enterprise*
Silver City (N.M.) *Herald*
Southwest Sentinel (Silver City, N.M.)
St. Louis Daily Globe–Democrat
St. Louis Post-Dispatch
Tombstone (Ariz.) *Epitaph*
Tombstone (Ariz.) *Republican*
Tucson Daily Star

Articles, Books, and Theses

Abel, Anna Heloise. "Indian Reservations in Kansas and the Extinguishment of Their Title." *Transactions of the Kansas State Historical Society* 8 (1903): 72–109.

Allen, R. S. "Pinos Altos, New Mexico." *New Mexico Historical Review* 23 (Oct. 1948): 302–32.

Anderson, Eugene Carter. *The Metal Resources of New Mexico and Their Economic Fea-*

tures through 1954. Bulletin 39. Socorro, New Mexico: State Bureau of Mines and Mineral Resources, 1957.

Andreas, A. T. *History of the State of Kansas.* Chicago: Published by the author, 1883.

Ball, Eve. "The Apache Scouts: A Chiricahua Appraisal." *Arizona and the West* 7 (Winter 1965): 315–28.

———. *In the Days of Victorio.* Tucson: University of Arizona Press, 1970.

———. *Indeh: An Apache Odyssey.* Provo, Utah: Brigham Young University Press, 1980.

Barbour, Barton H. *Reluctant Frontiersman: James Ross Larkin on the Santa Fe Trail, 1856–1857.* Albuquerque: University of New Mexico Press, 1990.

Barrett, S. M., ed. *Geronimo: His Own Story.* New York: Ballantine Books, 1971.

Basso, Keith H., ed. *Western Apache Raiding and Warfare.* Tucson: University of Arizona Press, 1971.

Berkow, Robert, ed. *The Merck Manual of Diagnosis and Therapy.* 15th ed. Rahway, N.J.: Merck and Company, 1987.

Berry, Susan, and Sharman Apt Russell. *Built to Last: An Architectural History of Silver City, New Mexico.* Silver City, New Mexico: Silver City Museum, 1986.

Betzinez, Jason. *I Fought With Geronimo.* Harrisburg, Pa.: Stackpole, 1959.

Bourke, John G. *An Apache Campaign in the Sierra Madre.* New York: Charles Scribner's Sons, 1958.

———. *On the Border with Crook.* New York: Charles Scribner's Sons, 1891.

Boyer, Ruth McDonald, and Narcissus Duffy Gayton. *Apache Mothers and Daughters.* Norman: University of Oklahoma Press, 1992.

Boyle, John. *Boyle Genealogy.* St. Louis, Missouri: N.p., 1909.

Buchanan, Kimberly Moore. *Apache Women Warriors.* El Paso: Texas Western Press, 1986.

Burnham, Frederick Russell. *Scouting on Two Continents.* Garden City, N.Y.: Garden City Publishing Company, 1926.

Christensen, Martin. "Fate of the McComas Family." *Frontier Times* 20 (Feb. 1943): 86.

Christopher, Adrienne. "The Life of Stephen Benton Elkins." *Westport Historical Quarterly* 4 (Dec. 1968): 28–32.

Cohn, Alfred, and Joe Chisholm. *"Take the Witness!"* Garden City, N.Y.: Garden City Publishing Company, 1934.

Comstock, Jun, ed. *The West Virginia Heritage Encyclopedia.* Richwood, West Virginia: Privately published, 1974.

Connell, Evan. *Son of the Morning Star.* San Francisco: North Point Press, 1984.

Connelley, William E. "Acceptance on Behalf of the Historical Society." *Collections of the Kansas State Historical Society, 1913–1914* 13 (1915): 42–51.

———. *A Standard History of Kansas and Kansans.* 5 vols. Chicago: Lewis Publishing Company, 1918.

Cook, Fleeta. *More Footprints: Mogollon Through Cook's Peak.* Silver City, New Mexico: Privately printed, n.d.

Cook, James H. *Fifty Years on the Old Frontier.* New Haven, Connecticut: Yale University Press, 1923.

Cory, C. E. "The Osage Ceded Lands." *Transactions of the Kansas State Historical Society, 1903–1904* 8 (1904): 187–99.

Cruse, Thomas. *Apache Days and After.* Lincoln: University of Nebraska Press, 1987.

Dacus, J. A., and James W. Buel. *A Tour of St. Louis, or, The Inside Life of a Great City.* St. Louis: Missouri Western Publishing Company, 1878.

Daly, H. W. "The Geronimo Campaign." *Arizona Historical Review* 3 (July 1930): 26–44.

Davis, Britton. *The Truth about Geronimo.* New Haven, Connecticut: Yale University Press, 1929.

Debo, Angie. *Geronimo, His Time, His Place.* Norman: University of Oklahoma Press, 1976.

Dixon, David. *Hero of Beecher Island: The Life and Military Career of George A. Forsyth.* Lincoln: University of Nebraska Press, 1994.

Dodge, Richard I. *Our Wild Indians.* Reprint ed. New York: Archer House, 1959.

Dunn, J. P., Jr. *Massacres of the Mountains.* Reprint ed. New York: Archer House, n.d.

Forsyth, George A. *Thrilling Days in Army Life.* New York: Harper, 1900.

Frazer, Robert W. *Forts of the West.* Norman: University of Oklahoma Press, 1965.

Giese, Dale F. *Echoes of the Bugles.* Silver City, New Mexico: Phelps Dodge Corporation, 1976.

Gillerman, Elliott. *Mineral Deposits of Western Grant County, New Mexico.* Bulletin 83. Socorro: New Mexico Institute of Mining and Technology, 1964.

Greene, A. C. *The Last Captive.* Austin: Encino Press, 1972.

Heitman, Francis B. *Historical Register and Dictionary of the United States Army.* 2 vols. Washington, D.C.: U.S. Government Printing Office, 1903.

Hill, Janaloo. *The Ranch on Whitewater Creek.* Silver City, New Mexico: Privately printed, 1984.

Hill, Rita. *Then and Now: Here and Around Shakespeare.* Lordsburg, New Mexico: Privately printed, 1963.

Hill, Rita, and Janaloo Hill. "Alias Shakespeare: The Town Nobody Knew." *New Mexico Historical Review* 41 (July 1967): 211–27.

Historical Encyclopedia of New Mexico. 2 vols. Albuquerque: New Mexico Historical Association, 1942.

Holmes, Kenneth L. *Ewing Young, Master Trapper.* Portland, Oregon: Binfords & Mort Publishers, 1967.

Hook, Jason. *Geronimo: Last Renegade of the Apaches.* Dorset, England: Firebird Books, 1989.

Hordes, Stanley, and Carol Joiner. *Historical Markers in New Mexico.* Santa Fe: Delgado Studios, 1984.

Hyde, George E. *Life of George Bent.* Norman: University of Oklahoma Press, 1967.

Johnson, Allen, ed. *Dictionary of American Biography.* 22 vols. New York: Charles Scribner's Sons, 1929–58.

King, James T. "George Crook, Indian Fighter and Humanitarian." *Arizona and the West* 9 (Winter 1967): 333–48.

Ladd, Horatio O. *Story of New Mexico.* Boston: D. Lothrop Company, 1891.

Lambert, Oscar Doane. *Stephen Benton Elkins: American Foursquare.* Pittsburgh, Pa.: University of Pittsburgh Press, 1955.

Lekson, Stephen H. *Nana's Raid.* El Paso: Texas Western Press, 1987.

Leyburn, James G. *The Scotch-Irish: A Social History.* Chapel Hill: University of North Carolina Press, 1962.

Lockwood, Frank C. *The Apache Indians.* Reprint ed. Lincoln: University of Nebraska Press, 1987.

———. *Pioneer Days in Arizona.* New York: Macmillan, 1932.

Lowry, Gracy. "Life of Eugene Ware." M.S. thesis, Kansas State Teachers College, Pittsburgh, Kansas, 1936.

"The Lost Apache Tribe." Undated story from *El Paso Times,* reprinted in *Frontier Times* 20 (Oct. 1942): 28.

Lundwall, Helen J., ed. *Pioneering in Territorial Silver City.* Albuquerque: University of New Mexico Press, 1983.

Lundwall, Helen J., et al. *This Is Silver City.* Silver City, New Mexico: Privately printed, 1970.

Mazzanovich, Anton. *Trailing Geronimo.* 3rd ed. Hollywood, Calif.: Privately printed, 1931.

McFarland, Elizabeth Fleming. *Wilderness of the Gila.* Albuquerque: University of New Mexico Publications Office, 1974.

McIntosh, Charles. *Past and Present of Piatt County, Illinois.* Chicago: S. J. Clarke Company, 1903.

Meed, Douglas V. *They Never Surrendered: Bronco Apaches of the Sierra Madres.* Tucson, Arizona: Westernlore Press, 1993.

Melody, Michael E. *The Apache.* New York: Chelsea House, 1989.

Miles, Nelson A. *Personal Recollections and Observations of General Nelson A. Miles.* Chicago: Werner Company, 1897.

Muir, Emma M. "The First Militia." *New Mexico Magazine* 30 (Oct. 1952): 19, 41, 44–46.

Myres, S. D. *Pioneer Surveyor, Frontier Lawyer: The Personal Narrative of O. W. Williams, 1877–1902.* El Paso: Texas Western Press, 1968.

Naegle, Conrad Keeler. "The History of Silver City, New Mexico, 1870–1886." M.A. thesis, University of New Mexico, Albuquerque, 1943.

———. "The Rebellion in Grant County, New Mexico, in 1876." *Arizona and the West* 10 (Autumn 1968): 225–40.

Nelson, Susan, and David Nelson, eds. *The Silver City Book.* Silver City, New Mexico: Silver Star Publications, 1978.

Nevins, Allan. *Ordeal of the Union.* 5 vols. New York: Charles Scribner's Sons, 1947.

Novack, George. *Genocide Against the Indians.* New York: Pathfinder Press, 1988.

Ogle, Ralph Hedrick. *Federal Control of the Western Apaches.* Albuquerque: University of New Mexico Press, 1970.

Opler, Morris. *An Apache Life-Way.* Chicago: University of Chicago Press, 1941.

———. "Chiricahua Apache." In *Handbook of North American Indians,* vol. 10: *Southwest,* edited by Alfonso Ortiz, 401–18. Washington, D.C.: Smithsonian Institution, 1983.

Perry, Richard J. *Western Apache Heritage.* Austin: University of Texas Press, 1991.

Piatt, Emma C. *History of Piatt County, Together with a Brief History of Illinois.* Evansville, Ind.: Privately printed, [ca. 1883].

Pierce, Michael D. *The Most Promising Young Officer: A Life of Ranald Slidell Mackenzie.* Norman: University of Oklahoma Press, 1993.

Porter, Joseph C. *Paper Medicine Man: John Gregory Bourke and His American West.* Norman: University of Oklahoma Press, 1986.

Ravenswaay, Charles van. *St. Louis: An Informal History of the City and Its People, 1746–1865.* St. Louis: Missouri Historical Society Press, 1991.

Rice, Otis K. *West Virginia: A History.* Lexington: University Press of Kentucky, 1985.

Richardson, James D. *A Compilation of the Messages and Papers of the Presidents.* 10 vols. Washington, D.C.: U.S. Government Printing Office, 1896–99.

Richmond, Mabel E., et al. *Centennial History of Decatur and Macon County, 1829–1929.* Decatur, Ill.: Decatur Review, 1930.

Ringgold, Jennie Parks. *Frontier Days in the Southwest.* San Antonio, Texas: Naylor Company, 1952.

Rowe, Jack, and Lynda A. Sánchez. "A Short Stay in Paradise." *Journal of Arizona History* 28 (Spring 1987): 1–16.

Rudisill, Richard, comp. *Photographers of New Mexico Territory, 1854–1912.* Santa Fe: Museum of New Mexico, 1973.

Sánchez, Lynda A. "The Lost Apaches of the Sierra Madre." *Arizona Highways* 62 (Sept. 1986): 25–27.

Schmitt, Martin F., ed. *General Crook: His Autobiography.* Norman: University of Oklahoma Press, 1946.

Scott, Franklin William. *Newspapers and Periodicals of Illinois, 1814–1879.* Springfield: Illinois State Historical Library, 1910.

Sherman, James E., and Barbara H. Sherman. *Ghost Towns and Mining Camps of New Mexico.* Norman: University of Oklahoma Press, 1974.

Shonkwiler, Francis. *Historical Encyclopedia of Illinois and History of Piatt County.* Chicago: Munsell Publishing Company, [ca. 1917].

Simmons, Marc. *Ranchers, Ramblers, and Renegades.* Santa Fe: Ancient City Press, 1984.

Skinner, Woodrow B. *The Apache Rock Crumbles.* Pensacola, Florida: Skinner Publications, 1987.

Smith, Cornelius C., Jr. *Fort Huachuca: The Story of a Frontier Post.* Washington, D.C.: U.S. Government Printing Office, 1981.

Smith, Ralph A. "Apache Plunder Trails Southward, 1831–1840." *New Mexico Historical Review* 37 (Jan. 1962): 20–42.

———. "The Scalp Hunters in the Borderlands." *Arizona and the West* 5 (Spring 1964): 5–22.

Sonnichsen, C. L. *The Mescalero Apaches.* Norman: University of Oklahoma Press, 1958.

Sparks, Edwin E. *The Lincoln-Douglas Debates of 1858*. Springfield: Illinois State Historical Library, 1908.

Spicer, Edward H. *Cycles of Conquest*. Tucson: University of Arizona Press, 1962.

St. Johns, Adela Rogers. *Final Verdict*. Garden City, N.Y.: Doubleday, 1962.

Stockel, H. Henrietta. *Women of the Apache Nation*. Reno: University of Nevada Press, 1991.

Stout, Joseph A., Jr. *Apache Lightning: The Last Great Battles of the Ojo Calientes*. New York: Oxford University Press, 1974.

Sweeney, Edwin R. *Merejildo Grijalva: Apache Captive, Army Scout*. El Paso: Texas Western Press, 1992.

Thompson, Jerry D., ed. "With the Third Infantry in New Mexico, 1851–1853: The Lost Diary of Private Sylvester W. Matson." *Journal of Arizona History* 31 (Winter 1990): 349–404.

Thrapp, Dan L. *Al Sieber, Chief of Scouts*. Norman: University of Oklahoma Press, 1964.

———. *Encyclopedia of Frontier Biography*. 3 vols. Glendale, Calif.: Arthur H. Clark Company, 1988.

———. *General Crook and the Sierra Madre Adventure*. Norman: University of Oklahoma Press, 1972.

———. *Juh: An Incredible Indian*. El Paso: Texas Western Press, 1973.

———. *Victorio and the Mimbres Apaches*. Norman: University of Oklahoma Press, 1974.

———, ed. *Dateline Fort Bowie: Charles Fletcher Lummis Reports on an Apache War*. Norman: University of Oklahoma Press, 1979.

Twitchell, Ralph E. *The Leading Facts of New Mexican History*. 5 vols. Cedar Rapids, Iowa: Torch Press, 1911–17.

Unger, Patti, ed. *True Tales*. Silver City, New Mexico: Sun Dog Publishing, 1991.

Wagoner, Jay J. *Arizona Territory, 1863–1912*. Tucson: University of Arizona Press, 1970.

Wallace, Lew. *An Autobiography*. 2 vols. New York: Harper and Brothers, 1906.

Ware, Eugene F. *The Indian War of 1864*. Lincoln: University of Nebraska Press, 1963.

Watson, Dorothy. *The Pinos Altos Story*. Silver City, New Mexico: The Enterprise, 1960.

Wellman, Paul. *Death in the Desert*. New York: Macmillan Company, 1935.

West, Elliott. *Growing Up with the Country*. Albuquerque: University of New Mexico Press, 1989.

West, Judson S. "Eugene Ware." In *Collections of the Kansas State Historical Society, 1913–1914* 13 (1915): 65–71.

Westphall, Victor. *Thomas Benton Catron and His Era*. Tucson: University of Arizona Press, 1973.

Wharfield, Col. H. B. *Cibicue Creek Fight in Arizona: 1881*. El Cajon, Calif.: Privately printed, 1971.

Worcester, Donald E. *The Apaches: Eagles of the Southwest*. Norman: University of Oklahoma Press, 1979.

❧ Index ❧